CompTIA® A+ Practice Tests: Exam 220-1101

D. M. O' Connell

CompTIA® A+ Practice Tests:

Exam 220-1101

Other titles in the CompTIA® A+ Practice Tests series:

CompTIA A+ Practice Tests: Exam 220-1102

First published in December 2018.

Country of First Publication: England, U.K.

Second Edition published in August 2023.

Contents

Attention!

Thank you for your purchase of CompTIA® A+ Practice Tests: Exam 220-1101.

As the reader of this book, the author and publisher welcome your constructive comments and feedback.

If you purchased this book via Amazon, please post a review on the relevant website at your convenience.

Foreword

This book is intended for readers currently studying for the official CompTIA® A+ Core 1 certification exam. It is assumed that the reader is presently undertaking or has already successfully completed a relevant course of study in preparation for the A+ exam. Accordingly, the practice tests in this book should prove tremendously constructive in affording the reader an opportunity to test his/her knowledge before presenting for the A+ exam.

This book comprises approximately 820 questions presented in a multitude of different formats, including multiple choice questions (MCQs), scenario-based troubleshooting questions, and true/false statements amongst others. However, it is worth bearing in mind that the A+ exam normally consists of 90 questions, predominantly MCQs with a small proportion of performance-based questions (PBQs).

The 820 practice questions are intentionally divided into manageable test sets. Each test set comprises approximately 20 multi-format questions covering a diverse array of examinable topics. Each question is accompanied by answers and, where applicable, annotated solutions.

Whilst the annotated solutions provided at the end of each test set are selective and not intended to be comprehensive study notes, it is anticipated that these succinct notes will prove to be very useful for revision purposes in advance of the A+ exam.

D. M. O' Connell

Liverpool, England, U.K.

December 2018

Fortuna Eruditis Favet

Fortune Favors the Prepared Mind

Exam 220-1101

Practice Tests

Each test set comprises 20 multi-format questions approximately. Answers and study notes are provided at the end of each test set.

Practice Test 1

1. True or False: A power surge suppressor uses a MOV to protect sensitive electronic equipment.

2. A Dell® PC workstation's memory is being upgraded. The PC workstation already has a 4 GB Corsair® memory module installed in Bank 1. A technician installs a new 4 GB Corsair® DIMM stick into the correct slot in Bank 2 on the ATX motherboard. However, when the computer workstation is rebooted, a memory error notification is displayed on the monitor.

Which of the following is the most likely explanation for this error?

(i) BIOS does not recognise the newly installed DIMM

(ii) The new memory module operates at a lower speed compared to the pre-existing DIMM in Bank 1

(iii) The new memory module is overheating

(iv) The RAM slot is dirty

3. True or False: If a technician installs a PostScript driver for a printer that only supports PCL, the printer will only print unintelligible text or gobbledegook.

4. A laser printer is printing lighter in random areas of each page. What should a maintenance technician do to resolve this printer issue?

(i) Clean the primary corona wire

(ii) Clean the fusing assembly

(iii) Clean the rubber rollers

(iv) Replace the toner cartridge

5. True or False: A PC is connected to a known working AC outlet. If you are troubleshooting what you believe to be a power issue affecting this PC, it is advisable to test the 24-pin PSU connector initially before checking the AC outlet, the IEC cable, or the actual PSU.

6. A computer operates normally for a few minutes, but then the system "freezes" or "crashes". What is the most likely cause?

(i) Case cooling fans are starting to fail

(ii) Device driver errors

(iii) Physical DIMM faults

(iv) Motherboard manufacturing defects

7. True or False: If a laser printer is printing out blurry and smudged pages, it is very likely that the fuser is not getting sufficiently hot.

8. A computer technician is troubleshooting a networking issue. She types ping 193.168.10.05 -l 1500 into the command shell. What does this command do?

(i) This command pings the specified IP address with 1,500 bytes of data 10 times

(ii) This command pings the specified IP address with 1,500 bytes of data 4 times

(iii) This command pings the specified IP address with 1 byte of data 1,500 times

(iv) This command pings the specified IP address with 1,500 bytes of data only once

(v) This command is incorrect. The correct command is: ping 193.168.10.05 -L 1500

9. Which statement most accurately describes the purpose and function of the netstat -n command? (Select two answers.)

(i) If a computer technician intends to submit a request to a DNS server to determine DNS details, including the IP address of host computers, he/she would enter netstat -n at the command prompt

(ii) Netstat -n displays network protocol statistics for a local computer that use NetBIOS over TCP/IP connections

(iii) Netstat -n shows the network statistics for a local computer in a numerical format only

(iv) The netstat -n command specifies the number of active connections open on a network at any given point in time

10. A company's IT technician is working on a Windows® 8.1 OS desktop computer in the main office. The office administrator asks the technician to securely erase the SATA hard drive so that the company can recycle it.

What should the technician do to securely erase this hard drive?

(i) Perform a low-level format on the hard drive

(ii) Use the **format** command with the **/p** parameter

(iii) Run Disk Cleanup utility

(iv) Use **defrag -f** command

11. Fill in the blank: There are two main types of optic fibres: Single mode (otherwise known as SMF) and ____.

12. Which of the following ethernet physical media would support the use of a fibre optic connection? (Select two answers.)

(i) An ethernet cable that supports a data transmission rate of 100 Mbps

(ii) A networking cable that supports a data transmission rate of 1,000 Kbps

(iii) An ethernet cable that is designed to a 1,000 Mbps specification

(iv) A networking cable that can transmit 10 Gbps

13. True or False: A DC jack is a laptop component that needs to be soldered in place when installed.

14. Which networking device has a demodulator?

(i) Hub

(ii) Modem

(iii) Switch

(iv) WAP

15. When a user turned on his computer workstation, the LCD monitor started to flicker and then became blank, and smoke started to come out of the PC case.

However, the user notices that the case fans are still working because he can hear their signature sound.

What is the most likely cause of this PC issue?

(i) Faulty inverter

(ii) Failed video card

(iii) Defective PSU

(iv) Faulty LCD monitor

16. Which of the following is the most common indication that a PC's PSU is starting to fail? (Select all applicable answers.)

(i) Smoke emanating from the computer case

(ii) The computer system repeatedly "freezes" or "crashes"

(iii) BSOD event

(iv) Repeated failure of the computer system's hard drives

17. The optical drive in a computer is no longer working. The PC user has decided to buy and install a new drive.

Which optical drive variety can be purchased to allow the user to record the most data on a single disc?

(i) BR-D

(ii) DVD-RW

(iii) DVD+RW

(iv) CD-ROM

18. A technician is troubleshooting a laptop. He decides to boot the computer into VGA mode from the ABOM.

What is the default display resolution for this mode?

(i) 1280 x 800

(ii) 1366 x 768

(iii) 640 x 480

(iv) 1920 x 1080

19. Which cable type is used for carrying satellite television signals?

(i) Coaxial

(ii) UTP

(iii) STP

(iv) Plenum-rated

20. Which of the following are the primary benefits of using static IP addressing? (Select all applicable answers.)

(i) Static IP addressing is a prerequisite when setting up and configuring a publicly accessible web server. Hence, a static IP address assigned to a web server makes it easier for computers to locate the server from anywhere in the world.

(ii) A system administrator can set up and configure PC workstations connected to a network that can be easily pinged and troubleshot from a central location.

(iii) Since static IP addresses are simpler to assign and maintain, it becomes easier for network administrators to monitor network traffic and assign network resource access to authorised users based on IP address identification.

(iv) Static IP addressing is regularly used when setting up and configuring computer workstations that allow remote access over a closed network. This allows different types of computers running different types of operating systems external to the closed network to access the host computer system by searching for the same IP address every time.

Practice Test 1			
MCQ Solutions			
1.	True	11.	See notes
2.	(ii)	12.	(iii), (iv)
3.	True	13.	True
4.	(iv)	14.	(ii)
5.	False	15.	(ii)
6.	(i)	16.	(ii), (iv)
7.	True	17.	(i)
8.	(ii)	18.	(iii)
9.	(iii), (iv)	19.	(i)
10.	(ii)	20.	(i), (ii), (iii), (iv)

1. True. MOV is an acronym for Metal Oxide Varistor.

2. Correct: (ii). If memory is added to a PC workstation and memory errors occur during boot-up, it is highly likely that the new RAM module runs at a lower speed than the pre-existing memory module in Bank 1.

3. True. PCL is an acronym for Printer Control Language. PostScript is also oftentimes referred to as PS. Both PCL and PS are the two most commonly used PDLs (Page Description Language). PDLs are special purpose languages or coding that translate various computer languages into a format that printing devices can understand. While PCL is trademarked by Hewlett Packard (HP), PostScript is a PDL that was originally developed by Adobe. PCL is device dependent which means that it uses the printer hardware to perform its printing tasks. Contrariwise, PostScript is device independent which means that this PDL performs its printing function without needing any hardware support.

4. Correct: (iv). It is highly likely that the toner cartridge needs to be replaced.

5. False. According to the scenario, the PC is connected to a known working AC outlet. Hence, it is not necessary to check the AC outlet as a potential cause of the power issue affecting the PC. Instead, it is recommended to test the IEC cable initially before checking the PSU, 24-pin ATX 12V 2.x power connector, voltage selector, etc.

6. Correct: (i). It is very likely that the air-cooling fans in the computer case are starting to fail.

7. True.

8. Correct: (ii). The ping [IP address] -l command and switch pings the specified IP address with X bytes of data packets (e.g. 1500 bytes) 4 times.

9. Correct: (iii) Netstat -n shows the network statistics for a local computer in a numerical format only and (iv) The netstat -n command specifies the number of active connections open on a network at any given point in time.

10. Correct: (ii) Use the format command with the /p parameter.

11. Multi-mode optic fiber (otherwise known as MMF).

12. Correct: (iii) and (iv). Any high-speed ethernet cable is compatible with fiber optic connectors, i.e. 1,000 Mbps (1 Gbps) and 10 Gbps ethernet cables, respectively.

13. True.

14. Correct: (ii) Modem.

15. Correct: (ii) Failed video card. A failed video card is the most likely cause of this particular issue. Since the technician can still hear the case fans, this indicates that the power supply (PSU) is still operational and providing power to the motherboard. A faulty inverter or burned-out backlight would cause the monitor to go blank without warning, but this event would not necessarily be accompanied by smoke emanating from the computer case. Thus, the most likely cause in this situation is a defective video card.

16. Correct: (ii) and (iv). A system repeatedly locking up or freezing is a common indication of a failing power supply unit (PSU). This is usually because of voltage spikes or sags due to the failing PSU. In some situations, repeated failure of a computer system's HDDs may indicate that the PSU is starting to become defective.

17. Correct: (i) BD-R (Blu-ray drive).

18. Correct: (iii) VGA mode: 640 x 480 pixels. ABOM is an acronym for Advanced Boot Options Menu. The other display resolutions listed in the question are commonly found in laptops: (a) WXGA (Widescreen Extended Graphics Array) 1280 x 800. (b) HD Ready (High Definition Ready) 1366 x 768. (c) Full HD (Full High Definition) 1920 x 1080. Full HD or 1080P is a common video resolution found on laptops nowadays.

19. Correct: (i) Coaxial cable.

20. Correct: (i), (ii), (iii), and (iv).

Practice Test 2

1. The LAN in a large workplace needs to be set up using the most common cabling and wiring standard.

What is the name of this TIA/EIA network standard?

(i) ANSI

(ii) T568A

(iii) T568B

(iv) 802.3af

2. The thermal printer module that forms part of a cash register at a service station has started to print light and barely readable text.

What is the most likely cause of this issue?

(i) High humidity

(ii) Moisture

(iii) Dirty heating element

(iv) Worn print ribbon

3. A maintenance technician has recently installed a duplexing assembly into an office laser printer.

What does the duplexing assembly enable the printer to do?

(i) A duplexing device enables a black-and-white laser printer to produce color printouts

(ii) High-speed data transmission between a network computer and a laser printer is permitted via the use of a duplexing assembly installed in the laser printer, thereby facilitating comparatively faster printing

(iii) A duplexing assembly enables a laser printer to print on both sides of paper

(iv) None of the above

4. A computer technician is reviewing the settings in a PC's BIOS. Which of the following changes can the technician make within the Integrated Peripherals section of the BIOS?

(i) Adjust the CPU's operating voltage

(ii) Change the CPU's permitted temperature threshold

(iii) Enable or disable on-board devices

(iv) Enable or disable virtualization support

5. Which of the following connections allow devices to be connected to a PC at distances greater than 20 feet (6 meters) using a single cable? (Select two answers.)

(i) IEEE 1394

(ii) Thunderbolt

(iii) USB 2.0

(iv) USB 3.0

6. What is the primary function of the Northbridge chipset on an ATX motherboard?

(i) The Northbridge chipset handles communications between the CPU, RAM, and PCIe (or AGP) video cards

(ii) The Northbridge is the chip that controls all of a computer's I/O functions, such as USB, audio, serial, ISA bus, interrupt controller, and IDE channels

(iii) The primary function of the Northbridge is to handle and store the BIOS configuration settings of the motherboard

(iv) None of the above

7. Which of the following IEEE Wi-Fi standards are most likely to be affected by the activity of wireless phones, Bluetooth devices, and microwaves?

(i) 802.11a

(ii) 802.11a and 802.11b

(iii) 802.11b and 802.11g

(iv) 802.11b, 802.11g, and 802.11n

8. Which type of networking cable would be the best choice to use underneath the floor of a building?

(i) Cat 3 UTP

(ii) Coaxial

(iii) Plenum-grade Cat 5e UTP

(iv) STP

9. A technician has been requested to troubleshoot a computer workstation that will not boot. However, the technician notices that the case fans are running as normal.

What is the most likely cause of this issue? (Select two possible answers.)

(i) Defective PSU

(ii) 24-pin ATX 12V 2.1 power connector is loose

(iii) Faulty CMOS battery

(iv) 24-pin ATX 12V 2.1 power connector is not seated properly

10. Which connection type is primarily used with a computer (as opposed to a TV) and carries both a digital and analog signal?

(i) DVI-A

(ii) DVI-D

(iii) DVI-I

(iv) micro-HDMI

11. Which media type is the best choice for large backups in a corporate environment?

(i) Blu-ray

(ii) CD-ROM

(iii) DVD

(iv) Tape

12. What is the maximum data transfer rate of a SATA 3.2 HDD?

(i) 1.5 Gbps

(ii) 5 Gbps

(iii) 6 Gbps

(iv) 16 Gbps

13. True or False: A 15-pin connector supplies power from the PSU to devices on an ATX motherboard such as case fans, optical drives, and IDE PATA hard drives.

14. A customer has informed their local PC repair shop that their flat panel LCD monitor has several faulty pixels. The customer complains that the faulty pixels are affecting her concentration as she can see them in her peripheral visual field as she works on an important project.

Which pixel color will most likely require the LCD display to be replaced?

(i) Black

(ii) Blue

(iii) Green

(iv) Yellow

(v) None of the above

15. What network cabling variety has four twisted pairs?

(i) EMI

(ii) MMF

(iii) SMF

(iv) UTP

16. An Apple® MacBook™ user recently purchased a new external SATA HDD. The user intends to back up important files and documents to this external HDD. However, he does not recognize the connector type.

What type of connector would the user most likely have encountered?

(i) eSATA

(ii) Thunderbolt

(iii) HDMI Type D

(iv) micro USB

17. Which unit of measurement is typically used to demonstrate the effectiveness and throughput speed of computer air cooling systems?

(i) CDMA

(ii) CFM

(iii) DTR

(iv) TDP

18. A Dell® Inspiron™ laptop user receives an on-screen notification stating "No connections are available" when he is trying to locate his usual wireless network.

What is the most likely cause as to why the laptop user is not finding the correct network?

(i) Hidden SSID

(ii) Wireless turned off

(iii) Disabled wireless NIC

(iv) Incorrect firewall settings

19. An English Literature student has noticed that whenever she puts her Android™ smartphone too close to her wallet, the smartphone makes a beeping sound. The student is concerned that her new smartphone is faulty, and therefore she visits a mobile phone repair shop for advice.

What do you think the technician is going to tell the student?

(i) Android™ OS is intermittently updating

(ii) NFC is enabled

(iii) NFC is disabled

(iv) Smartphone's antenna is faulty

20. A marketing executive has recently relocated from Europe to the United States as part of a corporate restructuring program. However, the executive has been unable to power up his PC since his arrival in

Seattle. The PC never posed any problems to the executive when he was working in Frankfurt, Germany.

What is the most likely issue with the PC?

(i) PSU has become defective

(ii) Dual voltage selector is improperly set

(iii) IEC cable has become loose

(iv) 24-pin ATX motherboard power connector is damaged

Practice Test 2			
MCQ Solutions			
1.	(iii)	11.	(iv)
2.	(iii)	12.	(iv)
3.	(iii)	13.	False
4.	(iii)	14.	(i)
5.	(i), (ii)	15.	(iv)
6.	(i)	16.	(ii)
7.	(iii)	17.	(ii)
8.	(iii)	18.	(i)
9.	(ii), (iv)	19.	(ii)
10.	(iii)	20.	(ii)

1. Correct: (iii) T568B. The TIA/EIA network cabling and wiring standards are devised by the Telecommunications Industry Association and Electronic Industries Alliance, respectively.

2. Correct: (iii). The thermal printer has a dirty heating element.

3. Correct: (iii) A duplexing assembly enables a laser printer to print on both sides of paper.

4. Correct: (iii) Enable or disable on-board devices.

5. Correct: (i) and (ii). IEEE 1394 (Firewire) and Thunderbolt.

6. Correct: (i) The Northbridge chipset of an ATX motherboard typically handles communications between the CPU, RAM, and PCIe (or AGP) video cards. The Northbridge may also have an EATX12V 4-pin or 8-pin CPU power connector. In actuality, most of today's ATX motherboards are equipped with this additional 4-pin or 8-pin 12 V power connector for the CPU. (Please note that AGP is an acronym for Accelerated Graphics Port and PCIe stands for Peripheral Component Interconnect Express.)

7. Correct: (iii) 802.11b and 802.11g.

8. Correct: (iii) Plenum-grade Category 5e UTP cable. UTP is an acronym for Unshielded Twisted Pair.

9. Correct: (ii) and (iv). In this scenario, it is very likely the main 24-pin power cable from the ATX 12V 2.x PSU to the motherboard is not seated properly or has become loose. The PSU seems to be functioning as per normal considering that the case fans are receiving power and are operating normally. The case fans normally receive power from the PSU by means of a 4-pin Molex connector. Molex connectors typically supply power to case fans, IDE hard drives, and some optical drives. Molex connectors have 4 wires: red (5 V), yellow (12 V), and two black ground wires (0 V).

10. Correct: (iii) DVI-I connector.

11. Correct: (iv) Tape. If a large organisation (such as a corporation) needs to back up several gigabytes of data on a regular basis, the best storage media to employ is tape storage media, such as LTO (Linear Tape-Open), or the older DLT (Digital Linear Tape).

12. Correct: (iv) The maximum data transfer rate (DTR) of SATA 3.2 is 16 Gbps (1969 MB/s). (1) The maximum DTR of SATA 1.0 is 1.5 Gbps (150 MB/s). (2) SATA 2.0 3 Gbps (300 MB/s). (3) SATA 3.0 6 Gbps (600 MB/s). (4) USB 3.0 (SuperSpeed USB) has a maximum DTR of 5 Gbps.

13. False. A 4-pin Molex power connector supplies power to case fans, optical drives, and older legacy IDE PATA hard drives. A 15-pin SATA power connector supplies power to SATA hard drives and, in some situations, optical drives.

14. Correct: (i) Black pixels, which are referred to as "dead pixels". Dead pixels are rarely fixable.

15. Correct: (iv) UTP. UTP is an acronym for Unshielded Twisted Pair network cabling.

16. Correct: (ii) Thunderbolt connector (otherwise known as a lightning connector). Thunderbolt connectors are commonly used with Apple computers and associated peripherals (e.g., external HDDs, etc.).

17. Correct: (ii) Cubic Feet per Minute (CFM).

18. Correct: (i) Hidden SSID. The wireless network's SSID (Service Set Identifier) is not being broadcast, therefore the user's laptop cannot detect the network in this scenario. Naturally, we are assuming that the user has turned on his laptop's wireless functionality and that the laptop's wireless NIC (Network Interface Controller) is operating as normal.

19. Correct: (ii) NFC is enabled. The smartphone is not faulty. The most likely reason for the beeping sound is that the phone's NFC (Near Field Communication) functionality is enabled. NFC is a set of communication protocols that enable two electronic devices, one of which is usually a portable device such as a smartphone, to establish communication by bringing the devices within 4 cm (1.6 inches) of each other. NFC-enabled devices are commonly used in contactless payment systems, similar to those used by credit/debit cards and electronic ticket smartcards, and therefore allow mobile contactless payment methods to pay for everyday transactions. In the scenario, assuming that NFC is enabled on the student's Android smartphone, the smartphone will try to read data encoded on any debit/credit cards in the student's wallet once the NFC-enabled phone is brought into close proximity with the wallet, resulting in a beeping sound.

20. Correct: (ii) The dual voltage selector on the PC's power supply unit (PSU) is improperly set.

Practice Test 3

1. Which motherboard technology divides the RAM slots into different colors?

(i) Single-channel

(ii) Dual-channel

(iii) Full duplex

(iv) FM2+

2. Which chipset determines where data will be stored in a computer's RAM?

(i) Southbridge

(ii) Northbridge

(iii) EEPROM

(iv) PROM

3. What tool can be used to numerically display the amount of voltage that comes from an AC outlet?

(i) Power supply tester

(ii) AC receptacle tester

(iii) Cable certifier

(iv) Multimeter

4. True or False: A brownout is a sudden and unexpected increase in voltage that can cause computers to shut down.

5. A technician working in a large distribution center has been asked to connect wireless earpieces to company-issued smartphones. This is to ensure that drivers can operate their articulated vehicles safely while speaking on the phone.

Which technology would you advise the technician to use in this situation?

(i) Wi-Fi

(ii) Bluetooth

(iii) NFC

(iv) WiMAX

6. How many colors, approximately, does a 32-bit Windows® OS have?

(i) 256

(ii) 65,536

(iii) 16.78 million

(iv) 4.29 billion

7. A very successful design studio located in London, England allows its employees to use their own mobile devices to carry out work-related tasks.

What is this organizational policy known as?

(i) BYOD

(ii) DRM

(iii) EULA

(iv) SSO

8. You are the senior IT technician for a large transnational company. The Director of IT has asked you if there are viable alternatives to the standard username and password when employees log on to their workstations.

Which of the following peripherals could potentially be used as alternative log-on methods for employees? (Select two answers.)

(i) Biometric device

(ii) KVM switch

(iii) Smart card reader

(iv) USB key

9. Which fiber optic cable connector has a bayonet tip?

(i) F-connector

(ii) LC

(iii) RJ45

(iv) ST

10. A company's LAN is set up on the basis of DHCP networking. Recently, new PC workstations have been added to the network. One user has reported to the IT department that her computer has generated a system error message:

Error: There is an IP conflict with another device on the network. Unable to access network resources. Please try again later.

The user also confirmed that her workstation operated properly up until recently.

(a) What is the most likely cause of this networking error? (Select the best answer.)

(i) DHCP server has "crashed" and needs to be power cycled

(ii) DNS resolver cache has become corrupt

(iii) The local computer's NetBIOS settings have become misconfigured

(iv) There is a duplicate IP address registered on the network

(b) How would you resolve this error?

(i) Ping the local computer before rebooting the system

(ii) Run the ipconfig /flushdns command using the CLI tool and then restart the computer

(iii) Run the ipconfig /release command using the CLI tool and then restart the computer

(iv) Troubleshoot and, if necessary, replace the local computer's NIC

11. Which wireless technology requires an unobstructed "line of sight" between devices?

(i) IR

(ii) NFC

(iii) Bluetooth

(iv) GSM

12. What type of network can be created by means of a Bluetooth connection?

(i) LAN

(ii) MAN

(iii) PAN

(iv) WLAN

13. An employee working for a prestigious software development firm reports that she is unable to decrypt email messages using her company-issued mobile device. The firm's IT technician has noticed that her mobile device does not have the correct digital certificate.

What else could be potentially missing from the user's mobile device? (Select one answer.)

(i) POP3

(ii) Private key

(iii) Public key

(iv) SSL certificate

14. A computer technician has installed a new 2 GB Corsair® DDR3 SODIMM module into a Samsung® Chromebook™ laptop which already has a pre-existing older generation 2 GB Corsair® memory stick. She confirms that the new SODIMM module is compatible with the motherboard.

However, when the computer is eventually rebooted and the technician reviews the BIOS settings, she discovers that the BIOS still only recognizes 2 GB RAM.

What do you think the technician should do to resolve the issue?

(i) Upgrade the CPU

(ii) Replace the RAM modules

(iii) Flash the BIOS

(iv) Re-seat the RAM modules

15. What type of laptop display uses a backlight?

(i) CRT

(ii) LCD

(iii) Plasma

(iv) VDU

16. Which device enables multiple PC workstations to be controlled from one keyboard, monitor, and mouse?

(i) Ethernet switch

(ii) KVM switch

(iii) STB

(iv) USB hub

17. Which type of video connector is primarily used with a computer (as opposed to a Smart TV) and carries an analog signal?

(i) DVI-A

(ii) DVI-I

(iii) HDMI Type A

(iv) M1-DA

18. Which of the following allows a mobile device (e.g., smartphone) to access 4G signals?

(i) Wi-Fi card

(ii) Cellular card

(iii) Bluetooth dongle

(iv) NIC

19. A technician is installing a new touchscreen monitor for a Windows® 8.0 OS workstation in a small bank branch.

Which of the following cable connections will be required to ensure that the touchscreen monitor will function properly? (Select three answers.)

(i) Ethernet

(ii) Power

(iii) USB

(iv) Video

20. A technician is configuring a router for an accountancy practice. In the interests of network security, the technician wants to ensure that the router assigns its public IP address to all data packets heading to external networks (e.g., Internet), thereby ensuring that the originating sources of data packets on the network (e.g., client workstations) remain hidden.

Which feature of the router should be enabled to enhance network security?

(i) Channel

(ii) NAS

(iii) NAT

(iv) WEP

Practice Test 3			
MCQ Solutions			
1.	(ii)	11.	(i)
2.	(ii)	12.	(iii)
3.	(iv)	13.	(ii)
4.	False	14.	(iii)
5.	(ii)	15.	(ii)
6.	(iv)	16.	(ii)
7.	(i)	17.	(i)
8.	(i), (iii)	18.	(ii)
9.	(iv)	19.	(ii), (iii), (iv)
10.	(a)(iv), (b)(iii)	20.	(iii)

1. Correct: (ii) Dual-channel RAM technology.

2. Correct: (ii) Northbridge. The northbridge chipset, specifically the memory controller chip, is responsible for transferring data to RAM and retrieving data from RAM. PROM is an acronym for Programmable Read Only Memory and EEPROM stands for Electrically Erasable Programmable Read Only Memory.

3. Correct: (iv) Multimeter.

4. False. A brownout is a sudden and unexpected drop in voltage that can cause computer systems to shut down.

5. Correct: (ii) Bluetooth.

6. Correct: (iv) Approximately 4.29 billion colors. An 8-bit color depth in Windows OS has 256 colors, 16-bit corresponds to 65,536 colors, 24-bit corresponds to approximately 16.78 million colors, and 32-bit color depth has approximately 4.29 billion colors.

7. Correct: (i) BYOD (Bring Your Own Device).

8. Correct: (i) Biometric device (e.g., fingerprint scanner, retinal scanner, etc.) and (iii) Smart card reader.

9. Correct: (iv) ST (Straight Tip) connector. (1) LC and ST are types of fiber optic connectors. The distinguishing characteristic of a ST connector is that it features a bayonet-like tip. (2) The F-connector is commonly used for "over the air" terrestrial television, cable television, and satellite television, as well as with cable modems for Internet access, typically using RG-6 coaxial cable or, in older installations, RG-59 coaxial cable. (3) RJ45 is the connector that is used on twisted-pair patch cables.

10. **(a)** (iv) In this scenario, it is very probable that there is a duplicate IP address registered on the network – in other words, two network devices have been inadvertently assigned the same IP address. Consequently, this duplicate IP addressing causes an IP conflict on the network. **(b)** (iii) Run the ipconfig/ release command using the CLI tool and then restart the computer.

11. Correct: (i) IR (infrared) technology. NFC refers to Near Field Communication and GSM is an acronym for Global System for Mobile Communication.

12. Correct: (iii) PAN (Personal Area Network).

13. Correct: (ii) Private key. The user's mobile device will require both a private key and a valid digital SSL certificate to download and decrypt email messages. SSL (Secure Sockets Layer) is a standard security technology for establishing an encrypted link between a server and a client computer – typically a web server and a browser (e.g., Google Chrome, Microsoft Edge, etc.), or a mail server and a mail client (e.g., Microsoft Outlook, Google Gmail, etc.). SSL certificates have a key pair: a public key and a private key. These keys work together to establish an encrypted, secure connection. The SSL certificate also contains "subject" information, which is the identity of the certificate or website owner.

14. Correct: (iii) Flash the BIOS. In this scenario, we are told that the new RAM module is supposedly compatible with the motherboard. However, the computer system does not recognize the new RAM version. Hence, the BIOS utility only shows 2 GB RAM even though the technician had increased the laptop's RAM capacity to 4 GB. In all probability, the RAM module is so new that the motherboard does not yet have the required firmware to recognize the new memory. So, it will be necessary to upgrade (or "flash") the BIOS firmware before re-booting the laptop.

15. Correct: (ii) LCD (Liquid Crystal Display).

16. Correct: (ii) KVM switch. KVM is an acronym for Keyboard, Video, and Mouse.

17. Correct: (i) DVI-A connector.

18. Correct: (ii) Cellular card.

19. Correct: (ii) Power cable, (iii) USB cable, and (iv) Video cable.

20. Correct: (iii) NAT (Network Address Translation).

Practice Test 4

1. A PC technician is in the process of installing a newly purchased ATX motherboard in a PC case. Before installing the motherboard, what would you recommend the technician to do first?

(i) Verify that the new motherboard is compatible with the specifications of the PC case

(ii) Install the CPU into the LGA socket before installing the motherboard into the PC case

(iii) Employ appropriate ESD prevention methods and tools

(iv) Test the motherboard with a multimeter

2. A typical Northbridge/Southbridge motherboard configuration is depicted in *Figure 1.*

Identify the components labelled A, B, C, and D.

3. True or False: Speakers are normally plugged into a type of port known as a 1/8-inch (3.5 mm) TRS mini-jack.

4. Fill in the missing space: An x16 card is normally plugged into an expansion slot on a motherboard called a ______.

5. What type of form factor normally uses a single 24-pin power connector?

(i) ATX

(ii) HTPC

(iii) Mobile-ITX

(iv) Pico-ITX

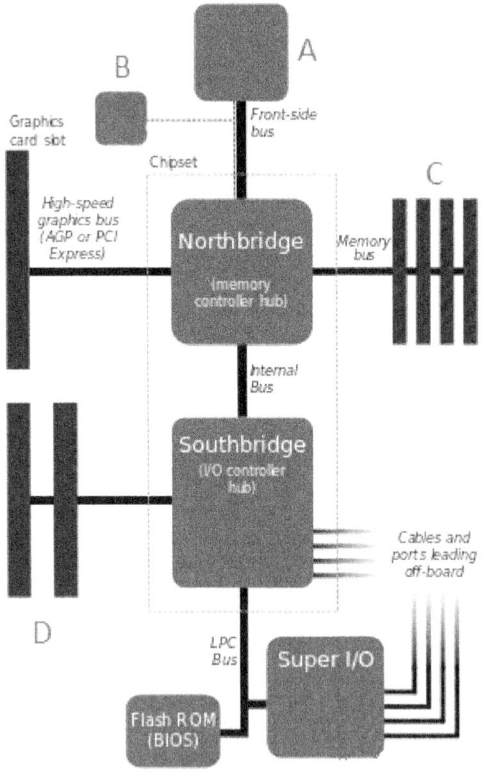

Figure 1

6. True or False: A PGA is a common type of CPU for a smartphone.

7. To prevent damage to a computer system and other sensitive electronic equipment, a computer should be connected to which of the following devices?

(i) Power strip

(ii) Power inverter

(iii) UPS unit

(iv) AC power conditioner

8. Which of the following is the default subnet mask for the IP address 192.162.1.10?

(i) 255.0.0.0

(ii) 255.255.255.0

(iii) FE80::/10

(iv) FF00::/8

9. How many pins does a SATA HDD data connector have?

(i) 4

(ii) 7

(iii) 15

(iv) 24

10. What is the maximum data transfer rate of USB 3.0?

(i) 400 Mbps

(ii) 480 Mbps

(iii) 5 Gbps

(iv) 10 Gbps

11. A PC user in a SOHO environment is installing a wireless keyboard to a computer.

What type of dongle does the PC require to enable connectivity to the wireless keyboard?

(i) Bluetooth

(ii) NFC

(iii) WiMAX

(iv) None of the above

12. What is the name of the networking device that connects multiple computer workstations together in a wired LAN environment?

(i) Cat 6

(ii) Ethernet switch

(iii) Network interface controller

(iv) Router

13. Which type of form factor is commonly found in HTPCs?

(i) ATX

(ii) micro-ATX

(iii) mobile-ITX

(iv) nano-ITX

14. What is the term that is used to describe the transmission and receiving of data at the same time?

(i) Duplexing

(ii) Half duplex

(iii) Full duplex

(iv) Simultaneous transfer

(v) None of the above

15. Which networking protocol uses port 3389?

(i) Telnet

(ii) RDP

(iii) SMTP

(iv) SSH

16. An IT technician has finished servicing a company laptop and he has certified that the Windows® 8.1 OS laptop is in perfect working condition. However, one week later, the Director of Quality Systems reports to the company's IT helpdesk that the laptop cannot access the wireless network. No other users within the company have reported experiencing any networking issues with their mobile devices.

What are the possible reasons for the laptop's inability to access the wireless network? (Select three answers.)

(i) Faulty network adapter

(ii) Airplane mode is on

(iii) "Forgotten" wireless network

(iv) WAPs are out of range

(v) Function key for wireless connectivity was accidentally pressed

17. A color laser printer has recently produced images that are tinted green.

What would you do initially to troubleshoot this specific issue?

(i) Calibrate the laser printer

(ii) Clean the imaging drum with a dry lint-free cloth

(iii) Replace the laser printer's duplexing assembly

(iv) Use isopropyl alcohol or another suitable solvent to clean the primary corona wire

18. True or False: UTP cables, coaxials, and Category 7 cables all have a gold transmission medium.

19. Which of the following items has the fastest data throughput?

(i) CD-ROM

(ii) USB 3.0

(iii) SATA HDD

(iv) RAM

20. Which statement regarding LGA and PGA sockets is correct? (Select one answer.)

(i) LGA is a type of CPU socket on a motherboard that uses "lands" to connect the socket to the CPU

(ii) LGA is a type of CPU socket on a motherboard that uses a series of moveable "levers" to embed the CPU in the motherboard

(iii) PGA sockets have a multitude of tiny protrusions that facilitate connectivity between the processor and the motherboard

(iv) PGA sockets are a type of specialized motherboard socket into which the Northbridge chipset is installed

Practice Test 4			
MCQ Solutions			
1.	(iii)	11.	(i)
2.	See notes	12.	(ii)
3.	True	13.	(ii)
4.	See notes	14.	(iii)
5.	(i)	15.	(ii)
6.	False	16.	(ii), (iii), (v)
7.	(iii)	17.	(i)
8.	(ii)	18.	False
9.	(ii)	19.	(iv)
10.	(iii)	20.	(i)

1. Correct: (iii). The technician should employ appropriate ESD prevention methods and tools: Before working with any computer components outside or inside a computer case, it is vitally important to always employ standard ESD prevention methods.

2. A = CPU. B = Clock generator (otherwise known as a Real-Time Clock or RTC). C = RAM memory slots. D = PCI slots.

3. True.

4. PCIe (Peripheral Component Interconnect Express).

5. Correct: (i) ATX. (1) An ATX 12V 2.x form factor (e.g., ATX 12V 2.1, ATX 12V 2.2, or higher) typically uses a 24-pin power connector. (2) Moreover, a smaller version of the standard ATX motherboard, known as microATX (mATX), is explicitly designed to be backward-compatible with ATX motherboards. The mounting points of microATX motherboards (9.6 x 9.6 inches) are a subset of those used on standard ATX motherboards, and the I/O panel is also identical on both mATX and full-size ATX motherboards. Hence, most microATX motherboards can be installed in full-size ATX computer cases since most microATX motherboards typically use the same power connectors as standard ATX motherboards. (3) Accordingly, both ATX and microATX motherboards use a 24-pin power connector (since full-size ATX power supplies are generally designed to be compatible with microATX boards).

6. False. A SoC (System on a Chip) is a common type of CPU for a smartphone.

7. Correct: (iii) UPS (Uninterrupted Power Supply) unit. An AC power conditioner is also known as a line conditioner.

8. Correct: (ii) 255.255.255.0. IP addresses in the range 192 to 223 are normally associated with SOHO (Small Office/Home Office) networks, and such IP addresses are classified as belonging to IP Class C. The default subnet mask for Class C IP addresses is 255.255.255.0 (net.net.net.node).

9. Correct: (ii) 7 pins.

10. Correct: (iii) 5 Gbps (gigabits per second). (1) IEEE 1394a (Firewire 400) has a maximum data transfer rate (DTR) of 400 Mbps (megabits per second) and IEEE 1394b (Firewire 800) has a maximum DTR of 800 Mbps. (2) USB 2.0 has a maximum DTR of 480 Mbps. (3) USB 3.0 (SuperSpeed USB) 5 Gbps. (4) USB 3.1 Gen 2 10 Gbps.

11. Correct: (i) Bluetooth dongle.

12. Correct: (ii) Ethernet switch.

13. Correct: (ii) micro-ATX. HTPCs (Home Theatre PCs) typically use a micro-ATX form factor.

14. Correct: (iii) Full duplex.

15. Correct: (ii) RDP (Remote Desktop Protocol).

16. Correct: (ii), (iii), and (v). (ii) The laptop's Airplane Mode has been accidentally activated. (iii) The wireless network was "forgotten" in the laptop's Windows OS. (v) The laptop's function key for wireless was accidentally pressed, thereby deactivating the laptop's NIC (Network Interface Controller).

17. Correct: (i) Calibrate the laser printer. In this scenario, the first troubleshooting step would be to calibrate the laser printer. If unsuccessful, the technician would have to consider other potential troubleshooting steps to remedy the issue.

18. False. UTP cables, coaxial cables, and Category 7 cables all have a copper transmission medium.

19. Correct: (iv) RAM (Random Access Memory).

20. Correct: (i) LGA means "Land Grid Array" and it is a type of CPU socket on a motherboard that uses "lands" to connect the socket to the CPU. PGA means "Pin Grid Array." PGA sockets are another type of motherboard socket into which the CPU is installed. PGA sockets have pinholes that ensure connectivity to the CPU's copper pins.

Practice Test 5

1. True or False: STP cable is not resistant to EMI.

2. What port number is used by HTTP?

(i) 23

(ii) 80

(iii) 427

(iv) 443

3. What is the name of the RAM module that is normally installed in tablet computers and smartphones?

(i) LPDDR

(ii) SODIMM

(iii) eMMC

(iv) SRAM

4. Which type of memory do most mobile devices, such as tablet computers and smartphones, store long-term data to?

(i) SATA HDD

(ii) SCSI

(iii) SoC

(iv) Solid-state flash memory

5. Fill in the missing space: Moving a CPU's processing speed beyond its normal operating range or frequency is called ______.

6. True or False: MIDI connections are used in conjunction with musical equipment.

7. Fill in the missing space: XPS and PRN are both examples of ______ printing.

8. Using the CLI tool, which command displays a NIC's MAC address?

(i) arp -a

(ii) ipconfig

(iii) ipconfig /all

(iv) netstat -a

9. True or False: IPv6 addresses use 32-bits.

10. A senior partner in a prestigious law office wants to rip the contents of an audio CD to a compressed file format that can be easily read using Windows® OS PCs, Linux® computers, and Apple® Mac™ computers.

Which file format should be selected in this situation?

(i) *.bmp

(ii) *.docx

(iii) *.jpeg

(iv) *.mp3

11. Which of the following tools can be used by a computer technician to test an AC outlet? (Select two answers.)

(i) Multimeter

(ii) POST card

(iii) PSU tester

(iv) Receptacle tester

12. A large manufacturing facility predominantly relies on its server room installations for computing resources and, as a result, is less dependent upon the computing power of its client workstations.

In this scenario, what term is commonly used to describe these client workstations?

(i) Thin clients

(ii) Thick clients

(iii) Virtual machines

(iv) Heavy clients

13. What type of cable should be used to directly connect a laptop to a PC?

(i) Cat 5e crossover cable

(ii) SMF

(iii) USB 3.1 cable

(iv) None of the above

14. A PC user observes that the lights on her computer's keyboard repeatedly flicker during POST.

What would this sequence of events tell a technician?

(i) Keyboard's USB cable is loose

(ii) BIOS firmware is automatically updating

(iii) Hardware error

(iv) Corrupt keyboard driver

15. A Windows® 8.0 OS computer is unable to access the Internet. However, all other PC users in the office report no difficulties connecting to the Internet.

Which of the following is the first step an IT technician should take when investigating this particular issue?

(i) Check Windows® firewall settings

(ii) Check the NIC driver

(iii) Check the patch cable

(iv) Check the NIC

16. Fill in the missing spaces: Historically, original ATX PSUs connected to the motherboard using a ______-pin connector. However, nowadays, newer ATX 12V 2.x

PSUs connect to the motherboard with a ______-pin connector.

17. True or False: 32-bit CPUs can only communicate with a maximum of 2 GB of RAM.

18. Which of the following are possible symptoms of a failing CPU? (Select all applicable answers.)

(i) System lockups

(ii) Singular BSOD event

(iii) CPU temperature in BIOS is beyond its recommended range

(iv) Beeping codes during POST

(v) Recurrent video card failure

(vi) CPU is operating beyond its recommended voltage range

Figure 2

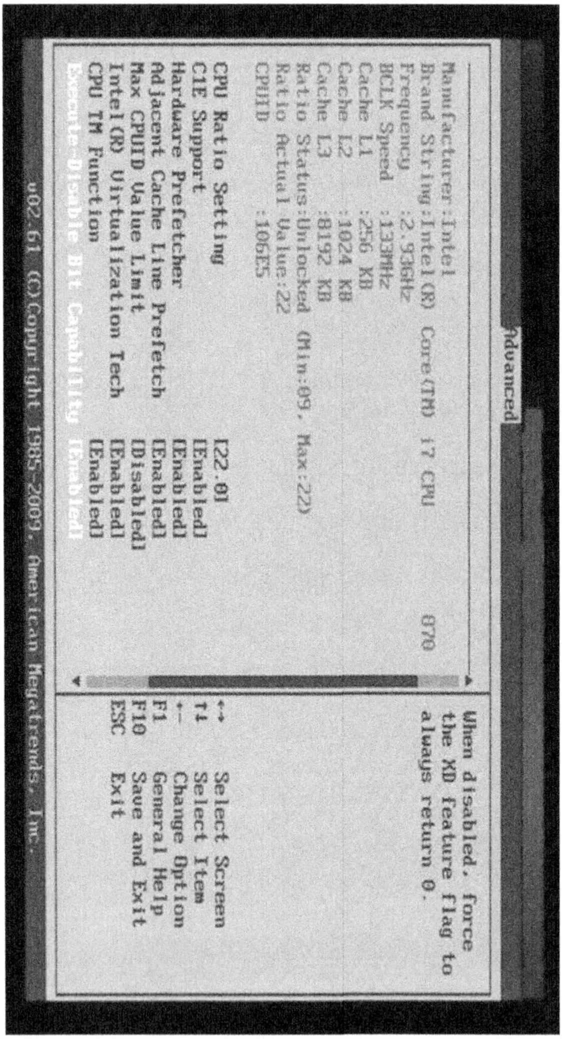
Advanced
Manufacturer:Intel
Brand String:Intel(R) Core(TM) i7 CPU 870
Frequency :2.93GHz
BCLK Speed :133MHz
Cache L1 :256 KB
Cache L2 :1024 KB
Cache L3 :8192 KB
Ratio Status:Unlocked (Min:09, Max:22)
Ratio Actual Value:22
CPUID :106E5
CPU Ratio Setting [22.0]
C1E Support [Enabled]
Hardware Prefetcher [Enabled]
Adjacent Cache Line Prefetch [Enabled]
Max CPUID Value Limit [Disabled]
Intel(R) Virtualization Tech [Enabled]
CPU TM Function [Enabled]
Execute-Disable Bit Capability [Enabled]
When disabled, force the XD feature flag to always return 0.
←→ Select Screen
↑↓ Select Item
+- Change Option
F1 General Help
F10 Save and Exit
ESC Exit
v02.61 (C)Copyright 1985-2009, American Megatrends, Inc.

19. On the basis of the information presented in *Figure 2*, answer the following questions.

(a) Identify the screen depicted in the figure.

(b) What is the name of the CPU installed on the motherboard?

(c) State the processing frequency of the CPU.

(d) State the capacity, in kilobytes, of the CPU's fastest cache memory.

(e) What is the computer's base clock speed?

(f) Does this computer have a hypervisor?

20. A PC repair technician is replacing the LCD screen of a laptop.

What tool should the technician use to minimise the risk of damage to the plastic casing when removing the LCD screen?

(i) Crimper

(ii) Phillips-head screwdriver

(iii) Plastic shim

(iv) Torx screwdriver

Practice Test 5			
MCQ Solutions			
1.	False	11.	(i), (iv)
2.	(ii)	12.	(i)
3.	(i)	13.	(i)
4.	(iv)	14.	(iii)
5.	See notes	15.	(iii)
6.	True	16.	See notes
7.	See notes	17.	False
8.	(iii)	18.	(i), (iii), (iv), (v)
9.	False	19.	See notes
10.	(iv)	20.	(iii)

1. False. STP (Shielded Twisted Pair) cable is resistant to EMI (Electromagnetic Interference). STP cables include special metal shielding over each pair of wires within each STP cable, thus reducing external EMI and the risk of unauthorized network access.

2. Correct: (ii) HTTP (Hypertext Transfer Protocol) uses port 80.

3. Correct: (i) LPDDR RAM. This RAM module is similar to the DDR standard that PCs use, but it has a much smaller form factor.

4. Correct: (iv) Solid-state flash memory. Mobile devices such as tablet computers and smartphones do not store long-term data to SATA magnetic disks or SATA SSDs (Solid State Disks). Instead, such mobile devices store long-term data to solid-state flash memory.

5. Overclocking. The completed statement should read: "Moving a CPU's processing speed beyond its normal operating range or frequency is called overclocking."

6. True. MIDI (Musical Instrument Device Interface) connectors are typically used with musical equipment.

7. Virtual. The completed statement should read: "XPS and PRN are both examples of virtual printing."

8. Correct: (iii). The ipconfig /all command displays a network interface card's MAC address.

9. False. IPv6 addresses use 128-bits.

10. Correct: (iv) *.mp3 file format.

11. Correct: (i) Multimeter and (iv) Receptacle tester.

12. Correct: (i) Thin clients. (1) In the given scenario, the client workstations are commonly referred to as thin clients, since most of the computing requirements of the manufacturing facility are handled by its server farm. (2) On the other hand, thick clients (otherwise known as fat clients or heavy clients) are fully featured computers that are connected to a network. Unlike thin clients, which lack hard drives and other functionality, thick clients are completely functional in their own right whether they are connected to the network or not. Many companies and organisations provide thick clients to their employees. This allows employees to access files and other shared network resources stored on a local server as well as use the computers offline. When a thick client is disconnected from a network, it is oftentimes referred to as a computer workstation. (3) A virtual machine (VM) is an operating system (OS) or application environment that is installed on a special powerful computer known as a virtualization workstation. The virtualization workstation can simultaneously host one or more VMs, depending upon the requirements of the company, etc. The virtualization workstation employs what is known as a hypervisor (or Virtual Machine Manager (VMM)), and it is the hypervisor feature of a virtualization computer that allows multiple VMs to run at the same time on a single computer.

13. Correct: (i) Cat 5e crossover cable. In actuality, any Ethernet cable (for example, Cat 5, Cat 5e or Cat 6 UTP cable) can be used as a crossover cable (or converted into a crossover cable using a suitable crossover adapter).

14. Correct: (iii) Hardware error. If the lights on a keyboard repeatedly flash or flicker during POST (Power-on Self Test), it is very likely that there is a hardware error that requires further investigation and troubleshooting.

15. Correct: (iii). Check the patch cable or ethernet cable initially to ensure that this cable is secured attached to the appropriate connector on the computer.

16. (i) 20-pin connector. (ii) 24-pin connector. Historically, original ATX PSUs connected to the motherboard using a 20-pin connector. However, nowadays, newer ATX 12V 2.x PSUs connect to the motherboard with a 24-pin connector.

17. False. 32-bit CPUs can only address a maximum of 4 GB of RAM.

18. Correct: (i), (iii), (iv), and (v). Possible symptoms of a failing CPU include: (1) System lockups or "freezes" immediately before the computer automatically shuts down. (2) If the BIOS/UEFI (or a third-party diagnostic utility) shows that the CPU's temperature is beyond its recommended range, this is a clear indication that the processor is overheating. CPU overheating may be attributable to a defective heat sink/fan assembly or perhaps the CPU fan has completely failed. Prolonged overheating can permanently damage the CPU. (3) During bootup, if the POST (Power-on Self Test) detects a problem with the CPU, the motherboard will generate beep codes. Beeping codes can be useful to a technician troubleshooting a potential CPU problem, and the meaning of the beeping codes can be determined using Google (or another search engine). (4) Another indication of a failing CPU is a charred motherboard and/or CPU. Severe CPU overheating can melt or leave a charred appearance on both the motherboard and the CPU. If the overheating is severe, the CPU may be permanently damaged and require replacement. In this situation, the motherboard may also be damaged and require further testing and troubleshooting. (5) The CPU is operating beyond its recommended voltage range, as specified by the CPU's manufacturer. A singular BSOD ("Blue Screen of Death") event does not necessarily imply a problem with the CPU or any other hardware component. However, if BSOD or "blue screen" events recurrently happen, it is very likely that there is a serious underlying hardware issue that needs further investigation and troubleshooting. In that event, it is vital for the technician to capture all information presented on the screen during a "blue screen" recurrent episode and research that information using Google, etc.

19. (a) BIOS (Basic Input/Output System) utility. **(b)** Intel Core i7 processor. **(c)** 2.93 GHz. **(d)** The fastest CPU cache memory is invariably L1 (Level 1) cache. According to the BIOS, the CPU has L1 cache capacity of 256 KB. The second fastest CPU cache memory is L2, followed by L3. However, even though L3 is the slowest CPU cache memory, it is still faster than DRAM (Dynamic RAM) memory modules installed on the motherboard. **(e)** 133 MHz. **(f)** Yes. According to the BIOS screen, the computer's processor is enabled to support virtualization. Virtualization workstations normally have an installed hypervisor, either a Type 1 hypervisor (otherwise known as a Native Hypervisor or "bare metal" hypervisor) or a Type 2 hypervisor (also called a Hosted Hypervisor).

20. Correct: (iii) A plastic shim.

Practice Test 6

1. Fill in the missing space: The standard voltages of a SATA HDD connection on an ATX power supply are 3.3v, ______, and 12v.

2. True or False: Voltage is defined as the movement of electric charge.

3. Which of the following networking protocols use port 53?

(i) DNS

(ii) HTTPS

(iii) SSH

(iv) TLS

4. What CLI command allows a network technician to view the current network sessions between a PC and the Internet?

(i) nbtstat -A

(ii) netstat

(iii) ipconfig /all

(iv) None of the above

5. DisplayPort is a type of video card connector. Which of the following video connectors was DisplayPort originally designed to replace? (Select two answers.)

(i) Component RGB

(ii) DVI

(iii) HDMI

(iv) VGA

6. True or False: HT technology enables a single-core CPU to calculate four instruction sets simultaneously.

7. What component on a motherboard typically supplies power to the CMOS after a computer is shut down?

(i) Li-ion battery

(ii) Li-ion polymer battery

(iii) NiCd battery

(iv) CR2032 battery

8. CompTIA recommends a six-step troubleshooting process that should be adhered to by PC technicians working in the field.

State all six steps of the prescribed CompTIA® A+ troubleshooting methodology.

9. True or False: DVI-I connectors are video connectors that only transmit analog and digital video signals.

10. A graphics designer sends a 3D image to the network laser printer. However, when collecting the printout, she notices that the printout only shows a ghosted image. An IT technician confirms that there are no networking issues to be concerned about.

What is the most likely cause of the ghosted image?

(i) Depleted toner cartridge

(ii) Faulty photosensitive drum

(iii) Transfer corona wire is not receiving sufficient voltage

(iv) Fusing assembly is not getting sufficiently hot

11. Laptops can communicate with other computers using wired connections such as ethernet cables and dial-up (RJ11) connections.

Which wireless connections enable laptops to communicate with other computers and devices? (Select all applicable answers.)

(i) Bluetooth

(ii) WLAN

(iii) NFC

(iv) Cellular WAN

(v) USB 3.0

12. Which of the following CLI tools can be used by a network technician to determine which router between his PC workstation and another computer on the network has failed?

(i) tracert

(ii) arp -a

(iii) nbtstat -a

(iv) ipconfig /?

13. While investigating the cause of a network issue, a technician notices that one set of LED lights on an ethernet switch is blinking rapidly. All other LED lights on the switch are blinking at a normal, intermittent rate.

Which of the following are the most likely reasons for the rapidly blinking LED lights on the switch? (Select two answers.)

(i) A network adapter card in a networked computer is defective

(ii) The firmware on the switch needs to be updated

(iii) A port on the switch is faulty

(iv) High-speed data transmission over the network

14. An inkjet printer is printing streaks on documents. What is the best first troubleshooting step to resolve this issue?

(i) Manually wipe the print heads with a clean, lint-free cloth

(ii) Replace the print ribbon

(iii) Use the printer's "Clean" option

(iv) Power cycle the printer

15. Sound does not emanate from a HTPC's integrated speakers. Which of the following are possible reasons for this specific issue? (Select two answers.)

(i) The sound card's driver needs to be installed

(ii) The volume is turned down or muted

(iii) Faulty speakers

(iv) Defective sound card

16. What term is used to describe the practice of sharing a mobile device's Internet connection with other Wi-Fi capable USB-connected devices?

(i) PAN

(ii) Synchronization

(iii) Wi-Fi tethering

(iv) None of the above

17. What troubleshooting command is very useful when a technician is trying to determine connectivity problems on a Windows® OS computer that is unable to connect to the Internet?

(i) ipconfig

(ii) nbtstat

(iii) netstat

(iv) None of the above

18. True or False: Apple® iPads™ typically have a lithium ion battery, which has the same specification as the battery that is found in most laptops.

19. A technician in a PC repair shop has been asked by a customer to add a second SODIMM memory module to his laptop. When the technician opens the memory compartment on the undersurface of the laptop, he notices that there is already a 2 GB DDR3 memory module installed to the only available slot. However, this laptop is specified to accommodate a maximum of 4 GB RAM.

Where should the technician look for a second memory slot?

(i) Underneath the keyboard

(ii) Behind the Li-ion battery compartment

(iii) Underneath the optical drive

(iv) Underneath the touchpad

20. A technician receives a call from a client who is attempting to set up a home theatre stereo system. The client has stated that she is unsure how to connect her HTPC's sound card to the stereo system.

What types of audio connections would you recommend to the client? (Select two answers.)

(i) Component RGB

(ii) M1-DA

(iii) TOSLINK™ optical audio

(iv) RCA

Practice Test 6			
MCQ Solutions			
1.	See notes	11.	(i), (ii), (iv)
2.	False	12.	(i)
3.	(i)	13.	(i), (iii)
4.	(ii)	14.	(iii)
5.	(ii), (iii)	15.	(i), (ii)
6.	False	16.	(iii)
7.	(iv)	17.	(i)
8.	See notes	18.	False
9.	True	19.	(i)
10.	(ii)	20.	(iii)

1. 5 volts. The standard voltages of a SATA HDD connection on an ATX power supply unit are 3.3v, 5v, and 12v.

2. False. Amperage is defined as the movement of electric charge through a circuit.

3. Correct: (i) DNS (Domain Name System).

4. Correct: (ii) Netstat.

5. Correct: (ii) and (iii). DisplayPort was originally designed to replace DVI (Digital Visual Interface) and HDMI (High Definition Multimedia Interface) video connectors.

6. False. HT (Hyper Threading) technology enables a single-core CPU to calculate two instruction sets simultaneously.

7. Correct: (iv) CR2032 lithium battery (also known as a CR2032 lithium coin cell).

8. Step 1: Identify the problem. Step 2: Establish a theory of probable cause. Step 3: Test the theory to determine cause. Step 4: Establish a plan of action to resolve the problem and then implement a solution. Step 5: Verify full system functionality and, if applicable, implement preventative measures. Step 6: Document findings, actions taken, and outcomes.

9. True.

10. Correct: (ii) Faulty photosensitive drum. It is very likely that the laser printer's photosensitive drum (imaging drum) has started to become defective. Consequently, the drum may need to be replaced.

11. Correct: (i), (ii), and (iv). Laptops can wirelessly communicate with other computers and devices by means of Bluetooth, WLAN (Wireless LAN), IR (infrared), and cellular WAN.

12. Correct: (i) tracert.

13. Correct: (i) A network adapter card (NIC) in a computer attached to the network is defective and (iii) A port on the ethernet switch is faulty.

14. Correct: (iii) Use the inkjet printer's "Clean" option. The easiest first troubleshooting step to take is to use the printer's "Clean" option. If that does not resolve the matter, the ink cartridge print heads can be manually wiped with a clean, lint-free cloth. Power-cycling (turning off and then on) the printer will be of limited utility in this particular scenario. An inkjet printer is not equipped with a print ribbon – ribbons are normally found in impact printers (or dot matrix printers).

15. (i) The sound card's driver needs to be installed. (ii) The volume is turned down or muted.

16. Wi-Fi tethering. The Wi-Fi capable device is connected to the primary mobile device (e.g., smartphone, tablet) using a USB cable, and the appropriate Wi-Fi tethering option is enabled within the Settings screen of the smartphone, etc.

17. Correct: (i) ipconfig (or ipconfig /all).

18. False. Apple iPads (and other tablet computers) usually have a lithium-ion polymer battery. These batteries are similar to the lithium-ion batteries that are commonly found in laptops. However, the polymer batteries can be molded into any shape. Lithium-ion polymer batteries last, on average, for 10 hours on a full charge, assuming typical iPad usage.

19. Correct: (i) Underneath the keyboard. SODIMM modules are usually located inside a compartment on the undersurface of most laptops and/or underneath the keyboard.

20. Correct: (iii) TOSLINK optical audio connection and (iv) RCA audio connection. TOSLINK is an acronym for Toshiba Link. TOSLINK (also known as an optical audio connection) is a standardized optical fiber connector system. TOSLINK is most commonly used in consumer audio equipment via a S/PDIF (Sony/Phillips Digital Interconnect Format) port (or "digital optical" port) where it transmits a digital audio stream from components such as CD and DVD players, DAT (Digital Audio Tape) recorders, computers, and video game consoles to an AV (audio/video) receiver. The transmitted digital optical signal is typically a red, laser-like light. By the same token, the S/PDIF optical port (on a computer, video game console, etc.) normally emits a red, laser-like light. When the digital optical port is not in use (e.g., TOSLINK audio cable is not plugged in), the red light should be obscured using the S/PDIF port's plastic cover.

Practice Test 7

1. True or False: When designing a RAID configuration for a computer system, HDD arrays (or SSD arrays) should always be built using identical drives.

2. A PC user in a large open-plan office is attempting to connect to a shared network printer designated as "printer 20" using the UNC path **\74.125.126.100\printer20.** Upon executing the said UNC path, an error message appears on the monitor.

Which of the following UNC paths would enable the PC user to successfully connect to "printer 20"? (Select two answers.)

(i) //74.125.126.100/printer20

(ii) http://74.125.126.100/printer20

(iii) https://74.125.126.100/printer20

(iv) ipp://74.125.126.100/printer20

3. Which type of cable connector is primarily used with a computer (as opposed to a Smart TV) and carries only a digital signal?

(i) DVI-D

(ii) DVI-I

(iii) HDMI Type A

(iv) M1-DA

4. A power outage occurs due to an electrical storm. The computer workstations in the administrative center shut down in an orderly manner because UPS units had been previously deployed. All 50 workstations connected to the LAN are configured to use a DHCP server.

However, upon rebooting the workstations, an IT technician notices that two computers are unable to reconnect to the network. Rebooting these two computers does not resolve the matter.

What do you think is the most likely cause of the network issue? (Select three answers.)

(i) The two computer workstations were previously assigned Static IP addresses

(ii) The ports on the switch connected to these two workstations have become defective

(iii) The ethernet cables connecting the two workstations to the switch have either become defective or loose

(iv) The DHCP server is not working properly

(v) The NIC drivers on the affected workstations need to be updated

5. A junior network technician is in the process of installing a new patch panel in a server room. A senior technician is supervising the installation and commissioning activities. Once the patch panel framework has been installed, the various ethernet cables must be attached to the relevant 110 punch blocks.

(a) Which of the following tools should the senior technician recommend to his subordinate when carrying out the cabling attachment activity?

(i) RJ45 crimper

(ii) Punch down tool

(iii) Punch-in tool

(iv) Torx screwdriver

(b) Briefly explain the purpose and function of a 110 punch block.

6. Which of the following connections offer the fastest data transfer rates? (Select one answer.)

(i) Thunderbolt

(ii) SuperSpeed USB

(iii) Firewire 800

(iv) Thunderbolt 3.0

7. Which of the following devices or installations is linked to a network and has the sole purpose of providing data to client workstations?

(i) Patch panel

(ii) Switch

(iii) NAS

(iv) Bridge

8. On which of the following computers is RAM capacity a very important consideration?

(i) AV workstation

(ii) Virtualization workstation

(iii) HTPC

(iv) Gaming PC

9. Which of the following actions helps to secure a router in a SOHO environment? (Select all correct answers.)

(i) Enable SSID broadcasting

(ii) Enable MAC filtering

(iii) Enable WEP 128 encryption

(iv) Change the SOHO router's default password

(v) Disable SSID broadcasting

(vi) Enable WPS

(vii) Select IEEE 802.11 b/g/n standard

10. What two steps can be performed to optimize an IR connection between a laptop and a HP® LaserJet Pro® printer? (Select two answers.)

(i) Install an IR booster

(ii) Maintain a clear and direct "line of sight" between both devices

(iii) Modify the laptop's power scheme to ensure that the laptop does not enter S3 state whilst using the IR-enabled printer

(iv) Shorten the distance between the laptop and the IR-enabled printer

11. Which of the following hardware cards enables the full functionality of Windows® Media Centre™ "Live TV" option?

(i) Network Adapter Card

(ii) GPU video card

(iii) TV tuner card

(iv) SDXC card

12. Name any five hand tools that are commonly found in a PC technician's computer repair toolkit.

13. What should be used to clean a laser printer's rubber rollers? (Select two answers.)

(i) Diluted boric acid

(ii) Lactic acid

(iii) Lint-free cloth

(iv) Isopropyl alcohol

(v) Vinegar

14. What is the third step of the CompTIA® A+ troubleshooting methodology?

(i) Question the user of the computer equipment being troubleshot

(ii) Establish a theory of probable cause

(iii) Verify full system functionality and, if applicable, implement preventative measures

(iv) Test the theory to determine cause

15. A network technician is troubleshooting a networking issue using a computer's Command Shell. The technician enters a command and the computer returns the following information, as shown in *Figure 3.*

(a) What command did the technician enter at the command line to generate the information displayed in the figure?

(b) What type of information is displayed in the figure?

(c) State the computer's IPv4 address.

(d) True or False: The computer the technician is troubleshooting is part of a SOHO network.

Figure 3

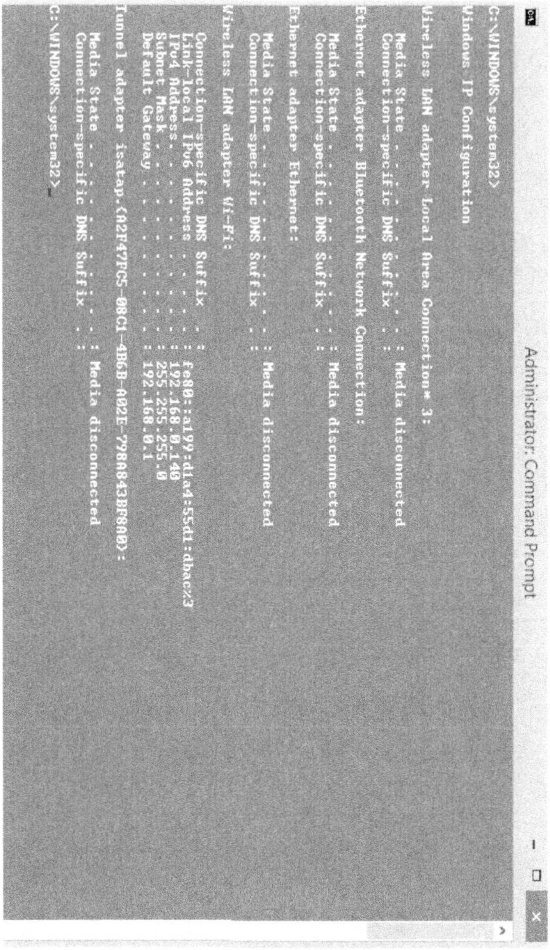
Administrator: Command Prompt
C:\WINDOWS\system32>
Windows IP Configuration
Wireless LAN adapter Local Area Connection* 3:
Media State . . . . : Media disconnected
Connection-specific DNS Suffix . :
Ethernet adapter Bluetooth Network Connection:
Media State . . . . : Media disconnected
Connection-specific DNS Suffix . :
Ethernet adapter Ethernet:
Media State . . . . : Media disconnected
Connection-specific DNS Suffix . :
Wireless LAN adapter Wi-Fi:
Connection-specific DNS Suffix . :
Link-local IPv6 Address . . . . . : fe80::a199:d1a4:55d1:dbac%3
IPv4 Address. . . . . : 192.168.0.140
Subnet Mask . . . . : 255.255.255.0
Default Gateway . . . . : 192.168.0.1
Tunnel adapter isatap.{A2F47FC5-08C1-4B6B-A02E-798A843BF8A0}:
Media State . . . . : Media disconnected
Connection-specific DNS Suffix . :
C:\WINDOWS\system32>

16. A Python developer working for a prestigious software development firm in London contacts the IT helpdesk explaining that his Dell® PC workstation requires additional memory. Frequently, the developer has numerous PaaS applications open on the screen, and he has noticed that the Dell® PC occasionally becomes non-responsive for a few moments or its performance is marginally slower than normal.

An IT technician confirms that the computer most likely needs additional DDR3 memory to be installed. According to the BIOS settings, the computer already has 4 GB Kingston® DDR3 memory installed. Also, the motherboard has dual-channel RAM architecture.

After prepping a vacant RAM slot on the motherboard, the technician carefully seats a new 4 GB Kingston® DDR3 memory module. However, when the computer is booted, a memory error is displayed on the display.

(a) Define the following terms:

(i) PaaS

(ii) DDR3

(iii) BIOS

(iv) Dual-channel RAM

(b) What is the most probable reason for a memory error occurring upon booting the computer?

(i) The new memory module has not been seated correctly in the corresponding slot

(ii) The new memory module is defective and needs to be replaced

(iii) The new memory module has been inserted into the incorrect RAM slot on the motherboard

(iv) Dirty RAM slot

17. An IT technician working for a large pharmaceutical company is reviewing several troubleshooting tickets at the start of her 12-hour shift.

One of the tickets reports that an employee in the Operations Team is having problems with the LCD display on his work laptop. The employee states that the LCD display shows intermittent lines on the screen while he is working, and that these lines become more pronounced when he moves his laptop around during shift.

The technician notes that the maintenance log shows that laptops used by the Operations Team were recently serviced.

What is the most likely reason for the issue raised in the ticket?

(i) Defective video card

(ii) LCD display cable is loose

(iii) Faulty LCD monitor

(iv) PSU is starting to fail

18. A router is a networking device that connects a SOHO network or LAN to other networks. Routers can also be used to connect a WAN (or WANs) to a LAN or connect dissimilar networks together.

(a) Explain the terms *SOHO, LAN,* and *WAN.*

(b) Which of the following are other notable functions of a router? (Select all applicable answers.)

(i) Limits network broadcasts

(ii) Segments IP address ranges

(iii) Allows different networked devices to communicate

(iv) Interconnects different physical media

(v) Filters and isolates network traffic

19. Which of the following RAID arrays is fault tolerant and permits mirroring combined with striping?

(i) RAID 0

(ii) RAID 1

(iii) RAID 5

(iv) RAID 10

20. Identify the connectors labelled A and B which are displayed in *Figure 4.*

Figure 4

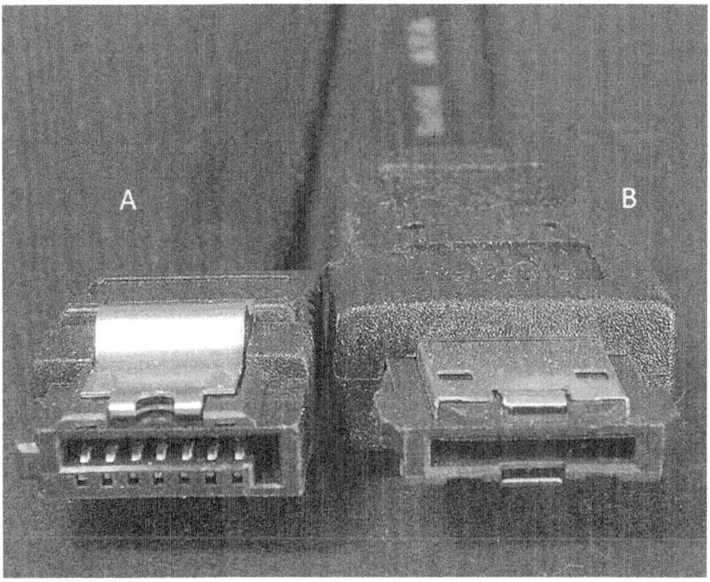

Practice Test 7			
MCQ Solutions			
1.	True	11.	(iii)
2.	(iii)	12.	See notes
3.	(i)	13.	(iii), (iv)
4.	(i), (ii), (iii)	14.	(iv)
5.	(a)(ii), (b) See notes	15.	(a)-(c) See notes, (d) True
6.	(iv)	16.	(a) See notes, (b)(iii)
7.	(iii)	17.	(ii)
8.	(ii)	18.	(a) See notes, (b)(i)(ii)(iv)(v)
9.	(ii), (iv), (v)	19.	(iv)
10.	(ii), (iv)	20.	See notes

1. True.

2. Correct: (iii) https:// (iv) ipp://. HTTPS is an acronym for Hypertext Transfer Protocol Secure. IPP means Internet Printing Protocol. IPP is a common standard used for remote printing, although some organisations prefer HTTPS to enable secure remote printing.

IPP is an Internet protocol that enables communication between client devices (such as PCs, mobile phones, tablet computers, etc.) and printers (or print servers). IPP allows the client send one or more print jobs to a printer (or print server) as well as carrying out other tasks such as querying the current status of a printer, determining the current status of print jobs, or cancelling individual print jobs. IPP can operate at a local level or over the Internet to perform printing-related tasks. Unlike other printing protocols, IPP also supports access control, authentication, and encryption, thereby facilitating more secure printing. IPP is supported by the vast majority of printers manufactured and sold nowadays.

3. Correct: (i) DVI-D connector.

4. Correct: (i), (ii), and (iii). Since most of the PC workstations are able to connect to the network upon rebooting, it is apparent that the DHCP server is operating as normal, therefore (iv) is not correct. Option (v) is not correct either, because we are assuming that all workstations are using the same NIC drivers before the power outage. Since most workstations are able to connect to the network upon rebooting, it is highly unlikely that updating the NIC drivers on the two errant workstations will resolve the networking issue.

5. (a) Correct: (ii) A punch down tool. **(b)** A 110 block is a type of punch block that is used to terminate runs of networking cables. In server rooms, these 110 punch blocks are often built into the back of patch panel installations to terminate cable runs. These 110 punch blocks (also referred to as 110-style IDC (Insulation Displacement Contact) connectors) may also be used with keystone modules which are typically attached to wall plates. 110 punch blocks are normally used in preference to older generation 66 blocks in high-speed networks because they minimise the possibility of signal interference (or "cross talk"). 110 blocks are commonly certified for use in Category 5, Category 6, and Category 6a network cabling systems, which also explains their common usage in high-speed networks.

6. Correct: (iv) Thunderbolt 3.0. Thunderbolt 3 has a data transfer rate of 20 Gbps. Thunderbolt (otherwise referred to as Thunderbolt 1.0) operates at 10 Gbps. SuperSpeed USB (otherwise known as USB 3.0) operates at 5 Gbps. Firewire 800 has a significantly slower data transfer rate of 800 Mbps.

7. Correct: (iii) NAS (Network Attached Storage).

8. Correct: (ii) Virtualization workstation. An AV workstation is used for audio visual editing and HTPC refers to Home Theatre PC.

9. Correct answers: (ii), (iv), and (v). Enable MAC filtering, change the SOHO router's default password, and disable SSID broadcasting.

10. Correct: (ii) Maintain a clear and direct "line of sight" between both devices. (iv) Shorten the distance between the laptop and the IR (infrared)-enabled printer.

11. Correct: (iii) TV tuner card.

12. (1) Flat-head screwdriver. (2) Phillips-head screwdriver. (3) Torx screwdriver. (4) Hex driver (otherwise known as a nut driver). (5) Needle-nose pliers. (6) Wire cutter. (7) Tweezers. (8) Extension magnet or part retriever. (9) Flashlight. (10) Wire stripper. (11) Crimper. (12) Punch-down tool.

13. Correct: (iii) and (iv). A lint-free cloth that has been moistened with isopropyl alcohol or clean water is preferable when cleaning a laser printer's rubber rollers.

14. Correct: (iv) Test the theory to determine cause.

15. (a) ipconfig. **(b)** The Internet Protocol Configuration command (ipconfig) displays the current TCP/IP network configuration parameters. The ipconfig command is one of the first CLI tools a technician should use when attempting to troubleshoot a network connectivity issue. A variant of the ipconfig command is ipconfig /all. **(c)** 192.168.0.140 **(d)** True. The computer is connected to a SOHO (Small Office/Home Office) network, because the subnet mask is 255.255.255.0 (net.net.net.node) and the computer's IPv4 address is in the 192 to 223 range, which is synonymous with SOHO networks.

16. (a) (A) PaaS (Platform as a Service) is a cloud-based service that provides various software solutions to companies and other corporate entities, particularly the ability to develop software solutions in a virtual environment. This virtual set up is advantageous because it allows companies (e.g., software houses) to develop software applications without the cost or administration of a physical platform. Such companies can gain access to easily configurable operating systems (e.g., Windows, Linux, Apple OS X) and other on-demand computing resources via "the cloud" without having to pay for maintenance of the underlying physical hardware (e.g., servers, HDD arrays, etc.). These companies therefore only pay for the actual cloud-based services that they use. (a) (B) DDR3 is a type of DIMM (or RAM module used in PCs) that was originally designed for lower power consumption, higher levels of performance and speed, and higher reliability. DDR3 DIMMs are similar to DDR2 DIMMs (both have 240-pins), but they are not backward compatible. (a) (C) BIOS (Basic Input Output System) is the first component of a motherboard that runs when a PC or laptop is booted. The purpose of the BIOS is to identify, check, and initialize various critical components of the computer system. Once the BIOS checks have been completed, the computer's primary OS will load up and take control of the entire system's management. Nowadays, BIOS settings are stored on an EEPROM (Electrically Erasable Programmable ROM) chip on the motherboard. (a) (D) Dual-channel RAM is a type of RAM architecture that essentially doubles the data throughput between the memory bank and the CPU. Two separate 64-bit data channels are used on the motherboard, resulting in a 128-bit bus between the memory bank and the memory controller chip (MCC). Motherboards that use dual-channel RAM technology have color-coded matching memory banks (e.g., 2 black slots and 2 blue slots). To effectively use dual-channel RAM technology, 2 RAM modules would need to be installed to matching colored slots (for example, the RAM sticks could be inserted into both blue slots, leaving the black slots empty, depending upon performance requirements). For optimal performance and to prevent memory errors, both

DIMMs must be identical, in terms of capacity or number of GBs, speed, and number of chips on each RAM stick. **(b)** (iii) Considering that the motherboard uses dual-channel RAM architecture, it is highly likely the technician inserted the new memory module into an incorrectly colored slot. It is very unlikely that the newly installed memory stick has not been seated correctly considering that the technician in this scenario has carefully inserted the new memory stick into a RAM slot on the motherboard and we are also told that the technician has "prepped" or cleaned the RAM slot prior to seating the new memory module. Hence, (iii) is the best answer in light of this particular scenario.

17. Correct: (ii) It is more likely that the LCD display cable is loose, as opposed to having an issue with a defective video card (or video card controller). Considering that this laptop was recently serviced, the maintenance technician may have accidentally neglected to check whether the display cable is seated correctly, and/or the cable became loose during routine servicing.

18. (a) SOHO is an acronym for Small Office/Home Office. A SOHO network (sometimes referred to as a "virtual office") is a small type of LAN. A LAN (Local Area Network) is a group of computers and other networked devices typically located in a small area, such as a house, a small office, or a single building. The computers and other devices that comprise the LAN are all connected to one or more ethernet switches, and a router allows the computers to access the Internet. A WAN (Wide Area Network) is a group of one or more LANs that cover a large geographical area. Such networks are commonly seen in a corporate environment, where a company or corporation connects branch offices or manufacturing facilities located in two different locales by means of a WAN. **(b)** Correct: (i), (ii), (iv), and (v). A router can be used to limit network broadcasts (or prevent what is known as "broadcast storms"), segment IP address ranges, interconnect different physical media connected to the network, as well as filter and isolate network traffic. However, an ethernet switch allows different networked devices to communicate with each other.

19. Correct: (iv) RAID 10.

20. (a) SATA (Serial Advanced Technology Attachment) connector. **(b)** eSATA (External SATA) connector. eSATA is an extension to the Serial ATA standard that enables SATA hard drives to be attached externally. Prior to eSATA, external hard drives were connected to a computer system by means of USB 2.0 or IEEE 1394 (Firewire).

Practice Test 8

1. Identify the connectors labelled A and B which are displayed in *Figure 5.*

2. True or False: PoE devices operate on the basis of IEEE 802.3an.

3. What is the standard printing resolution stated in DPI?

(i) 24

(ii) 72

(iii) 300

(iv) 600

4. True or False: A typical CD can hold up to 700 MB of data. The maximum read speed of a CD-ROM drive is 150 MB/s.

5. A prominent networking installation and engineering company has recently been awarded a US federal contract to install the Cat-6 networking cables in a purpose-built government research center.

An experienced network engineer and a team of technicians have also been appointed by the regional government to monitor the installation and commissioning work carried out by the network cabling company. The purpose of the audit is to ensure that all Cat-6 cable runs do not exceed a maximum length of

100 meters (328 feet) and that data transmission rates over the network will be within specified parameters.

What tool can be used by the audit team to carry out their assigned tasks in the most efficient manner possible?

(i) Use a patch cable tester to verify cable distance

(ii) Use a tone generator and probe to verify cable distance

(iii) Use a network multimeter to verify cable distance

(iv) None of the above

Figure 5

6. IEEE 802.11b and Bluetooth 3.0 provide wireless connectivity between devices in a networked environment. Which standard offers the fastest data transfer rate?

7. What are the Intel® and AMD® names for CPU virtualization using a hypervisor, respectively? (Select two answers.)

(i) AM3+

(ii) AMD-V

(iii) FM2+

(iv) VT-x

8. How many pins are normally found in the print head of a high-quality dot matrix printer?

(i) 15

(ii) 20

(iii) 24

(iv) 34

9. A PC repair technician has been requested to service a number of PCs that are used for inventory management and order processing purposes in a large grain storage depot. Warehouse staff report that the computers tend to shut down unexpectedly and this phenomenon has been occurring frequently over the last few weeks.

The technician notices that the PC cases are full of dust, with a lot of dust having accumulated in the exhaust vents. Also, the technician observes that some of the computers have no card slot covers.

(a) What are the most likely reasons for the warehouse computers shutting down unexpectedly? (Select two answers.)

(i) Computers are connected to faulty AC receptacles owing to an intermittent, undiagnosed problem with an electrical circuit (or circuits) within the warehouse facility

(ii) Inadequate air circulation within the computer cases

(iii) Malfunctioning or defective power supplies

(iv) Overheating CPUs

(b) What simple measures could the technician do to minimise the risk of this problem arising again in the future? (Select the best two answers.)

(i) Arrange for a licensed electrician to investigate and repair any electrical faults within the warehouse facility

(ii) Clean out the PC cases

(iii) Install a suitable liquid cooling system within the computer cases to minimise the risk of CPU overheating

(iv) Install slot covers to block the openings left by empty card slots

10. A large university hospital campus in New York is very reliant upon the computer resources provided by its dedicated server room.

The Chief Technical Officer (CTO) of the hospital board is formulating a plan to gradually replace the hard disk drives used by the servers with SSDs. Very confidential patient medical records and other sensitive hospital data are stored on the servers. Hence, the CTO wants to configure RAID arrays that will ensure data security and minimise the risk of data corruption or loss.

(a) Which of the following options would an IT consultant most likely recommend to the hospital board? (Select one answer.)

(i) IPsec

(ii) RAID 5

(iii) RAID 10

(iv) TLS/SSL

(b) Following on from part (a) above, briefly justify the IT consultant's choice.

Figure 6

11. What port number is typically associated with IMAP?

(i) 23

(ii) 143

(iii) 443

(iv) 3389

12. Identify the computer component shown in *Figure 6.*

13. A PC user notices that the on-screen cursor of a wireless optical mouse sometimes moves erratically around the screen. On other occasions, the cursor is intermittently non-responsive.

What are possible reasons for this phenomenon? (Select all applicable answers.)

(i) A loose Bluetooth dongle connection via a USB port on the computer

(ii) Defective or failing batteries installed in the wireless optical mouse

(iii) The wireless mouse is on an uneven surface

(iv) The optical eye on the bottom of the mouse is possibly dirty

14. A PC technician is troubleshooting a computer and he has opened the case. In the event of an unexpected power surge or electrical discharge, which of the following tools may be helpful in protecting the technician?

(i) Antistatic strap

(ii) Antistatic bag

(iii) Antistatic mat

(iv) Multimeter

15. What is user-replaceable memory in a PC called?

(i) SRAM

(ii) DRAM

(iii) SODIMM

(iv) Cache

16. Which of the following hardware components is the least likely to be replaced on a laptop?

(i) Keyboard

(ii) LCD display

(iii) SODIMM

(iv) CPU

17. What is the typical rotational speed of a SATA HDD?

(i) 5,400 RPM

(ii) 7,200 RPM

(iii) 10,000 RPM

(iv) 10,800 RPM

18. True or False: Use of cellular connectivity on a smartphone, tablet computer, or with a WAN card requires a subscription with a cellular provider.

19. A computer system in a server room is configured to house a RAID 5 HDD array. One of the drives in the 8-disk array has become defective. A technician is in the process of replacing the drive. According to the maintenance log, this specific computer has been affected by frequent failure of HDDs over the last 6 months.

(a) How many drives in a RAID 5 array can fail before the entire RAID configuration is rendered defective?

(i) 1

(ii) 2

(iii) 3

(iv) 5

(b) What other internal component of the computer system should the technician inspect whilst diagnosing the cause of the HDD failure?

(i) CPU

(ii) RAID controller

(iii) Southbridge chipset

(iv) PSU

(c) Why should the technician inspect and subsequently test this component?

(i) To ascertain if the driver associated with the RAID controller is compatible and functioning to specification

(ii) To check whether the voltages supplied by the power supply are normal and within tolerance

(iii) To determine if the voltages supplied by the motherboard are normal and within tolerance

(iv) To validate the functionality and performance of the Southbridge chipset

20. Identify the connectors labelled A and B which are displayed in *Figure 7.*

Figure 7

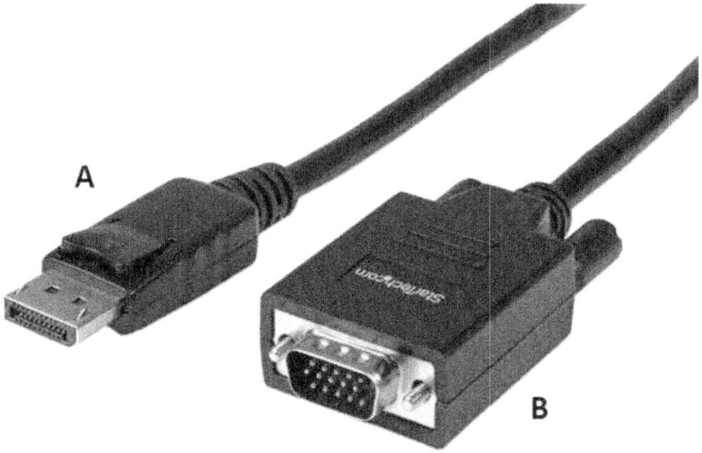

Practice Test 8			
MCQ Solutions			
1.	See notes	11.	(ii)
2.	False	12.	See notes
3.	(iv)	13.	(i), (ii), (iii), (iv)
4.	False	14.	(i)
5.	(iii)	15.	(ii)
6.	See notes	16.	(iv)
7.	(ii), (iv)	17.	(ii)
8.	(iii)	18.	True
9.	(a)(ii)(iv), (b)(ii)(iv)	19.	(a)(i), (b)(iv), (c)(ii)
10.	(a)(iii), (ii) See notes	20.	See notes

1. (a) USB connector. (b) HDMI connector.

2. False. PoE (Power over ethernet) devices operate on the basis of IEEE 802.3af. However, if a wired network is transmitting data at a maximum speed of 10 Gb/s over twisted-pair cable, the IEEE 802.3an classification applies.

3. Correct: (iv) 600 DPI (dots per inch).

4. False. A typical CD can hold up to 700 MB of data. However, the maximum read speed of a CD-ROM drive is 150 KB/s, not 150 MB/s.

5. Correct: (iii). It is more accurate and efficient to use a network multimeter to carry out this task, compared to a cable tester. A network multimeter is a multi-purpose device that can be used to test and certify an assortment of network components, such as cables, ports, and NICs. Another distinct advantage of using a network multimeter is that this versatile device can report the status of various network conditions, such as the data transmission speed of a cable, length of a cable, PoE (Power over Ethernet) voltage levels, and whether a particular cable is specified to allow full duplex or half duplex data transmissions.

6. Bluetooth 3.0 is relatively faster than IEEE 802.11b wireless networks. Bluetooth 3.0 has a theoretical maximum data throughput of 24 Mbps, but only when combined with IEEE 802.11 wireless technology. IEEE 802.11b wireless networks have a maximum data transfer rate of 11 Mbps and operate at a frequency of 2.4 GHz.

7. Correct: (ii) AMD-V and (iv) Intel VT-x.

8. Correct: (iii) 24.

9. (a) (ii) Inadequate air circulation within the computer cases and (iv) Overheating CPUs. In this scenario, the computers are shutting down unexpectedly due to overheating. Since the PC cases are full of dust and the exhaust vents are clogged, there is inadequate air flow through the PC cases. As a result, there is not sufficient air cooling to dissipate the heat generated by the CPU. When overheating occurs, the PCs automatically shut down to prevent irreversible damage to the CPU. **(b)** (ii) Clean out the PC cases and (iv) Install slot covers to block the openings left by empty card slots. After cleaning out the PC cases, the technician needs to install slot covers to block the openings left by empty card slots. Any card slot without a cover creates an opening for dust and other air-borne contaminants to be drawn into the PC case, which can accumulate inside the case, causing clogged up areas and limited air flow.

10. (a) (iii) RAID 10. **(b)** In this particular scenario, RAID 10 is the most appropriate and optimum RAID configuration. RAID 10 combines the advantages of RAID 0 ("striping") and RAID 1 ("mirroring"). RAID 10 is fault-tolerant, which means that the HDD array will continue to function as normal, even if there is a problem with one of the drives. RAID 10 configurations contain at least 2 mirrored HDDs that are then striped. However, a typical RAID 10 configuration will have 4 HDDs or more. Another option that the IT consultant could consider is a RAID 5 configuration, also known as "striping with parity". This RAID array is also fault tolerant and requires a minimum of 3 disks to function. However, in this particular scenario, where a large hospital campus would most likely be equipped with a correspondingly large server room and possibly multiple HDD banks, a RAID 10 configuration is considered the most effective solution. RAID 10 provides very fast read/write speeds, very fast recovery from HDD failure, and is more fault-tolerant than RAID 5 because RAID 10 can tolerate failure of multiple HDDs at the same time.

11. Correct: (ii) IMAP (Internet Message Access Protocol) uses port 143.

12. Network interface controller (also known as a network adapter card or NIC). This card is identifiable by its distinctly characteristic RJ45 ethernet port.

13. Correct: (i), (ii), (iii), and (iv). In summation, the main reasons why the on-screen cursor of a wireless Bluetooth-enabled optical mouse exhibits characteristics such as erratic on-screen movements independent of the user and/or intermittent non-responsiveness or inactivity are: (1) The optical eye on the bottom of the mouse is possibly dirty or partially obscured. (2) The wireless mouse is on an uneven surface. (3) The mouse is on a glossy surface, which affects the optical sensor's performance. (4) Poor wireless connection between the mouse and the USB receiver (or Bluetooth USB dongle) plugged into the PC. (5) Defective or failing batteries installed in the wireless optical mouse. (6) A loose Bluetooth USB dongle connection or a malfunctioning USB port on the PC. (7) An incorrect, out-of-date, or corrupt mouse driver installed on the computer.

14. Correct: (i) Antistatic strap.

15. Correct: (ii) DRAM. User-replaceable memory (RAM) in a PC is termed DRAM (Dynamic RAM).

16. Correct: (iv) CPU. Generally speaking, the CPU is the internal component that is least likely to be replaced. The hardware components of a laptop that are most prone to replacement include: keyboard, LCD display, optical drive, inverter, SODIMM modules (RAM) and network adapter card. Further, the various I/O ports (e.g., USB ports, etc.) on a laptop may become damaged or defective over time. However, this list is not intended to be exhaustive and it all depends on the specific working environment of a laptop.

17. Correct: (ii) 7,200 RPM. The magnetic platter in a typical SATA HDD (Hard Disk Drive) has a rotational speed of 7,200 RPM (revolutions per minute). However, other HDDs have rotational speeds of 5,400 RPM and 10,000 RPM, respectively.

18. True.

19. **(a)** (i) Although RAID 5 is fault tolerant, it only protects against one drive failure. If more than one drive should become defective, the entire RAID 5 array will fail. **(b)** (iv) PSU (Power Supply Unit). **(c)** (ii) To check whether the voltages supplied by the power supply are normal and within tolerance. Repeated failure of a computer system's HDDs may indicate that the PSU is starting to become defective. Hence, it will be necessary to test the PSU with a PSU tester or multimeter to check whether the voltages supplied by the PSU are normal and within tolerance.

20. **(a)** DisplayPort connector. **(b)** VGA connector.

Practice Test 9

1. Which of the following should a technician check first when a Windows® OS PC is unable to connect to the Internet?

(i) Patch cable

(ii) NIC driver

(iii) TCP/IP settings

(iv) Windows® Firewall settings

2. What is the minimum number of HDDs necessary to set up a RAID 5 array?

(i) Two

(ii) Three

(iii) Five

(iv) None of the above

3. True or False: Specialist data destruction companies typically use incineration and shredding to destroy HDDs and HHDs.

4. UDP is a networking protocol. Which of the following statements regarding UDP are correct? (Select all applicable answers.)

(i) Data packets may arrive out of order

(ii) UDP sessions are known as "connection-less sessions"

(iii) UDP sessions are known as "connection-oriented sessions"

(iv) UDP is used in streaming media sessions

(v) Every data packet sent is tracked and acknowledged

5. Identify the video connector adapter shown in *Figure 8.*

6. What precautionary step should be performed before removing a paper jam in a network printer?

(i) Employ appropriate anti-ESD measures

(ii) Reduce the fuser assembly's temperature

(iii) Disconnect the patch cable from the printer's RJ45 jack

(iv) Switch off the printer

7. Which of the following is <u>not</u> a possible reason explaining why a laptop's keyboard ceases to function? (Select one answer.)

(i) A damaged or defective Esc key

(ii) A loose keyboard ribbon cable

(iii) A warped keyboard

(iv) Liquid spillage over the keyboard

Figure 8

8. Which of the following commands will ping a specified IP address continuously until such time that a technician terminates the command?

(i) ping -t

(ii) ping -a

(iii) ping -6

(iv) ping -l

9. True or False: Compared to a single core processor, a multi-core processor has two cores, with separate caches, on the same physical chip.

10. What is the main difference between a router and an ethernet switch?

(i) An ethernet switch is designed to interconnect computers on the same network so that they can communicate with each other. A router interconnects one or more networks

(ii) A router is designed to interconnect computers on the same network so that they can communicate with each other. An ethernet switch interconnects one or more networks

(iii) Both an ethernet switch and a router are designed to interconnect computers on the same network so that they can communicate with each other

(iv) An ethernet switch is simply a router that is equipped with multiple ports

11. According to the CompTIA® A+ troubleshooting methodology, what should a technician do initially before making any adjustments to a computer system? (Select two answers.)

(i) Identify the problem

(ii) Establish a theory of probable cause

(iii) Implement effective anti-ESD measures

(iv) Perform a system backup

(v) Consult the manufacturer's documentation

12. Motherboards normally contain a component known as CMOS.

(a) Define the term *CMOS.*

(b) What is the primary function of this component?

(i) CMOS is an alternative name for the Southbridge chipset and therefore controls all of a computer system's I/O functions, such as USB, audio, serial, ISA bus, interrupter controller, and IDE channels

(ii) The CMOS manages data transmissions between the CPU, RAM, and PCIe video card

(iii) The CMOS stores the BIOS settings

(iv) The CMOS temporarily stores data required by the CPU

13. What command can be entered at the command prompt to find out which ports are open in Windows® Firewall?

(i) arp -a

(ii) ipconfig /all

(iii) netstat -an

(iv) ping /?

14. A documentation specialist working for a pharmaceutical company has noticed that when she prints short documents, the network laser printer is very efficient and fast. However, when she tries to print larger SOP manuals, the printer is non-responsive.

An IT technician has confirmed that all printer cables and settings are correct. Also, the technician has verified the spooler settings are properly configured.

(a) What is the most likely cause of this particular problem?

(i) Obsolete or corrupted printer driver

(ii) Printer's in-built memory is inadequate

(iii) Faulty RJ45 jack on printer

(iv) Defective imaging drum

(b) What should the technician do to resolve the issue?

(i) Add more physical memory to the printer

(ii) Modify the print spooler settings

(iii) Replace the imaging drum

(iv) Update the printer's driver and other ancillary software components

Figure 9

15. Fill in the missing space: IEEE 802.11a is a wireless networking standard that operates at ______ GHz only.

16. AFP is a common networking protocol that is employed by Apple® Mac™ computers and associated devices.

(a) What port number is normally associated with AFP?

(i) 25

(ii) 443

(iii) 548

(iv) 3389

(b) Explain the term AFP.

17. Which of the following are examples of cellular technologies? (Select all applicable answers.)

(i) GSM

(ii) TDMA

(iii) CDMA

(iv) TDP

18. True or False: WEP, WPA2, and AES are wireless encryption protocols. WEP/AES offers the most secure encryption method. WPA2/AES is another very secure encryption method, but it is slightly weaker than the WEP/AES encryption combination.

19. A CPU socket is an electrical interface between the processor and the motherboard. LGA and PGA are two common types of socket.

(a) What are the main functions of a CPU socket? (Select two answers.)

(i) A CPU socket insulates and therefore protects the processor from drastic changes in ambient temperatures

(ii) A CPU socket physically supports an installed processor and heat sink assembly

(iii) A CPU socket protects the processor from EMI and extraneous signal interference

(iv) The main function of a CPU socket is to house the processor on the motherboard without the necessity to solder the CPU in situ

(b) Identify the type of socket shown in *Figure 9.*

(c) True or False: The socket type shown in the figure is commonly used to support AMD® processors.

20. Computer workstations in a small office are connected to a surge protector. All PC workstations seem to be operating as normal. During the course of the working day, a brownout event occurs. When the SOHO administrator subsequently checks to determine if any workstations are affected, he observes that only one PC's monitor has no display. However, the LED light on the monitor appears to be functional.

(a) Explain the terms *surge protector* and *brownout.*

(b) What is the first action to be taken to troubleshoot the monitor issue?

(i) Modify the ACPI settings in the BIOS

(ii) Open the computer case and inspect the PCIe video card connection

(iii) Reboot the PC

(iv) Use a multimeter or PSU tester to validate the voltages supplied by the power supply

Practice Test 9			
MCQ Solutions			
1.	(i)	11.	(iii), (iv)
2.	(ii)	12.	(a) See notes, (b)(iii)
3.	True	13.	(iii)
4.	(i), (ii), (iv)	14.	(a)(ii), (b)(i)
5.	See notes	15.	See notes
6.	(iv)	16.	(a)(iii), (b) See notes
7.	(i)	17.	(i), (ii), (iii)
8.	(i)	18.	False
9.	False	19.	(a)(ii)(iv), (b) See notes, (c) True
10.	(i)	20.	(a) See notes, (b)(iii)

1. Correct: (i) Patch cable.

2. Correct: (ii) Three.

3. True. Incidentally, the acronym HHD refers to Hybrid Hard Drive. HHD, sometimes known as a solid-state hybrid drive (SSHD), is a mass storage device that combines a conventional magnetic hard disk drive (HDD) and a NAND flash module. A HHD affords the storage capacity, cost, and performance of magnetic disk storage with the accelerated performance of flash.

4. Correct: (i), (ii), and (iv). UDP (User Datagram Protocol) is a type of networking protocol. Its main characteristics are: (1) Data packets may arrive out of order. (2) UDP is connectionless. (3) UDP is oftentimes used in streaming media sessions. (4) UDP does not use acknowledgments and is usually used in network sessions where a few lost datagrams (or data packets) do not matter. (5) The primary uses for UDP include service advertisements (such as routing protocol updates and server availability), one-to-many multicast applications, and streaming applications (such as voice and video) where a lost datagram is far less important than an out-of-order datagram.

5. DisplayPort (Left) to HDMI (Right) adapter.

6. Correct: (iv) Switch off the printer.

7. Correct: (i) A damaged or defective Esc key. In brief, possible reasons for a defective or dysfunctional laptop keyboard are: (1) A cluster of "stuck" or damaged keys (although one stuck or damaged key will not cause the entire keyboard to stop functioning). (2) A disconnected or loose keyboard ribbon cable. (3) A warped keyboard. (4) Liquid spillage over the body of the keyboard may irreversibly damage the key contacts. (5) Physical damage to the keyboard, as may happen if the laptop is inadvertently dropped on to the ground by the user, or otherwise impacted.

8. Correct: (i) ping -t. Ping -t continuously pings a specified IP address until such time that the command is terminated using the Ctrl+C keystroke.

9. False. The correct statement should read: "Compared to a single core processor, a dual-core processor has two cores, with separate caches, on the same physical chip."

10. Correct: (i). An ethernet switch is designed to interconnect computers on the same network so that they can communicate with each other. A router interconnects one or more networks.

11. Correct: (iii) and (iv). The technician should implement effective anti-ESD measures before opening the computer case and touching or removing any internal component (e.g., RAM modules, video card, network adapter card, etc.). Also, the technician should always perform a backup of any critically important data stored on the computer drive <u>before</u> making any changes to the system.

12. (a) CMOS is an acronym for Complementary Metal-Oxide Semiconductor. It is also known as an RTC (Real-Time Clock), NVRAM (Non-volatile RAM), or CMOS RAM. **(b)** (iii) The CMOS stores the contents of the BIOS, such as the type and speed of the CPU, the capacity of the hard disk drive, and the current time and date.

13. Correct: (iii) netstat -an.

14. **(a)** (ii) There is clearly an issue with the laser printer's integrated memory – in other words, the printer's memory is inadequate to store large documents. **(b)** (i) Add more physical memory to the printer.

15. 5 GHz. The completed statement should read: "IEEE 802.11a is a wireless networking standard that operates at 5 GHz only."

16. **(a)** (iii) 548. **(b)** AFP is an acronym for Apple Filing Protocol. AFP is a networking protocol used by Apple Mac computers and associated devices that have Apple OS X installed. This protocol allows for the transfer of files across a network. AFP predominately uses port 548 (and occasionally 427) for establishing intercommunication between two networked computer systems.

17. Correct: (i), (ii), and (iii). CDMA (Code Division Multiple Access), GSM (Global System for Mobile Communication), and TDMA (Time Division Multiple Access) are all examples of cellular technologies. Other examples include GPRS (General Packet Radio Services), EDGE (Enhanced Data Rates for GSM Evolution), 4G, and LTE.

18. False. The correct statement should read: "WEP (Wired Equivalent Privacy), WPA2 (Wi-Fi Protected Access version 2), and AES (Advanced Encryption Standard) are wireless encryption protocols. WEP is deprecated and is no longer available. Since 2006, all new Wi-Fi certified network devices must use WPA2 encryption protocol, or a more secure wireless encryption method (e.g. WPA2-PSK (TKIP) or WPA2-PSK (AES). WPA2/AES is a very secure encryption method and is the strongest encryption combination currently available."

19. (a) (ii) A CPU socket physically supports an installed processor and heat sink assembly and (iv) The main function of a CPU socket is to house the processor on the motherboard without the necessity to solder the CPU in situ. A CPU socket is directly attached to the motherboard and its primary function is to house the processor. Therefore, it physically supports an installed processor and heat sink while also enabling easy replacement of the CPU (in light of the fact that the CPU is not soldered in situ on the motherboard). **(b)** PGA (Pin Grid Array) socket. **(c)** True. It is common to find PGA sockets on motherboards that are designed to support AMD processors. LGA (Land Grid Array) sockets are usually found on motherboards compatible with Intel processors.

20. (a) (1) A surge protector (otherwise known as a surge suppressor) is effectively a power strip that has an integrated metal oxide varistor (MOV). The primary function of the surge protector is to safeguard computer and other sensitive equipment against power surges and spikes. (2) A brownout is a sudden drop in voltage within the electrical grid that can cause computer systems to shut down. **(b)** (iii) The first troubleshooting step is to power cycle the PC – in other words, re-boot the PC.

Practice Test 10

1. True or False: The most common CPU cooling method is the CPU/heat sink/fan combination. Liquid-based cooling systems are sometimes used to dissipate heat generated by the processor. However, such systems are slightly less efficient compared to the conventional heat sink/fan combination.

2. An Apple® iPad™ Air tablet is wirelessly connected to a local Bluetooth-enabled printer.

What is the name of the app on the tablet that permits the user to print documents?

(i) AirPrint™

(ii) APNS

(iii) Bonjour™

(iv) None of the above

3. The laser printing process normally comprises seven distinct steps. State each of these steps in the correct sequential order.

4. A junior computer technician is troubleshooting a virtualization workstation that is unable to complete the booting process. He has devised a series of theories regarding the probable cause of the issue and he has tested the theories. However, his endeavors to identify the root cause of the booting problem have been unsuccessful.

What should the technician do next?

(i) Establish another theory of probable cause

(ii) Document findings, actions taken, and outcomes

(iii) Implement a temporary solution

(iv) Escalate the matter to a more experienced technician

5. True or False: SSH uses port 22 and HTTPS uses port 80.

6. Which type of external connection permits the fastest hard drive data transfer rate?

(i) HDMI

(ii) HHD

(iii) eSATA

(iv) USB 3.0

7. True or False: WiMAX, satellite, and mobile cellular connections are all examples of wireless Internet services.

8. A computer technician has installed a new NIC into an ASUS® laptop.

(a) What CLI command can the technician use to test the functionality of the new NIC? (Select two answers.)

(i) netstat -a FF::/8

(ii) ping ::1

(iii) ping 127.0.0.1

(iv) ping FE80::/10

(b) What is the main disadvantage of using the CLI commands referred to in part *(a)* above? (Select the best answer.)

(i) Any replies generated by these commands do not prove that the network adapter is functioning to the manufacturer's specification

(ii) It does not prove that TCP/IP settings have been correctly configured on the computer for connection to a particular network

(iii) The information generated by these commands can sometimes be too complex for a computer technician to interpret, thus requiring referral to an appropriately certified network engineer or IT specialist for analysis

(iv) The responses generated by these Command Shell diagnostic tools do not prove TCP/IP has been correctly installed on the computer

(c) What physical tool can the technician use to test NIC functionality?

(i) KVM switch

(ii) LAN adapter

(iii) Loopback plug

(iv) POST card

9. True or False: The maximum data transfer rate of wireless networks operating on the basis of IEEE

802.11g is 54 Mbps. However, the data throughput of such networks can be increased to 1.7 Gbps using Super G technology.

10. An ATX motherboard is shown in *Figure 10.* Identify the components labelled A to G.

11. Which connector can transmit uncompressed digital video?

(i) VGA

(ii) DVI

(iii) S-video

(iv) HDMI

Figure 10

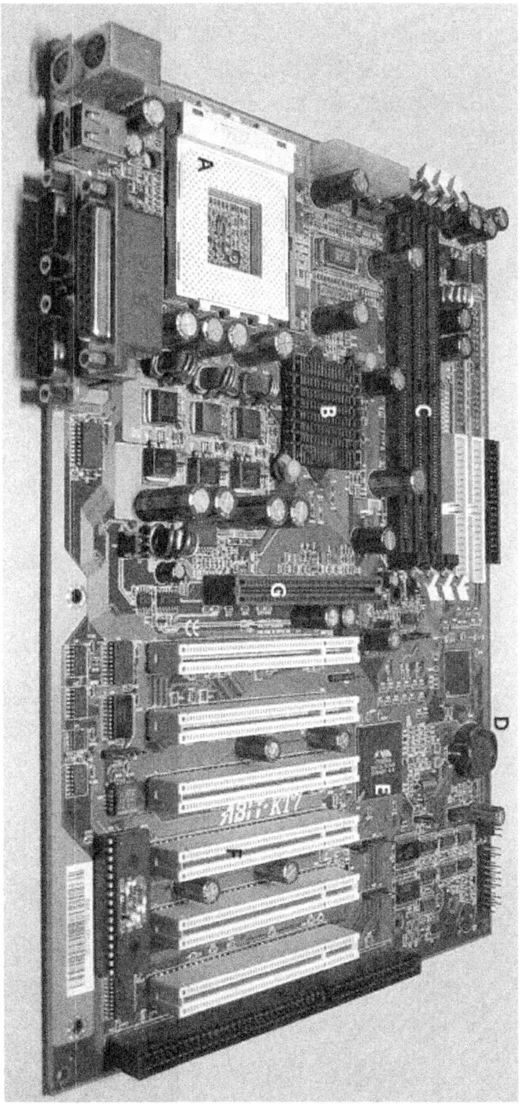

12. A small architectural design firm has a color laser printer that was purchased a few years ago. Historically, the printer has seldom given any problems, normally being fast and efficient. The printer is mainly used to print out large architectural schematics and large documents occasionally embedded with color images.

Recently, one of the architects has reported that the printer spontaneously pauses and resumes printing several times when large print jobs are sent to the printer.

What is the most likely cause of this issue?

(i) The printer's memory is not sufficient to handle large print jobs

(ii) The cable connections to the printer are loose

(iii) The printer is overheating

(iv) The pickup rollers are partially "jammed"

13. An IT technician has been called to a server room to troubleshoot a web server that has "crashed" and is now unresponsive.

The technician decides to take the server off-line and shut down the system. However, upon powering on the server, it does not boot into Windows® Server 2012™ OS. The technician now decides to reboot the system to access the BIOS settings. He discovers that the server has two resident HDDs, SATA 1 and SATA 2, configured into a RAID 1 array.

(a) What is the most likely reason for the server "crashing" in the first instance?

(i) HTTP settings are not correctly configured

(ii) Faulty patch cable

(iii) One of the resident HDDs has become defective

(iv) GbE NIC is starting to malfunction

(b) Briefly explain the purpose and function of a RAID 1 array.

(c) What is the easiest and most efficient way to allow the server to boot again and operate as normal?

(i) Designate the remaining functional hard disk as "active" within the BIOS

(ii) Open the computer case and disconnect the defective hard disk's SATA cable from the motherboard

(iii) No further troubleshooting action is needed to reboot the server since the RAID controller on the motherboard automatically manages the RAID 1 array on behalf of the user

(iv) Power down the server, open the system's outer casing, and remove the defective hard disk from the RAID array

14. The Command Shell can prove to be very useful when troubleshooting certain categories of networking issues.

Answer the following questions.

(a) What command can be entered into the Command Shell that will allow a specified number of bytes of data to be sent only four times to a specified IP address?

(i) ping -4

(ii) ping -l

(iii) ping -n

(iv) ping -t

(b) Which statement most accurately reflects the typical application of the command referred to in part *(a)* above?

(i) Diagnosing and troubleshooting issues with SCSI technology oftentimes involves the use of this CLI tool

(ii) Network technicians typically use this command to determine which router between a specific computer workstation in a LAN environment and another computer has failed and requires troubleshooting

(iii) This command has limited practical utility in diagnosing and troubleshooting network connectivity issues and thus is not normally used nowadays

(iv) This command is very useful in general network troubleshooting routines because it can be used as a diagnostic aid

15. Which of the following environmental factors is most likely to affect a thermal printer?

(i) Cold weather

(ii) High ambient temperatures

(iii) ESD

(iv) Moisture

16. A network technician working for a large BPO company has been requested by the Director of IT to create additional mapped network drives to support the business's ongoing client onboarding process. The technician opens the Command Shell and types a series of commands.

(a) What command should the technician enter at the command prompt to view any currently mapped network drives set up on the company's LAN?

(i) net use

(ii) net view

(iii) netstat

(iv) net start

(b) Which of the following commands should the technician enter at the command prompt if he wants to map a network drive S: to a shared resource called data$, located on a remote computer called PC-140?

(i) net use C: \\PC-140\data$

(ii) net start S: PC-140\data$

(iii) net use S: \\PC-140\data$

(iv) net view S: \\PC-140\data$

Figure 11

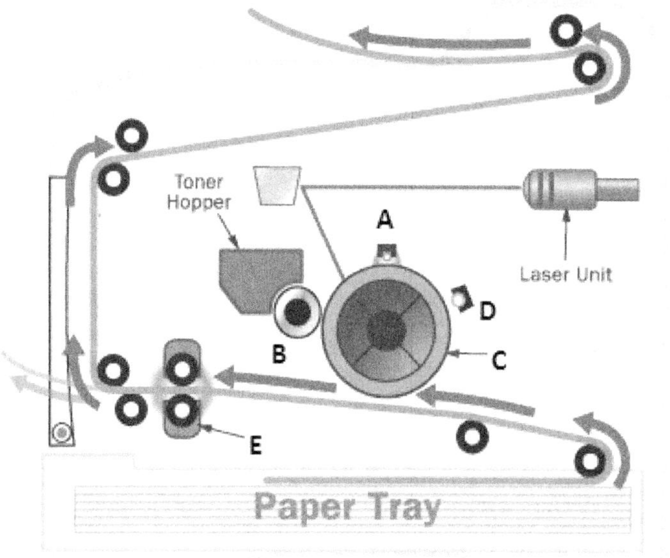

17. The schematic, as depicted in *Figure 11,* gives a succinct overview of the laser printing process.

Identify the components labelled A to E.

18. A computer technician is upgrading an ATX motherboard. He has successfully installed new DDR3 memory modules and a high-end graphics card. The technician has also flashed the BIOS to ensure that the reconditioned motherboard is compatible with Intel® processors. Finally, he installs an Intel® Core™ i5 CPU into the processor socket.

However, upon booting the computer, the technician hears a sequence of high and low beeps. Eventually the computer automatically shuts down.

(a) Which of the newly installed components are most likely the cause of this particular issue?

(i) BIOS

(ii) CPU

(iii) Graphics card

(iv) RAM

(b) What is the most likely reason for the reconditioned computer automatically shutting down only after a short period of operation?

(i) A manufacturing defect has precipitated the unexpected failure of the ATX motherboard

(ii) High-end graphics card is not properly seated in the PCIe slot

(iii) Misconfigured BIOS settings

(iv) Overheating processor

(c) What can the technician do to prevent this issue from arising again once the computer is rebooted? (Select two answers.)

(i) Ensure that the computer system has sufficient thermal paste between the relevant internal components

(ii) Flash the BIOS firmware again to ensure compatibility with the installed processor and accordingly adjust the BIOS settings

(iii) Reseat the high-end PCIe graphics card on the ATX motherboard whilst ensuring the stability of all on-board connections

(iv) Verify that the heat sink and CPU fan are correctly installed

19. Match the following descriptions to the correct video connector type listed below.

(i) This video connection typically sends analog or digital signals over 3 wires – red, green, and blue – with each wire terminating in an RCA plug. Also, this video connection is able to transmit HD digital signals.

(ii) This video connection is able to transmit SD video. It uses a mini-DIN connector which can have either 4, 6, 7, or 9 pins.

(iii) This video connection is only able to transmit SD video. It typically uses a single yellow RCA port for video, with white and red RCA ports for audio.

DisplayPort / S-video / Composite Video / HDMI / Component Video / USB 3.0

20. The component displayed in *Figure 12* is normally inserted into a laptop motherboard.

(a) Which of the following accurately describes the type of laptop component displayed in the figure?

(i) DIMM

(ii) NIC

(iii) SODIMM

(iv) SRAM

(b) How many pins does this component have?

(i) 200

(ii) 204

(iii) 240

(iv) 260

(c) What is the capacity, in gigabytes, of this component?

(d) What is the component's nominal data transfer rate, in megabytes per second (MB/s)?

(e) Which of the following represents the nominal number of mega-transfers per second (MT/s) that this component can potentially perform?

(i) 800

(ii) 1,600

(iii) 3,200

(iv) None of the above

(f) Which of the following represents the component's I/O clock speed, in mega-hertz (MHz)?

(i) 800

(ii) 1,600

(iii) 3,200

(iv) None of the above

Figure 12

Practice Test 10			
MCQ Solutions			
1.	False	11.	(ii)
2.	(i)	12.	(iii)
3.	See notes	13.	(a)(iii), (b) See notes, (c)(i)
4.	(iv)	14.	(a)(ii), (b)(iv)
5.	False	15.	(ii)
6.	(iii)	16.	(a)(i), (b)(iii)
7.	True	17.	See notes
8.	(a)(ii)(iii), (b)(ii), (c)(iii)	18.	(a)(ii), (b)(iv), (c)(i)(iv)
9.	False	19.	See notes
10.	See notes	20.	(a)(iii), (b)(ii), (c) See notes, (d) See notes, (e)(ii), (f)(i)

1. False. Of all the CPU cooling systems available nowadays, liquid-based cooling systems can dissipate heat generated by the processor the most efficiently. Therefore, the statement should have read: "The most common CPU cooling method is the CPU/heat sink/fan combination. Liquid-based cooling systems are sometimes used to dissipate heat generated by the processor. Of all the CPU cooling methods, liquid-based cooling can dissipate heat generated by the processor the most efficiently.

2. Correct: (i) AirPrint.

3. (1) Processing. (2) Charging. (3) Exposing. (4) Developing. (5) Transferring. (6) Fusing. (7) Cleaning.

4. Correct: (iv) Escalate the matter to a more experienced technician.

5. False. SSH (Secure Shell) uses port 22 and HTTPS (Hypertext Transfer Protocol Secure) uses port 443.

6. Correct: (iii) eSATA. The maximum data transfer rate of eSATA is 6 Gbps (600 MB/s).

7. True.

8. (a) (ii) and (iii). The technician can use the **ping 127.0.0.1** command for an IPv4 address and **ping ::1** for an IPv6 address. These IP addresses are known as loopback addresses and can be used in conjunction with the ping command for diagnostic and troubleshooting purposes. Any replies generated by these commands prove that the NIC is functioning properly and that TCP/IP (Transmission Control Protocol/Internet Protocol) has been correctly installed on this computer. **(b)** (ii) Pinging these loopback addresses does not prove that TCP/IP has been correctly configured on the computer for connection to a particular network (e.g., SOHO or LAN). **(c)** (iii) Loopback plug.

9. False. The correct statement should read: "The maximum data transfer rate of wireless networks operating on the basis of IEEE 802.11g is 54 Mbps. However, the data throughput of such networks can be increased to 108 Mbps using Super G technology." For the purposes of clarification, the wireless standard IEEE 802.11ac operates at a frequency of 5 GHz and has a maximum data throughput of 1.7 Gbps.

10. (A) PGA socket (that is used to house the CPU). (B) Heat sink covering the Northbridge chipset. (C) Memory slots (into which are inserted RAM modules). (D) CR2032 lithium battery. (E) Southbridge chipset. (F) PCI expansion bus slots. (G) PCIe expansion bus slot.

11. Correct: (ii) DVI. DVI (Digital Visual Interface) is an interface that is designed to transmit uncompressed digital video and can be configured to support multiple modes such as DVI-A (analog only), DVI-D (digital only), or DVI-I (analog and digital). Considering that DVI-A and DVI-I support analog connections, these modes are also compatible with the VGA interface.

12. Correct: (iii) The printer is overheating.

13. (a) (iii) It is highly likely that one of the resident HDDs, either SATA 1 or SATA 2, became defective and failed. **(b)** Since the BIOS settings show that the computer has a RAID 1 array, if one HDD fails, the other HDD would be expected to operate as normal since the data on one HDD is copied to the other disk (in a process known as "mirroring"). Therefore, RAID 1 arrays are fault-tolerant and prevent data loss or corruption by providing for redundancy of data. **(c)** (i) The easiest and most effective way to allow the server to boot again is to mark the remaining functional HDD (for example, SATA 2) as "active" within the BIOS. Of course, we are assuming that SATA 1 has failed and is no longer on-line.

14. **(a)** (ii) ping [IP address] -l [number of bytes]. For example, ping 192.168.10.12 -l 1500 will send 1500 bytes of data only 4 times to the device identified by the IP address 192.168.10.12. **(b)** (iv) This command is very useful in general network troubleshooting routines because it can be used as a diagnostic aid.

15. Correct: (ii) High ambient temperatures – in other words, hot environmental conditions.

16. **(a)** (i) net use. **(b)** (iii) net use S: \\PC-140\data$. If the network technician wants to create additional mapped network drives, s/he will use the UNC file path \\computername\sharename. Hence, the full generic command is net use drivename: \\computername\sharename. UNC is an acronym for Universal Naming Convention.

17. (A) Primary corona wire. (B) Developing roller. (C) Photosensitive drum (or imaging drum). (D) Cleaning unit. (E) Fusing assembly.

18. **(a)** (ii) CPU. A computer that has an Intel-compatible motherboard and Intel-based BIOS settings will normally generate a series of high and low beeping sounds during boot-up whenever there is a problem with the CPU. **(b)** (iv) It is most likely that the CPU started to overheat. **(c)** (i) and (iv). To prevent this issue from arising again, the technician should verify that the

CPU is seated correctly in the corresponding socket on the motherboard. He should also verify that the heat sink and CPU fan are installed correctly and operating to specification. Finally, the technician should ensure that there is sufficient thermal paste (thermal interface material) between the CPU and the heat sink, and that the paste is evenly spread.

19. (i) Component Video (RGB connector). (ii) S-video (Separate video). (iii) Composite Video (using RCA connectors).

20. **(a)** (iii) SODIMM (Small Outline Dual In-Line Memory Module). **(b)** (ii) 204 pins. Upon reading the information printed on the memory stick's adhesive label, we can see the text "PC3-12800S". The "PC3" signifies that the memory module is DDR3. SODIMM DDR3 modules have 204 pins. SODIMM DDR and DDR2 have 200-pins. SODIMM DDR4 has 260 pins. **(c)** 4 GB. **(d)** 12,800 MB/s. Once again, upon reading the information on the component's adhesive label, we can see the text "PC3-12800S". This information means that the memory module can potentially transfer 12,800 megabytes of data per second. Hence, the DTR (Data Transfer Rate) is 12,800 MB/s. **(e)** (ii) 1,600 MT/s. To calculate the maximum theoretical mega-transfers per second (MT/s), use the equation: Data Transfer Rate (in megabytes per second)/8 bytes = MT/s. Hence, 12,800 MB/s divided by 8 bytes = 1,600 MT/s. Since DDR versions are designed with a 64-bit wide bus, this means that only 8 bytes of data can be transferred per cycle, which explains why the DTR (in MB/s) is divided by 8 bytes. Since the SODIMM module given in the figure is designed to potentially allow 12,800 megabytes of data to be transferred per second, we can easily calculate the mega-transfers per second to be 1,600 MT/s. This SODIMM PC3-12800 module can also be referred to as a DDR3-1600 module. **(f)** (i) 800 MHz. The memory module's I/O clock speed can be calculated using the following equation: DTR (in MB/s) divided by (8 bytes x 2) = I/O clock speed (in MHz). Therefore, 12,800 MB/s divided by (8 bytes x 2) = 800 MHz. DDR (Double Data Rate) memory modules allow twice the data to be transferred but at the same clock speed. Since DDR memory is designed with a 64-bit wide bus, meaning that 8 bytes of data can be transferred per cycle, the DDR designation means that this data transfer happens twice each second (i.e., 8 bytes x 2) at the same clock speed. Accordingly, the DTR in megabytes per second is divided by 16, not 8 bytes, if we want to calculate the I/O clock speed (in MHz).

Practice Test 11

1. What is the standard connection type of a contemporary Apple® smart device?

(i) HDMI

(ii) micro-USB

(iii) USB Type C

(iv) Thunderbolt

2. Which of the following is the maximum speed of a USB 3.0-compatible ExpressCard device that uses a USB 2.0 bus?

(i) 400 Mbps

(ii) 480 Mbps

(iii) 5 Gbps

(iv) 10 Gbps

3. Answer the following questions with respect to DVD technology.

(a) What is the most common DVD format currently available?

(i) DVD-5

(ii) DVD-9

(iii) DVD-10

(iv) DVD-18

(b) What is the typical storage capacity of this DVD format?

(i) 1.5 GB

(ii) 4.7 GB

(iii) 5 GB

(iv) 9.4 GB

Figure 13(a)

Figure 13(b)

4. Identify the video connectors displayed in *Figure 13(a)* and *Figure 13(b).*

5. Fill in the missing spaces: A ______ workstation is a computer that hosts one or more virtual (or guest) operating systems. The guest operating systems are called ______ ______. These workstations use what is known as a ______. There are two main types: (a) Type 1 (Native or ______ ______), which directly uses the host computer's hardware, and (b) Type 2 (______), which means that the ______ operates within (or "on top of") the host operating system.

6. An IT engineer has set a new BIOS "Supervisor Password" for two web servers in a client's server room after carrying out routine maintenance. A few weeks later, the web servers are shut down and re-started as part of a security patch installation. However, the client's Senior Technician has mislaid the password and he is unable to boot the web servers into Windows® Server 2012 R2™.

How should the technician reset the BIOS password?

(i) Update BIOS firmware

(ii) Remove CMOS battery

(iii) Remove Northbridge chipset

(iv) Un-install and re-install Windows® Server 2012 R2™

7. An IT technician working for a prominent contract manufacturing company is notified that a critical server system in one of its manufacturing facilities is frequently rebooting itself without being instructed to do so. The exhaust vent fans are operating as normal. The technician determines that the fault is a hardware issue.

Which two components of the server system are most likely responsible for this fault?

(i) CPU cooling fan

(ii) KVM switch

(iii) RAID controller

(iv) PSU

8. Which CLI tool can be used to determine the MAC address of a computer's NIC?

(i) netBIOS

(ii) netstat

(iii) ipconfig

(iv) ping -a

9. Liquid cooling systems are sometimes employed in CPU-intensive computer systems to dissipate the heat generated by the processor.

Which of the following are typical components of a liquid-based cooling system? (Select all applicable answers.)

(i) CR2032 battery

(ii) Hollow metal block

(iii) Pump

(iv) PVC tubing

10. Fill in the missing spaces: Fiber optic cables transmit data by way of ______ signals instead of electricity. Hence, fiber optic is much faster and is not affected by ______. Fiber optic cables can also send data much further than ______-based telecommunication cables. There are two main types of fiber optic cables: ______ and ______. Fiber optic cables mainly use ______, SC, and ______ connectors. ______ connectors resemble SC connectors in physical appearance.

11. An IT help desk receives a call from an irate customer. The customer angrily explains that he has recently purchased a relatively expensive wireless inkjet printer. However, when he attempts to print a document using an application on his laptop, the wireless printer produces unintelligible text.

The customer confirms that the laptop and printer are correctly paired via Bluetooth connectivity, and that the printer is in close proximity to the laptop.

Which of the following options is the best first troubleshooting step to effectively resolve this issue? (Select one option.)

(i) Update the printer's driver

(ii) Clean the print heads

(iii) Ensure that the inkjet printer is correctly paired to the laptop

(iv) Power cycle the printer

12. Fill in the missing spaces: ______ technology operates at virtually the same ______ GHz frequency used by IEEE 802.11 b/g/n wireless networks. However, this technology uses a spread-spectrum "frequency hopping" signaling system to help minimise interference from the said wireless networks.

13. The IT department in a large pharmaceutical manufacturer has purchased a new high-end computer system for the Operations Team. The computer will be mainly used for data analytics and temporary storage of batch manufacturing records. The computer has several HDDs already installed.

The IT technician has been asked to configure the HDDs into a "striped set" for faster read/write speeds.

(a) What type of RAID configuration has the technician been asked to set up?

(i) RAID 0

(ii) RAID 1

(iii) RAID 5

(iv) RAID 10

(b) Where can this type of RAID set up be configured and implemented? (Select the correct option.)

(i) Device Manager

(ii) Control Panel

(iii) BIOS/UEFI

(iv) Disk Management console

(c) State <u>one</u> advantage of the RAID array that the technician has been asked to set up.

(d) State <u>one</u> significant disadvantage of using this RAID array.

14. Fill in the missing spaces: _____ is a type of video connection that is specifically used for SD video. It uses a 4, 6, 7, or 9-pin ______ connector.

15. A Xerox® maintenance technician is servicing a laser printer in a large open-plan office. There is one other laser printer in the office which is currently being used by staff. However, one member of staff is very annoyed because this other laser printer has mildly creased some pages in her printout.

What should the maintenance technician do to resolve this printer issue? (Select the best two answers.)

(i) Replace the pickup rollers

(ii) Adjust the humidity level to 5%

(iii) Adjust the humidity level to 35%

(iv) Inspect the laser printer and remove any unnoticed paper jams

16. A network technician is carrying out some modifications to a SOHO network on behalf of a small accountancy and taxation practice. The technician has opened the CLI tool and he enters a variant of the Ipconfig command at the command prompt. The computer generates the information shown in *Figure 14.*

On the basis of the information presented in the figure, answer the following questions.

(a) What variant of the ipconfig command did the technician enter at the command prompt to generate the information displayed in the figure?

(b) What type of information is presented in the figure?

(c) Does this SOHO network use DHCP?

(d) State the MAC address of the computer's NIC.

(e) What is the DNS server's IP address?

(f) Define the term DNS and briefly explain its function.

Figure 14

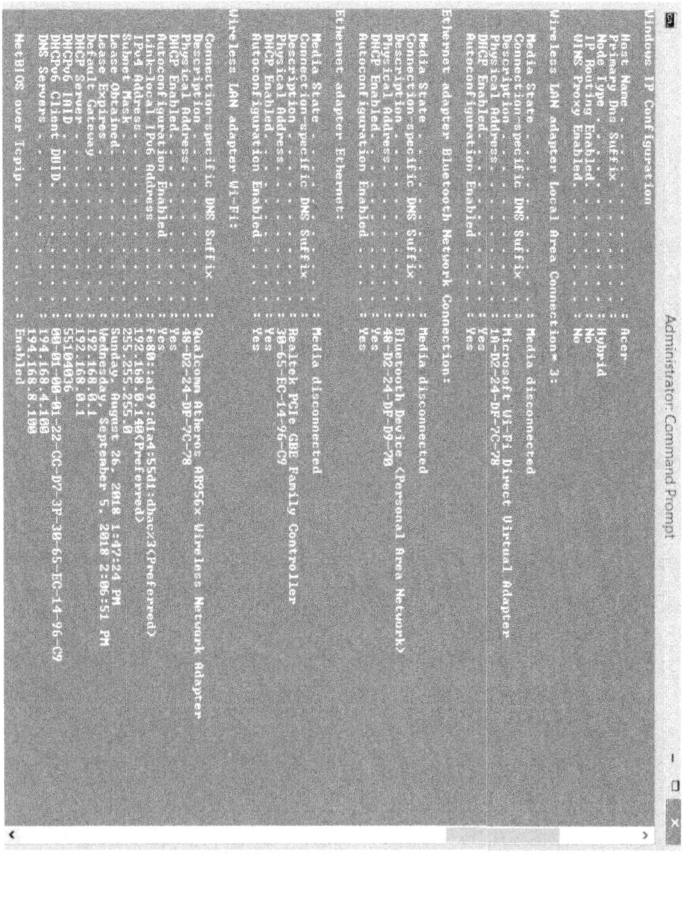
Administrator: Command Prompt
Windows IP Configuration
Host Name . . . . : Acer
Primary Dns Suffix . . . . :
Node Type . . . . : Hybrid
IP Routing Enabled. . . . . : No
WINS Proxy Enabled. . . . . : No
Wireless LAN adapter Local Area Connection* 3:
Media State . . . . : Media disconnected
Connection-specific DNS Suffix . :
Description . . . . : Microsoft Wi-Fi Direct Virtual Adapter
Physical Address. . . . . : 1A-D2-24-DF-7C-78
DHCP Enabled. . . . . : Yes
Autoconfiguration Enabled . . . . : Yes
Ethernet adapter Bluetooth Network Connection:
Media State . . . . : Media disconnected
Connection-specific DNS Suffix . :
Description . . . . : Bluetooth Device (Personal Area Network)
Physical Address. . . . . : 48-D2-24-DF-D9-70
DHCP Enabled. . . . . : Yes
Autoconfiguration Enabled . . . . : Yes
Ethernet adapter Ethernet:
Media State . . . . : Media disconnected
Connection-specific DNS Suffix . :
Description . . . . : Realtek PCIe GBE Family Controller
Physical Address. . . . . : 30-65-EC-14-96-C9
DHCP Enabled. . . . . : Yes
Autoconfiguration Enabled . . . . : Yes
Wireless LAN adapter Wi-Fi:
Connection-specific DNS Suffix . :
Description . . . . : Qualcomm Atheros AR956x Wireless Network Adapter
Physical Address. . . . . : 48-D2-24-DF-7C-78
DHCP Enabled. . . . . : Yes
Autoconfiguration Enabled . . . . : Yes
Link-local IPv6 Address . . . . . : fe80::a199:d1a4:55d1:dbac%3(Preferred)
IPv4 Address. . . . . : 192.168.0.140(Preferred)
Subnet Mask . . . . : 255.255.255.0
Lease Obtained. . . . . : Sunday, August 26, 2018 1:47:24 PM
Lease Expires . . . . : Wednesday, September 5, 2018 2:06:51 PM
Default Gateway . . . . : 192.168.0.1
DHCP Server . . . . : 192.168.0.1
DHCPv6 IAID . . . . : 55104036
DHCPv6 Client DUID. . . . . : 00-01-00-01-22-CC-D7-3F-30-65-EC-14-96-C9
DNS Servers . . . . : 194.168.4.100
194.168.8.100
NetBIOS over Tcpip. . . . . : Enabled

17. Which of the following connections provide the fastest data transfer rates? (Select one answer.)

(i) SuperSpeed USB

(ii) USB 3.1 Gen 2

(iii) eSATA

(iv) Bluetooth 3.0

18. Which of the following encryption protocol combinations offers the most secure form of wireless encryption?

(i) WPA2-PSK (TKIP)

(ii) WPA-PSK (TKIP)

(iii) WPA2-PSK (AES)

(iv) WEP

19. Select the correct options: A (Phillips/Torx) screwdriver is predominantly used by computer technicians to remove screws from the outside of a PC case or from within a laptop. However, on occasion, a (Phillips/Torx) screwdriver can also be used as an alternative.

20. Which of the following network devices allows a remote device (e.g., VoIP phone) to receive both data connectivity and electrical power?

(i) PoE injector

(ii) Repeater

(iii) Router

(iv) WAP

Practice Test 11			
MCQ Solutions			
1.	(iv)	11.	(iv)
2.	(ii)	12.	See notes
3.	(a)(i), (b)(ii)	13.	(a)(i), (b)(iii), (c) See notes, (d) See notes
4.	See notes	14.	See notes
5.	See notes	15.	(iii), (iv)
6.	(ii)	16.	See notes
7.	(i), (iv)	17.	(ii)
8.	(iii)	18.	(iii)
9.	(ii), (iii), (iv)	19.	See notes
10.	See notes	20.	(i)

1. Correct: (iv) Thunderbolt connector (otherwise known as a lightning connector).

2. Correct: (ii) 480 Mbps (or 480 Mb/s). In the scenario, the ExpressCard device is USB 3.0 compatible. In theory, this device can transmit data at USB 3.0 rates of 5 Gbps. However, the user has plugged the ExpressCard into a USB 2.0 port. Accordingly, the ExpressCard will only operate at the maximum data transfer speed permitted by the USB 2.0 port (480 Mbps).

3. Correct: **(a)** (i) At the date of publication of this book, DVD-5 is recognised as being the most common DVD format (1 side/1 layer). **(b)** (ii) 4.7 GB.

4. (A) DVI-A connector. (B) DVI-D (Dual Link) connector.

5. (1) Virtualization. (2) Virtual machines. (3) Hypervisor. (4) "bare metal". (5) Hosted. (6) Hypervisor. The completed statement should read: "A virtualization workstation is a computer that hosts one or more virtual (or guest) operating systems. The guest operating systems are called virtual machines. These workstations use what is known as a hypervisor. There are two main types: (a) Type 1 (Native or "bare metal"), which directly uses the host computer's hardware, and (b) Type 2 (Hosted), which means that the hypervisor operates within (or "on top of") the host operating system."

6. Correct: (ii) The technician can reset the BIOS "supervisor password" by removing the CMOS battery from the motherboard. The CMOS battery is generally a CR2032 lithium coin cell.

7. Correct: (i) CPU cooling fan and (iv) PSU. (1) The technician needs to open the server case to determine if the CPU fan is operating as normal. If the CPU fan is not working, any heat generated by the CPU will not be dissipated and the computer system will shut down automatically to prevent irreversible damage to the CPU. (2) The PSU may be defective or starting to fail. The PSU, also located within the computer case, may lose some of its ability to sustain a full power load over time. The failing PSU may not be able to consistently supply the correct voltage to the motherboard. If the computer system's motherboard does not receive the proper signal strength or voltage from a weakened PSU, the system will reboot itself. The only way to remedy this particular problem is to replace the PSU.

8. Correct: (iii) ipconfig.

9. Correct: (ii), (iii), and (iv). Typical components of a liquid-based cooling system are hollow metal block, radiator, pump, CPU fan, PVC tubing, drain valve, and a suitable coolant.

10. (1) Light. (2) EMI (Electromagnetic Interference). (3) Copper. (4) Single mode. (5) Multi-mode. (6) ST. (7) LC. (8) LC. The completed statement should read: "Fiber optic cables transmit data by way of light signals instead of electricity. Hence, fiber optic is much faster and is not affected by EMI. Fiber optic cables can also send data much further than copper-based telecommunication cables. There are two main types of fiber optic cables: single-mode and multi-mode. Fiber optic cables mainly use ST, SC, and LC connectors. LC connectors resemble SC connectors in physical appearance."

11. Correct: (iv) Power cycle the printer. Power cycling resolves many printer-related issues, and therefore is the best first troubleshooting step to take. However, if power cycling does not resolve the matter, the other options (i), (ii), and (iii) become viable troubleshooting opportunities worth exploring.

12. Bluetooth. 2.4 GHz. The correct completed statement should read: "Bluetooth technology operates at virtually the same 2.4 GHz frequency used by IEEE 802.11 b/g/n wireless networks. However, this technology uses a spread-spectrum frequency hopping signaling system to help minimise interference from the said wireless networks."

13. **(a)** (i) RAID 0 (otherwise known as "disk striping"). Data is striped across multiple HDDs in an attempt to increase performance. A minimum of 2 HDDs is required to set up this RAID array. **(b)** (iii) BIOS/UEFI settings. **(c)** This RAID configuration allows for fast read/write speeds and therefore enhanced performance of the computer system. **(d)** RAID 0 is not fault tolerant because it does not offer any type of data redundancy.

14. S-video. Mini-DIN connector. The correct completed statement should read: "S-video is a type of video connection that is specifically used for SD video. It uses a 4, 6, 7, or 9-pin mini-DIN connector."

15. Correct: (iii) Inspect the laser printer and remove any unnoticed paper jams, and (iv) Adjust the humidity level to 35%.

16. **(a)** ipconfig /all. **(b)** The ipconfig /all command displays a more detailed version of the computer's current TCP/IP network configuration parameters, as well as stating whether or not DHCP (Dynamic Host Configuration Protocol) is being used, the DNS server address, and the physical address (or MAC address) of the computer's network card (NIC). Hence, this command can offer a lot of useful information when troubleshooting a specific network issue. **(c)** DHCP Enabled: Yes. **(d)** Physical address: 48-D2-24-DF-7C-78 **(e)** 192.168.0.1 **(f)** DNS is an acronym for Domain Name System. A DNS server is responsible for resolving domain names to IP addresses – in other words, converting a website's (or network resource's) alphanumeric name into a numerical IP address. This translation using DNS is very important because networking devices only communicate with each other over a network via numerical IP addresses, not alphanumeric domain names (e.g., website addresses, etc.). In smaller networks such as SOHO networks, the DNS server is typically located at the ISP (Internet Service Provider). However, an organization with a large LAN may operate an internal DNS server, instead of relying on the server provided by the ISP.

17. Correct: (ii) USB 3.1 Gen 2 (otherwise simply known as USB 3.1) has a data transfer rate of 10 Gbps. eSATA 6 Gbps. SuperSpeed USB (USB 3.0) 5Gbps. Bluetooth 3.0 is the slowest.

18. Correct: (iii) WPA2-PSK (AES).

19. (1) Phillips. (2) Torx. The correct full statement should read: "A Phillips screwdriver is predominantly used by computer technicians to remove screws from the outside of a PC case or from within a laptop. However, on occasion, a Torx screwdriver can also be used as an alternative."

20. Correct: (i) PoE injector. A PoE (Power over Ethernet) injector is a network device that sends electrical power along with data packets over a single twisted pair ethernet cable to remote devices (e.g., wireless access points (WAPs), IP cameras, and VoIP phones). PoE network devices are designed to comply with the IEEE 802.3af standard and are normally "grounded" (or "earthed").

Practice Test 12

1. What type of computer display has the highest contrast ratio?

(i) LCD

(ii) LED

(iii) OLED

(iv) Plasma

2. An internationally renowned Internet technology company is planning to construct a new state-of-the-art data center in Finland. Ultimately, the data center will comprise a multitude of secure server rooms. A team of network engineers have been contracted to design these server rooms.

Which of the following devices should the engineers include in the design of each server room to ensure ease of administration for data center personnel?

(i) Ethernet switch

(ii) KVM switch

(iii) Linux® workstation

(iv) MIDI

3. A common networking device is displayed in *Figure 15.*

(a) State the name of the device labelled A in the figure.

(i) Ethernet switch

(ii) KVM switch

(iii) NAS drive

(iv) Rack server

(b) What is the primary function of this device? (Select two answers.)

(i) It is a specialized computer system used in a network environment to provide specific services to client computers; consequently, this device has significantly more processing power, memory, and storage capabilities relative to client computers

(ii) It serves as a central connecting device to which all networked computers are attached

(iii) This device provides data access and storage services to a heterogenous group of client computers

(iv) This device regenerates the signals it receives from other computers connected to the network and then sends the regenerated signals to the correct computers on the LAN

4. Which of the following connection types provides the fastest data transfer rates? (Select one answer.)

(i) Firewire 800

(ii) Firewire 400

(iii) eSATA

(iv) USB 2.0

Figure 15

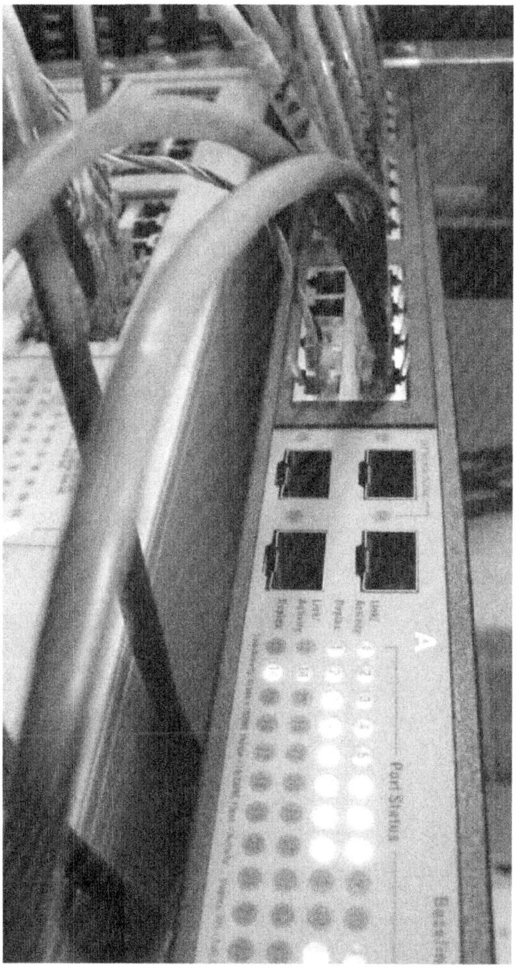

5. Select the correct option: (UTP/STP) and Fiber Optic cables are two types of cable that offer protection from EMI.

6. While troubleshooting a network issue, a computer technician types *net view* into the Command Shell.

What type of information does this command present on the screen?

(i) Net view displays network protocol statistics and current TCP/IP connections that use NetBIOS

(ii) Net view is used to show a list of computers and network devices connected to a specific network

(iii) The command net view specifies the number of active connections open on a network at any particular moment in time

(iv) None of the above

7. According to an ipconfig statement, a computer workstation in a LAN environment has been assigned the IP address 169.254.0.140. This Windows® OS computer is unable to access shared resources on the network or the Internet. Other computers on the network also have limited or no Internet connectivity.

(a) What is the significance of the IP address 169.254.0.140?

(i) The default gateway address applicable to the network is 169.254.0.140

(ii) The local computer has been previously configured to use a static IP address as opposed to using a dynamic IP address

(iii) The IP address 169.254.0.140 indicates that the local computer can no longer implement the APIPA protocol because it is unable to access the relevant server system

(iv) The IP address 169.254.0.140 indicates that Windows® OS on the local computer has implemented APIPA

(b) In the context of aforementioned scenario, which of the following network devices is most likely to be dysfunctional?

(i) DHCP server

(ii) Ethernet switch

(iii) Network firewall

(iv) Router

(v) Web server

Figure 16

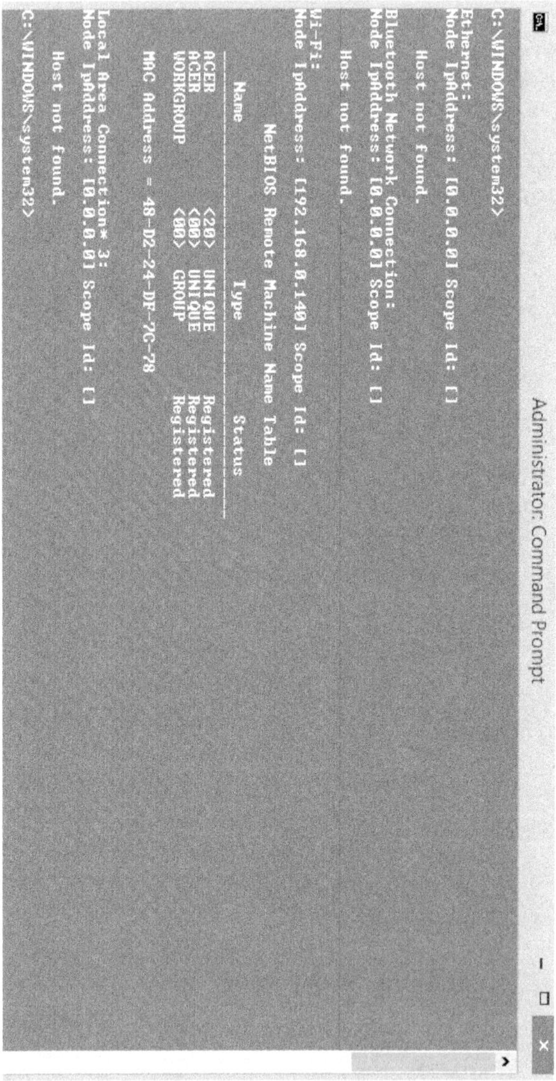
Administrator: Command Prompt
C:\WINDOWS\system32>
Ethernet:
Node IpAddress: [0.0.0.0] Scope Id: []
Host not found.
Bluetooth Network Connection:
Node IpAddress: [0.0.0.0] Scope Id: []
Host not found.
Wi-Fi:
Node IpAddress: [192.168.0.140] Scope Id: []
NetBIOS Remote Machine Name Table
Name Type Status
ACER <20> UNIQUE Registered
ACER <00> UNIQUE Registered
WORKGROUP <00> GROUP Registered
MAC Address = 48-D2-24-DF-7C-78
Local Area Connection* 3:
Node IpAddress: [0.0.0.0] Scope Id: []
Host not found.
C:\WINDOWS\system32>

8. A PC user intends to expand the peripheral devices of his Acer® Aspire™ desktop computer. However, the system does not have sufficient on-board ports.

What type of card should be installed to remedy this problem?

(i) SATA card

(ii) USB card

(iii) SDXC

(iv) SDHC

9. True or False: The maximum data transfer rate of IEEE wireless protocol 802.11n is 1,000 Mbps.

10. A technician is configuring a SOHO network on behalf of a client. He opens the CLI tool and enters a command. The information shown in *Figure 16* displays on the screen.

(a) Which of the following commands did the technician enter at the command prompt?

(i) nbtstat -A

(ii) netbios

(iii) netstat -n

(iv) nslookup

(b) Briefly explain the type of information that this command generates.

(c) What is the IP address of the remote computer?

(d) What is the physical address of the remote computer?

(e) What is the name of the network to which the remote computer is connected?

11. Which of the following is a common charging port that is built into an Android™ smartphone?

(i) USB Type B

(ii) Micro USB Type B

(iii) Mini USB Type B

(iv) Lightning

12. Which of the following is the maximum data transfer rate of SATA 3.0?

(i) 150 MB/s

(ii) 300 MB/s

(iii) 6 Gbps

(iv) 16 Gbps

13. A very experienced PC technician is installing a new kit of 2 Kingston® 2 GB DDR4 memory sticks into a Lenovo® laptop on behalf of a customer. The customer purchased the laptop almost 2 years ago.

According to the laptop manufacturer's website, the new memory sticks are compatible with the laptop's motherboard. However, when the technician boots the laptop, an error message appears on the screen:

Memory not recognised. Press any key to continue.

(a) What is the most likely cause of the memory error?

(i) New RAM modules not correctly seated

(ii) Dirty RAM slots

(iii) Memory modules were damaged by ESD during installation

(iv) UEFI BIOS does not recognize newly installed RAM

(b) What action should the technician take to remedy this fault?

14. What is the minimum category networking cable required for a 1000Base-T network?

(i) Cat 3

(ii) Cat 5

(iii) Cat 5e

(iv) Cat 7a

Figure 17

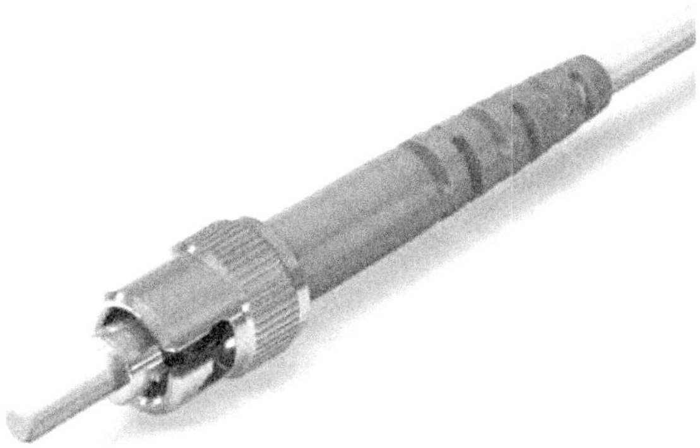

15. Identify the fiber optic connector shown in *Figure 17.*

16. A network technician is troubleshooting a LAN connectivity issue. She opens the Command Shell and enters a sequence of commands while reviewing the consequent networking information presented on the screen. The last command she enters generates the information displayed in *Figure 18.*

(a) Which of the following commands did the technician enter at the command prompt to generate the information displayed in the figure?

(i) netstat -an

(ii) netstat -n

(iii) netdom

(iv) nslookup

(v) tracert

(b) What type of information does this command generate?

(c) Which of the following port numbers is associated with HTTPS?

(i) 139

(ii) 443

(iii) 5228

(iv) 50108

Figure 18

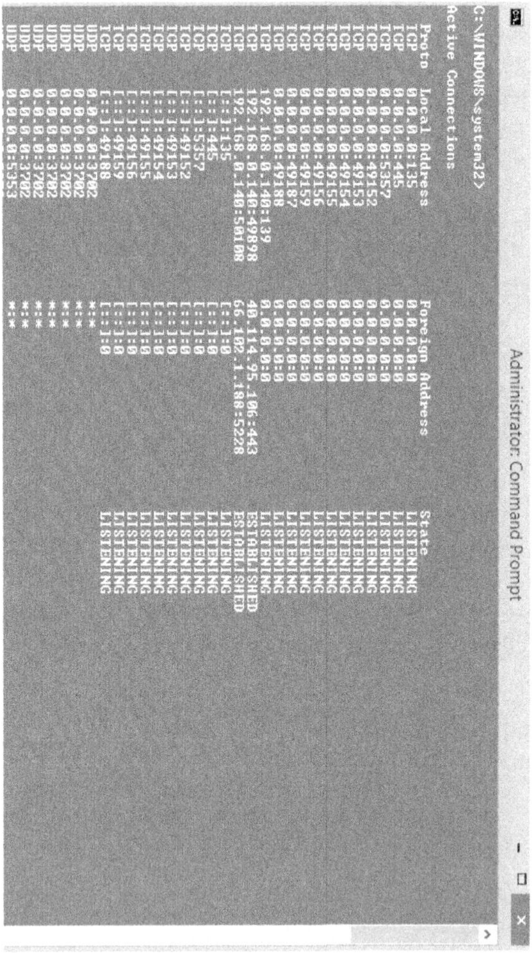

Administrator: Command Prompt
C:\WINDOWS\system32>
Active Connections
Proto Local Address Foreign Address State
TCP 0.0.0.0:135 0.0.0.0:0 LISTENING
TCP 0.0.0.0:445 0.0.0.0:0 LISTENING
TCP 0.0.0.0:5357 0.0.0.0:0 LISTENING
TCP 0.0.0.0:49152 0.0.0.0:0 LISTENING
TCP 0.0.0.0:49153 0.0.0.0:0 LISTENING
TCP 0.0.0.0:49154 0.0.0.0:0 LISTENING
TCP 0.0.0.0:49155 0.0.0.0:0 LISTENING
TCP 0.0.0.0:49156 0.0.0.0:0 LISTENING
TCP 0.0.0.0:49159 0.0.0.0:0 LISTENING
TCP 0.0.0.0:49187 0.0.0.0:0 LISTENING
TCP 0.0.0.0:49188 0.0.0.0:0 LISTENING
TCP 192.168.0.140:139 0.0.0.0:0 LISTENING
TCP 192.168.0.140:49898 40.114.95.106:443 ESTABLISHED
TCP 192.168.0.140:50108 66.102.1.188:5228 ESTABLISHED
TCP [::]:135 [::]:0 LISTENING
TCP [::]:445 [::]:0 LISTENING
TCP [::]:5357 [::]:0 LISTENING
TCP [::]:49152 [::]:0 LISTENING
TCP [::]:49153 [::]:0 LISTENING
TCP [::]:49154 [::]:0 LISTENING
TCP [::]:49155 [::]:0 LISTENING
TCP [::]:49156 [::]:0 LISTENING
TCP [::]:49159 [::]:0 LISTENING
TCP [::]:49188 [::]:0 LISTENING
UDP 0.0.0.0:3702 *:*
UDP 0.0.0.0:3702 *:*
UDP 0.0.0.0:3702 *:*
UDP 0.0.0.0:3702 *:*
UDP 0.0.0.0:3702 *:*
UDP 0.0.0.0:3702 *:*
UDP 0.0.0.0:5353 *:*

17. Fill in the missing spaces: A ______ printer should never be connected to a UPS unit due to the printer's high current requirements. Also, a ______ or ______ should never be connected to a UPS to prevent the power backup unit from being ______ and creating a ______ hazard.

18. A network technician is troubleshooting a Lenovo® PC workstation. The PC workstation's network connection seems to be operating at a slower speed than usual.

Using the Command Shell, he has already run an **ipconfig /all** statement and he has determined that the TCP/IP configuration settings for this workstation seem to be normal. He now wants to know how many SMB data packets are currently being received by this workstation.

What command should he enter at the command line?

(i) arp -a

(ii) nbtstat

(iii) netstat

(iv) ping -t

19. True or False: 120 V AC and 12 V DC are the standard voltages in Europe with respect to the internal workings of a computer in a SOHO environment.

Figure 19

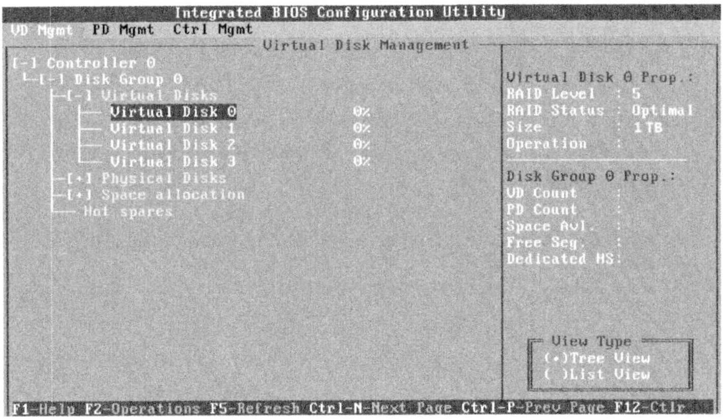
Integrated BIOS Configuration Utility
VD Mgmt PD Mgmt Ctrl Mgmt
Virtual Disk Management
[-] Controller 0
[-] Disk Group 0
[-] Virtual Disks
Virtual Disk 0 0%
Virtual Disk 1 0%
Virtual Disk 2 0%
Virtual Disk 3 0%
[+] Physical Disks
[+] Space allocation
Hot spares
Virtual Disk 0 Prop.:
RAID Level : 5
RAID Status : Optimal
Size : 1 TB
Operation :
Disk Group 0 Prop.:
VD Count :
PD Count :
Space Avl. :
Free Seg. :
Dedicated HS:
View Type
(•)Tree View
( )List View
F1-Help F2-Operations F5-Refresh Ctrl-N-Next Page Ctrl-P-Prev Page F12-Ctlr

20. A network technician is installing a new Seagate® 1 TB HDD into a Netgear® NAS system to increase the storage capacity of a pharmaceutical company's on-site network. The technician also inserts a new HP® RAID controller card into the motherboard. After the technician successfully installs the new HDD and RAID adapter card, he reboots the NAS system and re-configures the HDD array using the BIOS utility.

(a) Briefly explain the term *NAS* with reference to its purpose and function within a networked environment.

(b) What level of RAID is currently set up on the NAS BIOS utility shown in *Figure 19?*

(c) Which of the following is the minimum number of hard drives necessary to allow this RAID configuration to function?

(i) 2

(ii) 3

(iii) 4

(iv) 5

(d) Which of the following statements most accurately describes this RAID configuration? (Select one answer.)

(i) The RAID array does not stripe parity

(ii) The RAID level shown in the figure is not fault tolerant

(iii) The RAID configuration currently set up on the NAS system combines the advantages of mirroring and striping

(iv) The RAID array stripes data and parity

(e) After the technician re-configures the RAID settings in the BIOS utility (see *Figure 19*), he exits the BIOS and allows the NAS system to complete the boot-up process.

However, when the technician opens Windows® Disk Management utility, he is unable to see the newly installed Seagate® hard drive. Also, he notices a yellow warning icon on the screen indicating that the entire RAID array has failed.

Which of the following should the technician check first? (Select two answers.)

(i) Verify that the correct driver for the RAID controller is installed and updated

(ii) Check if any of the hard drives have failed

(iii) Check the RAID controller to determine if it has failed

(iv) Check whether the RAID controller card is securely plugged into the motherboard

(v) Check whether the hard drives are securely connected to the RAID controller

(f) The technician troubleshoots the NAS system in accordance with the CompTIA® A+ six-step troubleshooting methodology. However, he is still unable to diagnose the reason for the RAID array's sudden and unexpected failure.

He decides to escalate the matter to another more experienced technician. Upon reviewing the BIOS settings, the technician's colleague discovers that the NAS system's motherboard already has built-in RAID functionality.

Which of the following should she do to restore functionality to the Seagate® HDD array? (Select one answer.)

(i) Upgrade the newly installed RAID controller card

(ii) Disable the motherboard's RAID functionality within BIOS

(iii) Enable the motherboard's RAID functionality within BIOS

(iv) Update the drivers for both motherboard RAID and RAID adapter card

Practice Test 12			
MCQ Solutions			
1.	(iv)	11.	(ii)
2.	(ii)	12.	(iii)
3.	(a)(i), (b)(ii)(iv)	13.	(a)(iv), (b) See notes
4.	(iii)	14.	(iii)
5.	See notes	15.	See notes
6.	(ii)	16.	(a)(i), (b) See notes, (c)(ii)
7.	(a)(iv), (b)(i)	17.	See notes
8.	(ii)	18.	(iii)
9.	False	19.	False
10.	(a)(i), (b)-(e) See notes	20.	(a)-(b) See notes, (c) (ii), (d)(iv), (e)(iv)(v), (f)(ii)

1. Correct: (iv) Plasma screen.

2. Correct: (ii) KVM switch.

3. **(a)** (i) Network switch (ethernet switch). **(b)** (ii) and (iv). A switch is a central connecting device to which all networked computers are attached. In this way, a LAN is set up typically using a network design known as a star topology. The switch regenerates the signals it receives from other computers connected to the network, and then sends the regenerated signals to the correct computers on the LAN instead of transmitting the signals to every port on the network. The switch is able to route data to the correct computers because it identifies the MAC (physical) address of each computer, and therefore knows the destination computer for each signal or data packet.

4. Correct: (iii) eSATA. The data transfer rate of eSATA is 6 Gbps. The next fastest is Firewire 800 at 800 Mbps, followed by USB 2.0 at 480 Mbps and Firewire 400 at 400 Mbps.

5. STP (Shielded Twisted Pair). Full correct statement: "STP and Fiber Optic cables are two types of cable that offer protection from EMI." EMI is an acronym for Electromagnetic Interference.

6. Correct: (ii) The command net view is used to show a list of computers and network devices (e.g., servers) connected to a specific network.

7. **(a)** (iv) The IP address 169.254.x.x indicates that Windows OS on the local computer has implemented APIPA (Automatic Private IP Addressing). APIPA is a Windows OS function that provides DHCP autoconfiguration IP addressing to the local networked computer when a DHCP server is either permanently or temporarily unavailable. APIPA assigns a Class B IP address from 169.254.0.0 to 169.254.255.255 to the local computer when the computer is unable, for whatever reason, to contact a DHCP server to obtain an IP address. **(b)** (i) DHCP server.

8. Correct: (ii) USB card. USB (Universal Serial Bus) ports are predominantly used by many peripheral devices, including keyboards, mice, printers, cameras, dictation devices, etc. Nowadays, it is a standard feature of many PC motherboards to be equipped with a number of USB 3.0 ports that have a maximum data transfer rate of 5 Gbps. Motherboards will also be equipped with several USB 2.0 ports that have a maximum data transfer rate of 480 Mbps. However, if the motherboard does not have sufficient USB ports, a USB card can be installed. (For purposes of clarification, SDHC stands for Secure Digital High Capacity and SDXC means Secure Digital Extended Capacity. SDHC and SDXC cards are a type of insertable storage card that utilizes solid state technology and NAND memory.)

9. False. The maximum data transfer rate of IEEE wireless protocol 802.11n is 600 Mbps.

10. (a) (i) nbtstat -A. The computer technician entered the command nbtstat -A [IP address] at the command prompt. **(b)** The command nbtstat displays network protocol statistics and current TCP/IP connections that use NetBIOS (Network Basic Input/Output System) over TCP/IP (Transmission Control Protocol/Internet Protocol). Nbtstat can be used to show the services currently running on the local computer or a remote computer (in a format known as the NetBIOS Name Table), provided that the corresponding IP address is entered in conjunction with the appropriate nbtstat switch. For instance, typing the command nbtstat – A [IP address] into the Command Shell allows a technician to determine what services are currently running, what the local (or remote) computer's name is, and what network does the computer belong to (e.g., WORKGROUP, SOHO, etc.). The command nbtstat -a [computer name] shows the exact same information as the -A switch, but this information is generated using the computer's name as opposed to its IP address (e.g., nbtstat -a ACER). **(c)** 192.168.0.140 **(d)** MAC (physical) address: 48-D2-24-DF-7C-78. **(e)** WORKGROUP.

11. Correct: (ii) Micro USB Type B.

12. Correct: (iii) 6 Gbps (600 MB/s).

13. (a) (iv) The BIOS (or UEFI) settings do not recognize the new memory modules. (It is being assumed that: (1) the technician has employed appropriate ESD preventive measures during installation of the new memory modules; (2) the memory modules are not defective or faulty; (3) the RAM modules have been correctly seated on the motherboard; and (4) the technician prepped and cleaned the RAM slot before seating the new memory modules on the motherboard.) **(b)** Update the BIOS settings. This is achieved by "flashing" the BIOS.

14. Correct: (iii) Category 5e cable. 1000Base-T is a type of gigabit ethernet networking technology that utilizes copper cables as the medium of transmission. 1000Base-T uses four pairs of Category 5e UTP (Unshielded Twisted Pair) cables to attain gigabit data rates. The 1000Base-T standard is designated by the Institute of Electrical and Electronics Engineers (IEEE) as IEEE 802.3ab. This standard allows data transmission rates of 1 Gbps (1,000 Mbps) over distances of up to

330 feet. 1000Base-T can be used in data centers for fast server switching or in desktop PCs for broadband applications. The main advantage of 1000Base-T is that it can use existing copper cabling, thus negating the need to rewire the ethernet system with newer generation fiber optic cables.

15. ST connector.

16. (a) (i) netstat -an. **(b)** The command netstat shows the network statistics for a local computer. More specifically, netstat displays any active network connections between the local computer and remote computers using TCP/IP (Transmission Control Protocol/Internet Protocol), IPv4 and IPv6 routing tables, as well as providing useful information and statistics regarding other protocols in use (e.g., UDP or User Datagram Protocol). If a technician wants to see all currently active TCP and UDP sessions on a local computer, s/he would use the command netstat -a. However, to see TCP and UDP sessions in numerical format only, use the -an switch (i.e. netstat -an). **(c)** (ii) HTTPS (Hypertext Transfer Protocol Secure) is normally associated with port number 443.

17. (1) Laser. (2) Surge protector. (3) Power strip. (4) Overloaded. (5) Fire. The completed statement should read: "A laser printer should never be connected to a UPS unit due to the printer's high current requirements. Also, a surge protector or power strip should never be connected to a UPS to prevent the power backup unit from being overloaded and creating a fire hazard."

18. Correct: (iii) netstat. SMB is an acronym for Server Message Block which is a type of networking protocol.

19. False. The correct statement should read: "120 V AC and 12 V DC are the standard voltages in the United States with respect to the internal workings of a computer in a SOHO environment."

20. (a) NAS is an acronym for Network Attached Storage. A NAS box or NAS system is essentially a self-contained computer containing one or more hard drives that is connected to a network. The primary purpose of the NAS device is to provide file-based data storage services to other devices attached to the network. The shared file (and folder) resources on the NAS box can be accessed by means of network browsing or as a mapped network drive from any computer on the network. NAS boxes are normally connected to the network via an RJ45 ethernet port, oftentimes at speeds of 1,000 Mbps. However, a NAS box can also be directly attached to a computer by mean of a USB connection. **(b)** RAID 5. **(c)** (ii) 3. A RAID 5 array requires a minimum of 3 hard drives in order for the array to function properly. **(d)** (iv) RAID 5 arrays stripe data and fault-tolerant parity data is also written to each disk in the HDD array. **(e)** (iv) and (v). If a RAID array ceases to function for whatever reason and/or the OS does not recognize the RAID array, (1) a technician should initially check whether the hard drives are securely connected to the RAID controller (either a built-in RAID controller on the motherboard or a RAID adapter card). Then, if applicable, (2) the technician can check whether the RAID controller card is securely plugged into the motherboard. If the aforesaid connections are correct, (3) the technician can then verify that the correct driver for the RAID controller is installed and updated. (4) Finally, the technician can check if any of the hard drives or RAID controller has become defective. If the RAID controller is built into the motherboard and becomes defective, the only easiest and most practical option is to buy and install a RAID adapter card. **(f)** (ii) Disable the motherboard's RAID functionality within BIOS. If a computer system has a RAID adapter card installed, but the computer's motherboard also has integrated RAID functionality which is enabled within the BIOS, this potentially could cause a conflict thereby affecting the performance of a RAID array. In such circumstances, it is recommended to disable the motherboard RAID functionality within the BIOS.

Practice Test 13

1. Which networking device can be used to connect multiple network segments?

(i) Router

(ii) Switch

(iii) Cable modem

(iv) NAS

2. Why would a computer manufacturer incorporate a "dual rail" PSU into a system designed for high-end gaming? (Select two answers.)

(i) To enhance the current flowing through each power supply wire in order to optimize the performance of components on the motherboard that have a relatively high voltage load requirement

(ii) To improve the quality of power that is supplied to the various componentry on the motherboard

(iii) To monitor individual power circuits on the motherboard

(iv) To restrict the current flowing through each power supply wire to prevent system overheating and possible fire

3. True or False: HDMI connectors are primarily used for HD television. HDMI connections can carry both audio and video signals.

4. Which of the following is a critical component of Step 4 in the six-step CompTIA® A+ troubleshooting methodology?

(i) Question the user of the computer equipment being troubleshot

(ii) Establish a theory of probable cause

(iii) Implement a solution

(iv) Document findings, actions taken, and outcomes

(v) If necessary, escalate the computer problem to another technician

5. A PC technician has decided to upgrade the RAM modules in a HP® ProDesk® PC and a Samsung® laptop to optimize performance. The technician installs a DRAM memory stick into the relevant slot on the PC's motherboard. He also installs a new memory module into the relevant compartment on the undersurface of the laptop.

(a) What is user-replaceable memory in a laptop called?

(i) DRAM

(ii) SODIMM

(iii) SDXC

(iv) eMMC

(b) Explain the difference between DRAM and SRAM.

6. Which type of processor is commonly found in smartphones and tablet computers?

(i) AMD®

(ii) FM2+

(iii) ARM®

(iv) Intel® Core™ i3

7. True or False: If a computer displays the error message, "BIOS logged a chassis intrusion" during boot up, it is very likely that the computer case is damaged or insecure.

8. A customer brings a defective laptop to a PC repair shop. The technician states that he is unable to repair the faulty PGA socket on the motherboard. Since the laptop is still covered by a warranty certificate, the technician decides to raise an RMA with the OEM.

(a) Explain the terms PGA, RMA, and OEM.

(b) What critical step should the technician take before shipping the customer's laptop to the OEM?

(i) Remove the LCD screen

(ii) Remove the HDD

(iii) Remove the Li-ion battery

(iv) Disconnect all internal cables from the motherboard

Figure 20

9. Match the following descriptions to the correct technology or connector listed below.

(i) This wireless technology can be used to create PANs.

(ii) This medium of communication requires uninterrupted line of sight.

(iii) This connector is typically used to charge Android™ smartphones.

(iv) This wireless technology can be utilized to transfer data by touching two devices together.

(v) This connector is mainly used with LCD displays to provide a high-quality video connection.

NFC / Micro-USB / Mobile Tethering / IR / S-video / RGB / Bluetooth / DVI / Satellite

10. Identify the video connection ports labelled A, B, and C which are shown in *Figure 20.*

11. A PC technician was asked by a client to install a new PCIe graphics card and additional memory into her Acer® laptop.

The technician installs an Intel® HD Graphics 4000 card and another 4 GB Kingston® DDR3 bringing the total memory capacity to 8 GB DDR3. According to the laptop manufacturer's website, both the newly installed graphics card and RAM are compatible with the motherboard's specification.

However, upon booting the laptop, an error message is displayed on the screen:

Unable to read memory! Please any key to continue.

(a) Which of the following is the most probable cause for this error message? (Select the best two answers.)

(i) New DDR3 module is not seated correctly

(ii) Intel® HD graphics card is incompatible with newly installed RAM

(iii) New DDR3 module is faulty

(iv) MCC has become defective

(b) How should the technician troubleshoot this error? (Select one answer.)

(i) Apply thermal compound between the heat sink and the processor

(ii) Clean the CPU socket with compressed air and a dry, lint-free cloth and then reseat the processor in situ

(iii) Inspect the PCIe slot on the motherboard for dirt or other residue before re-inserting the graphics card

(iv) Open the laptop case and reseat the RAM module

12. A PC technician has inadvertently dropped a Phillips-head screw into an open computer case while troubleshooting a video card issue. The screw has rolled out of reach.

(a) Assuming that the technician has already implemented anti-ESD prevention techniques, what is the first step the technician should take in this particular situation?

(i) All jewelry should be removed from the technician's fingers and wrists

(ii) The technician should remove the video card

(iii) Unplug the computer's power cord from the AC outlet

(iv) Whilst attempting to retrieve the Phillips-head screw, the technician should regularly touch the inside of the computer's metal chassis

(b) Which of the following is the best tool to reach and remove the screw from the case?

(i) Pliers

(ii) Extension magnet

(iii) Tweezers

(iv) Small Phillips-head screwdriver

Figure 21

13. See *Figure 21* and answer the questions that follow.

(a) What term is used to describe the room shown in the figure?

(b) What is the purpose and function of this room?

(c) Which of the following devices or physical hardware are commonly found in this room? (Select all applicable answers.)

(i) Ethernet switches

(ii) KVM switches

(iii) Rack-mounted servers

(iv) SOHO routers

(d) The room shown in the figure typically requires adequate environmental controls to be installed. In this context, what is the purpose and function of a HVAC system? (Select the best two answers.)

(i) To provide an appropriate ambient temperature

(ii) To maintain humidity at an appropriate level

(iii) To minimise the risk of microbial and fungal contamination

(iv) To enhance security protocols

14. Select the correct options: The minimum number of disks in a (RAID 0/RAID 5) HDD array is three: two disks for data and one disk for parity. In theory, the maximum number of drives in a (RAID 0/RAID 5) array is (10/unlimited). Although (RAID 0/RAID 5) is fault tolerant, it only protects against (one/two) drive failure(s).

Figure 22

P/N: 78.C1GM0.AF10B
S/N: 2S1407100001
8GB ECC REG PC4-17000 CL15
Apacer

15. A common computer component is displayed in *Figure 22.*

(a) Which of the following most accurately describes the PC component shown in the figure?

(i) 8 GB DIMM DDR3

(ii) 8 GB DIMM DDR4

(iii) 8 GB SODIMM DDR3

(iv) SODIMM ECC DDR4

(b) How many pins does this PC component have?

(i) 184

(ii) 204

(iii) 240

(iv) 288

(c) What is the maximum theoretical data transfer rate, in megabytes per second, of this PC component?

(d) How many mega-transfers per second can this PC component perform? (Select the best approximate answer.)

(i) 2,100

(ii) 1,066

(iii) 8,500

(iv) 17,000

(e) This PC component is equipped with a technology known as ECC. Explain the term ECC and briefly state its primary function.

(f) According to the adhesive label on the PC component, the module has a CL15 rating. What does this mean?

(i) CL15 signifies the bus speed of the module

(ii) CL15 means that the PC component can transmit 15 bytes of data for every I/O clock cycle

(iii) CL15 refers to the latency setting of the module

(iv) The CL rating denotes the number of extra bits of data, known as parity bits, that are stored on the module and used for error correction

16. Which of the following UTP cable categories is suitable for 1,000 Mbps networks? (Select all applicable answers.)

(i) Cat 3

(ii) Cat 5

(iii) Cat 5e

(iv) Cat 6

17. During boot up, which process of a computer checks all its internal components and installed devices?

(i) Boot Manager

(ii) CMOS

(iii) POST

(iv) UEFI

18. What term is used to describe the delay in the RAM's response to a request from the MCC?

(i) Deferment

(ii) Lag time

(iii) Latency

(iv) None of the above

19. Which of the following respective frequencies in GHz does IEEE 802.11g and IEEE 802.11n normally operate at?

(i) 1, 2.4/5

(ii) 2.4, 2.4

(iii) 2.4, 2.4/5

(iv) 5, 2.4

20. A video connection adapter is shown in *Figure 23.*

Identify the ports labelled A, B, and C.

Figure 23

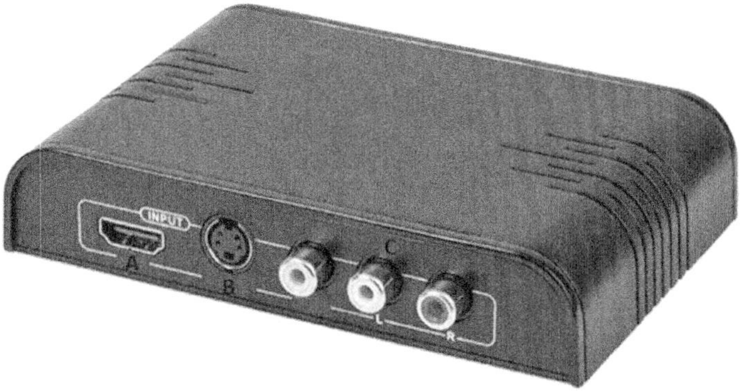

Practice Test 13			
MCQ Solutions			
1.	(i)	11.	(a)(i)(iii), (b)(iv)
2.	(iii), (iv)	12.	(a)(iii), (b)(ii)
3.	True	13.	(a)-(b) See notes, (c)(i)(ii)(iii), (d)(i)(ii)
4.	(iii)	14.	See notes
5.	(a)(ii), (b) See notes	15.	(a)(ii), (b)(iv), (c) See notes, (d)(i), (e) See notes, (f)(iii)
6.	(iii)	16.	(iii), (iv)
7.	False	17.	(iii)
8.	(a) See notes, (b)(ii)	18.	(iii)
9.	See notes	19.	(iii)
10.	See notes	20.	See notes

1. Correct: (i) Router.

2. Correct: (iii) and (iv). The purpose of "dual rail" PSUs is to separate and restrict the current flowing through each wire to prevent overheating and possible fire. Dual-rail or multi-rail PSUs are important in computer systems that are reliant on a lot of power (e.g., gaming computers and multimedia systems). This PSU architecture allows the computer system to monitor power circuits individually as opposed to collectively (which is seen in single-rail PSUs), therefore helping to prevent system overheating and fire hazards by shutting down the PSU if a certain threshold is reached.

3. True.

4. Correct: (iii). Step 4 of the CompTIA A+ troubleshooting methodology recommends establishing a plan of action to resolve the problem and then implementing a solution.

5. **(a)** (ii) SODIMM (Small Outline Dual In-Line Memory Module). **(b)** SRAM is an acronym for Static Random Access Memory. DRAM means Dynamic Random Access Memory. SRAM is RAM that does <u>not</u> need to be periodically refreshed. SRAM is typically located within the CPU where it is used as CPU cache memory (viz. L1, L2, and L3 cache). DRAM is RAM that does require periodic refreshing. Memory refreshing is effectively the act of reading data from a specific area of the memory module and then immediately rewriting that information back to the same area without any data modification.

6. Correct: (iii) ARM.

7. False. The correct statement should read: "If a computer displays the error message, "BIOS logged a chassis intrusion" during boot up, it is very likely that the computer case has been previously opened."

8. (a) PGA is an acronym for Pin Grid Array. RMA stands for Return Merchandise Authorization. OEM means Original Equipment Manufacturer. **(b)** (ii) The technician should remove the hard drive (HDD) from the laptop. The customer's laptop may contain data of a confidential, sensitive, and/or personal nature stored on the HDD. Therefore, in the interests of data privacy, it is fundamentally important to remove the HDD before shipping the laptop to the manufacturer for repair.

9. Correct answers: (i) Bluetooth. (ii) IR (infrared). (iii) Micro-USB. (iv) NFC (Near Field Communication). (v) DVI (Digital Visual Interface).

10. (A) VGA port. (B) Component video (or Component RGB) connections. (C) HDMI port.

11. (a) (i) and (iii). It is highly probable that the new DDR3 module is not seated correctly in the relevant motherboard RAM slot, or the newly installed DDR3 module is faulty or defective. MCC is an acronym for Memory Controller Chip. **(b)** (iv) Open the laptop case and reseat the DDR3 module or replace the module if necessary.

12. (a) (iii) It is always advisable to unplug the computer's power cord from the AC outlet to prevent "shorts". **(b)** (ii) Extension magnet.

13. (a) Server room. **(b)** A server room is a special room that is used to store, power, and operate computer servers and associated networking devices. The server room usually houses several physical servers organised together in different form factors, such as rack mounted servers, or the servers and associated devices may be stored in tower or blade enclosures. Server rooms resemble a small data center, and they can range in size from a closet to the full floor of a building. It is common for offices, schools, hospitals, and other facilities such as manufacturing facilities to have a dedicated server room. **(c)** (i), (ii), and (iii). Common elements of a server room include servers and data storage devices, racks for stacking and storing computer hardware so that space is used efficiently, KVM switches, ethernet switches, routers, UPS units, HVAC system, and data backup facilities. (SOHO routers are not found in server rooms considering that these routers are commonly designed for very small, privately-owned businesses or home office environments. In consequence, such network environments would not normally require the use of a server room.) **(d)** The purpose of a HVAC (Heating, Ventilation, and Air Conditioning) system in a server room environment is: (i) to provide an appropriate ambient temperature, and (ii) to maintain humidity at an appropriate level.

14. (1) RAID 5. (2) RAID 5. (3) Unlimited. (4) RAID 5. (5) One. The correct statement should read: "The minimum number of disks in a RAID 5 HDD array is three: two disks for data and one disk for parity. In theory, the maximum number of drives in a RAID 5 array is unlimited, although in practice the storage array is likely to have built-in limits. Although RAID 5 is fault tolerant, it only protects against one drive failure."

15. **(a)** (ii) 8 GB DIMM DDR4. According to the information on the adhesive label of the memory module, the component is described as "PC4-17000". The "PC4" signifies that the DIMM (Dual In-Line Memory Module) stick, which is normally inserted into PC motherboards, is designed to DDR4 specifications. We can also see that the capacity of the memory module is 8 GB. **(b)** (iv) 288 pins. DIMM DDR has 184 pins. DIMM DDR2 and DDR3 have 240 pins. DIMM DDR4 has 288 pins. **(c)** 17,000 MB/s. According to the information on the adhesive label, the component is a "PC4-17000" memory module. The 17,000 MB/s signifies the maximum theoretical data transfer rate (DTR), in megabytes per second, of this memory stick. **(d)** (i) 2,100 MT/s. To calculate the mega-transfers per second, use the equation: DTR (in MB/s) divided by 8 bytes. Hence, 17,000 MB/s divided by 8 bytes = 2,100 MT/s approximately. **(e)** ECC is an acronym for Error Correction Code. ECC is a RAM technology that is used to detect and correct errors. Additional bits of information need to be stored on the memory module in order for ECC RAM to be effective. However, ECC RAM is the slowest and most expensive type of memory. Nowadays, most new PCs do not need ECC RAM owing to the low possibility of data corruption and loss affecting newer generation RAM modules. If ECC RAM is supported by a computer, this option can be disabled in the BIOS, especially if newer generation RAM is being installed. **(f)** (iii) CL15 refers to the latency setting of the module. Memory latency refers to the very slight delay (usually measured in nanoseconds) that occurs when the memory controller chip (MCC) communicates with a memory stick in order to access data stored on that stick. Memory latency is commonly given a CL rating – the higher the CL number, the relatively longer the delay in accessing data on the memory module. DDR3 memory typically has a CL rating between 5 and 10. DDR4 memory typically has a CL rating of 14 or 15, meaning that DDR4 modules have marginally slower data access times compared to DDR3 modules. For most regular PC users, the CL rating of a memory module is largely irrelevant. However, CL ratings are important to bear in mind by PC users who run memory-intensive applications (e.g., AutoCAD and other CAD/CAM software, video editing and graphics rendering applications, online games, etc.).

16. Correct: (iii) and (iv). Category 5e and Category 6 UTP cables are designed for 1000Base-T networks – in other words, networks that permit data transmission rates of 1,000 Mbps (or 1 Gbps) over distances of up to 330 feet. Category 6 cables are also suitable for 10 Gbps networks. Category 3 cables are only designed for 10 Mbps networks. Category 5 cables are designed for 100 Mbps networks.

17. Correct: (iii) POST (Power-on Self Test).

18. Correct: (iii) Latency. MCC refers to the Memory Controller Chip.

19. Correct: (iii) 2.4, 2.4/5. IEEE 802.11g operates at a frequency of 2.4 GHz. IEEE 802.11n operates at a frequency in the range 2.4 GHz to 5 GHz.

20. (A) HDMI port. (B) S-video port. (C) Composite video or RCA port.

Practice Test 14

1. Which of the following networking protocols use port 21?

(i) AFP

(ii) FTP

(iii) SSH

(iv) Telnet

2. Which tool is normally used to test the actual amount of voltage that emanates from a 24-pin ATX 12V power connector?

(i) Receptacle tester

(ii) PSU tester

(iii) Ohmmeter

(iv) Multimeter

3. A SOHO network environment in a small real estate office comprises 5 Dell® PC workstations, 2 Samsung® laptops, and a wireless Samsung® Xpress® laser printer. However, the office administrator has noticed that connectivity to the wireless printer seems to be intermittent during peak times when employees are using all available computer workstations, including the portable devices.

An IT technician has been called to troubleshoot the issue and he discovers that only 7 IP addresses have been set up on the router. The office administrator tells the technician that the SOHO network has never given any problems in the past, with the exception of the recurrent connectivity issues affecting the wireless printer.

(a) What is the most likely cause of the intermittent wireless connectivity affecting the printer?

(i) Faulty RJ45 jack on the printer

(ii) Insufficient physical memory installed on the printer

(iii) There is no available IP address to assign to the printer during peak office times

(iv) Wrong virtual COM port has been assigned to the printer

(b) What can the technician do to prevent this issue from recurring?

(i) Update the printer driver

(ii) Show the office administrator how to power cycle the router

(iii) Assign a static IP address to the printer

(iv) Assign a static IP address to each PC

4. Which of the following is the most important item of information required to connect to a specific wireless network?

(i) QoS

(ii) Channel

(iii) SSID

(iv) MAC

5. What is the typical storage capacity of DVD-5 and DVD-18 formats, respectively? (Select two answers.)

(i) 4.7 GB

(ii) 5 GB

(iii) 9.4 GB

(iv) 17 GB

(v) 18 GB

6. Which of the following connection types is the slowest in terms of its data transfer rate?

(i) USB 3.0

(ii) Thunderbolt 1.0

(iii) USB 2.0

(iv) Firewire 400

7. Which of the following internal components of a computer could cause the POST to fail during boot up? (Select two answers.)

(i) CPU

(ii) LCD

(iii) Windows® OS

(iv) RAM

Figure 24

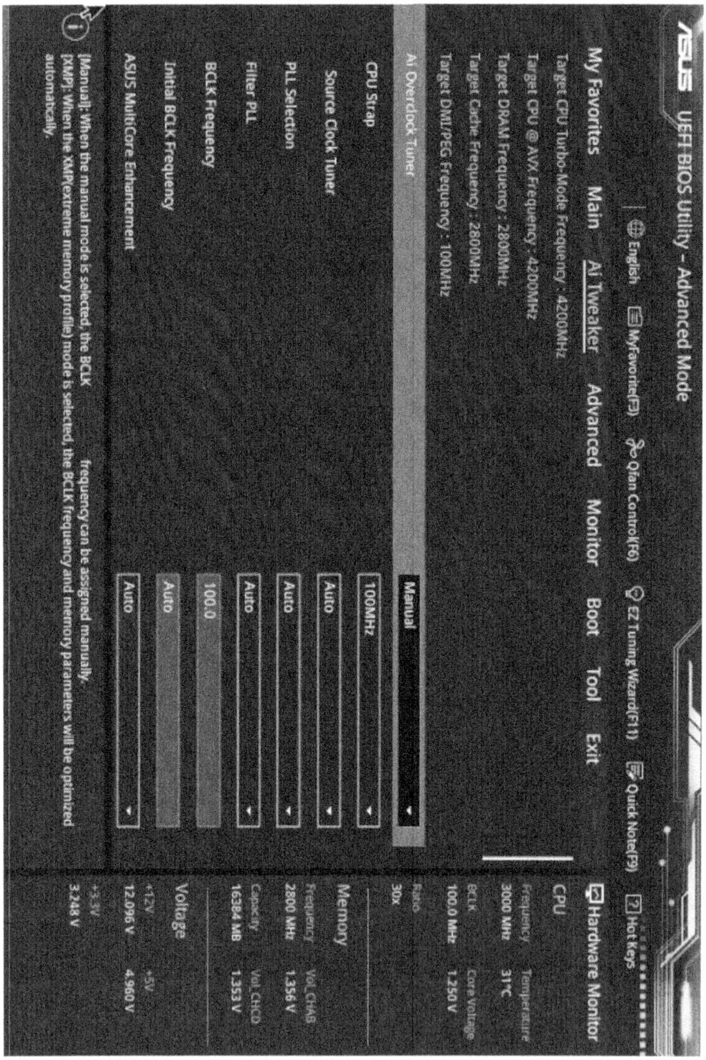
UEFI BIOS Utility – Advanced Mode
English
MyFavorite(F3)
Qfan Control(F6)
EZ Tuning Wizard(F11)
Quick Note(F9)
Hot Keys
My Favorites
Main
Ai Tweaker
Advanced
Monitor
Boot
Tool
Exit
Hardware Monitor
Target CPU Turbo-Mode Frequency : 4200MHz
Target CPU @ AVX Frequency : 4200MHz
Target DRAM Frequency : 2800MHz
Target Cache Frequency : 2800MHz
Target DMI/PEG Frequency : 100MHz
Ai Overclock Tuner
Manual
CPU Strap
100MHz
Source Clock Tuner
Auto
PLL Selection
Auto
Filter PLL
Auto
BCLK Frequency
100.0
Initial BCLK Frequency
Auto
ASUS MultiCore Enhancement
Auto
[Manual]: When the manual mode is selected, the BCLK frequency can be assigned manually.
[XMP]: When the XMP(extreme memory profile) mode is selected, the BCLK frequency and memory parameters will be optimized automatically.
CPU
Frequency
Temperature
3000 MHz
31°C
BCLK
Core Voltage
100.0 MHz
1.250 V
Ratio
30x
Memory
Frequency
Vol_CHAB
2800 MHz
1.356 V
Capacity
Vol_CHCD
16384 MB
1.353 V
Voltage
+12V
+5V
12.096 V
4.960 V
+3.3V
3.248 V

8. A PC technician is upgrading an ASUS® desktop computer. Once the new hardware components have been successfully installed, she reboots the computer and opens the UEFI BIOS utility, which is shown in *Figure 24.*

(a) What is the operating frequency, in gigahertz, of the processor?

(i) 3

(ii) 100

(iii) 30x

(iv) 3,000

(b) State the processor's current temperature and voltage.

(c) Which of the following is the base clock speed, measured in megahertz?

(i) 30x

(ii) 100

(iii) 2,800

(iv) 3,000

(d) What is the main function of the UEFI BIOS (or Legacy BIOS)?

(e) What are the main differences between Legacy BIOS and UEFI BIOS?

(f) Which of the following settings can be modified from within the UEFI BIOS (or Legacy BIOS) utility? (Select all applicable answers.)

(i) Time and Date

(ii) Boot Device Priority

(iii) APM/ACPI

(iv) WoL

(v) Temperature thresholds

(vi) Chassis intrusion detection

(vii) Screen resolution

9. Which one of the following IEEE 802.11 wireless standards has a maximum data transmission rate of 11 Mbps and uses the 2.4 GHz frequency range?

(i) 802.11a

(ii) 802.11b

(iii) 802.11g

(iv) 802.11n

(v) 802.11ac

10. Identify the fiber optic connector shown in *Figure 25.*

Figure 25

11. Read the following statement and select the correct options:

There are two main types of optic fiber cables: single mode and (dual mode/multi-mode). Single-mode optic fiber cables are a (cheaper/more expensive) option, but such cables can be run longer distances and offer (lower/higher) signal attenuation. On the other hand, (dual mode/multi-mode) fiber cables are the most popular amongst networking and telecommunications companies. These fiber cables have a (smaller/larger) diameter compared to single-mode fiber cables, and light signals are transmitted through the optic fibers at (the same angle/different angles). Unlike single-mode fiber cables, these fiber cables can only be run shorter distances.

12. Which of the following encryption protocols offer the strongest form of wireless encryption? (Select two answers.)

(i) WEP 64

(ii) WPA

(iii) WPA2

(iv) TKIP

(v) AES

(vi) WEP 128

13. A network technician is troubleshooting a newly installed Dell® desktop PC. The computer does not have any access to shared resources on the network or

Internet connectivity. The technician observes that the ethernet port light on the rear of the computer case is not active.

Which of the following indicates the most likely cause of this networking issue? (Select two answers.)

(i) The ethernet cable is disconnected

(ii) The network adapter is faulty

(iii) The ethernet cable is loose

(iv) BIOS firmware does not recognize the NIC

14. Which of the following cards is normally plugged into a PCIe x16 adapter card slot?

(i) ExpressCard

(ii) Network adapter card

(iii) RAID controller card

(iv) Video card

15. Answer the following questions relating to the laser printing process.

(a) What should be used to clean a laser printer's transfer corona wire? (Select two answers.)

(i) Cotton swab

(ii) Isopropyl alcohol

(iii) Small sponge

(iv) Urea

(b) Briefly describe the cleaning procedure.

16. A computer workstation in a LAN environment is able to boot off the network and possesses the ability to be brought out of sleep mode over the network.

(a) Which two technologies does the computer have? (Select two answers.)

(i) PXE

(ii) UEFI

(iii) TLS

(iv) WinRe

(v) WoL

(b) What computer utility was originally used to implement these technologies?

(i) ABOM

(ii) Device Manager

(iii) UEFI BIOS

(iv) Windows® Explorer

(c) What physical hardware item was originally installed in the computer to ensure that these two technologies can be implemented?

(i) NIC

(ii) RJ11 jack

(iii) RJ45 jack

(iv) Thunderbolt 3.0 port

17. A PC technician is custom-building a gaming PC on behalf of her client. Which of the following are the most important system requirements to ensure optimum performance? (Select all that apply.)

(i) HD audio card

(ii) Type 2 hypervisor

(iii) Powerful multi-core CPU

(iv) High-end graphics card with a specialized GPU

(v) High-speed RAM

(vi) One or more SATA HDDs

(vii) DSL internet connection

18. What term is used to describe the time delay it takes for a HDD to access a particular data sector on the magnetic platter?

(i) Latency

(ii) CAS

(iii) Lag time

(iv) Standard deviation

19. Why is it important not to plug an RJ11 phone line into an RJ45 port on a computer?

(i) Electric currents flowing through a computer's ethernet equipment can cause serious damage to telecommunication cables

(ii) Electric currents flowing through a computer's network adapter can amplify signal propagation along a phone line inadvertently inserted into the computer's RJ45 port, ultimately leading to permanent signal distortion along the phone line

(iii) Inserting an RJ11 phone line into a computer's RJ45 port affects the real-time performance of the computer, but without causing any long-lasting detrimental damage to the computer system

(iv) Phone line voltages can cause serious damage to a computer's ethernet equipment

20. An IT technician working on the night shift in a large university hospital complex in New York receives a troubleshooting ticket. A clinician complains that the computer she is using has lost its connectivity to the network. The technician subsequently visits the relevant hospital department to investigate the matter further.

(a) Which of the following should the technician do first?

(i) Check the patch cable

(ii) Ping 127.0.0.1

(iii) Enter ipconfig /all at the command prompt

(iv) Update the computer's network card driver

(b) Which of the following tools, if any, should the technician use to diagnose the issue?

(i) Continuity tester

(ii) Patch cable tester

(iii) Loopback tester

(iv) Command Shell

(v) None of the above

Practice Test 14			
MCQ Solutions			
1.	(ii)	11.	See notes
2.	(iv)	12.	(iii), (v)
3.	(a)(iii), (b)(iii)	13.	(i), (iii)
4.	(iii)	14.	(iv)
5.	(i), (iv)	15.	(a)(i)(ii), (b) See notes
6.	(iv)	16.	(a)(i)(v), (b)(iii), (c)(i),
7.	(i), (iv)	17.	(i), (iii), (iv), (v)
8.	(a)(i), (b) See notes, (c)(ii), (d)-(e) See notes, (f)(i)-(vi)	18.	(i)
9.	(ii)	19.	(iv)
10.	See notes	20.	(a)(i), (b)(ii)

1. Correct: (ii) FTP (File Transfer Protocol).

2. Correct: (iv) Multimeter. The multimeter is the only testing tool that can display the exact voltage supplied by the PSU to the ATX motherboard in a numerical format. For purposes of clarification, an ohmmeter is an electrical instrument that measures the amount of electrical resistance in a circuit, in other words, the opposition to an electric current. The SI unit of resistance is the ohm (Ω), compared to the unit of voltage which is the volt (v).

3. (a) (iii) When the SOHO network was originally set up, only 7 IP addresses were configured on the router even though there are 8 devices, including the wireless printer, connected to the network. Assuming that DHCP is enabled on the router, only 7 IP addresses can be assigned to active devices on the network. Hence, when all computers are being used during peak times, it is possible that the SOHO network does not recognize the printer because there is no available IP address to assign to the printer. As a result, the printer loses connectivity to the network and is unable to perform its printing function. **(b)** (iii) To prevent this issue from recurring in the future, configure the SOHO router so that a static IP address is assigned to the wireless printer.

4. Correct: (iii) SSID (Service Set Identifier). If the SSID a person requires does not appear when he/she scans for wireless networks, it will be necessary to manually enter the SSID. For purposes of clarification, QoS refers to "Quality of Service" and MAC refers to the physical address of the networked computer that is impressed on its NIC.

5. Correct: (i) DVD-5: 4.7 GB (1 side/1 layer) and (iv) DVD-18: 17 GB (2 sides/4 layers).

6. Correct: (iv) Firewire 400. Firewire 400 is the slowest at 400 Mbps. USB 2.0 has a data transfer rate of 480 Mbps. USB 3.0 (SuperSpeed USB) operates at 5 Gbps and Thunderbolt 1.0 operates at 10 Gbps.

7. Correct: (i) and (iv). Typically, problems with the CPU and memory (RAM) could cause the POST to fail. Other reasons that could cause the POST to fail during boot-up include a defective motherboard, a faulty or incompatible video card, or a failing power supply (PSU).

8. (a) (i) 3 GHz (3,000 MHz). **(b)** CPU temperature: 31 degrees Celsius. CPU core voltage: 1.250 V. **(c)** (ii) 100 MHz. **(d)** UEFI (Unified Extensible Firmware Interface) BIOS and Legacy BIOS (which is still commonly used in most PCs and laptops) are two firmware interfaces for computers which work as an interpreter between the operating system (OS) and the motherboard firmware. UEFI BIOS (or Legacy BIOS) is normally invoked once the computer is powered on to initialize the various hardware components and start the OS which is stored on the HDD. **(e)** (1) Legacy BIOS uses an MBR (Master Boot Record) to save information about hard drive data, so that the BIOS knows what to do when the computer system is powered on. When a computer is powered on, Legacy BIOS reads the first sector of the HDD and, in that way, the BIOS knows which components (e.g., CPU, RAM, etc.) to initialize and which additional code to execute. BIOS also knows which boot device needs to be initialized first (in accordance with BIOS Boot Device Priority) so that the OS can be ultimately loaded on to the computer system and take over control from the BIOS. Legacy BIOS still operates in a limited 16-bit mode, thereby restricting the amount of code that can be read and executed from the firmware ROM. (2) UEFI BIOS performs the same tasks as Legacy BIOS during computer startup, but it does so in a completely different manner. UEFI BIOS stores all relevant information regarding initialization and startup in an *.efi file as opposed to using a firmware ROM. This *.efi file is stored on the hard drive within a special partition known as an EFI System Partition (ESP). This ESP partition also contains the boot loader programs for the OS installed on the computer system. While Legacy BIOS uses an MBR (Master Boot Record) to save information about various hard drive data relevant to the initialization and startup process, UEFI BIOS uses a GUID partition table (GPT). **(f)** Correct: (i), (ii), (iii), (iv), (v), and (vi). The following computer settings can be adjusted within the UEFI BIOS (or Legacy BIOS) utility: (1) Time and Date. (2) Boot Device Priority (otherwise known as BIOS boot order). This setting determines which storage media is booted first (e.g., hard drive, optical drive, USB flash drive, or "over-the-network" using the PXE (Pre-boot Execution Environment) specification on PXE-enabled client computers.) (3) User and Supervisor (or Administrator) Passwords. (4) Power Management. This setting allows the selection or de-selection of either APM or ACPI power management options. APM (Advanced Power Management) is a legacy power management option that enables the OS to work with the BIOS to manage the power resources of the computer system. Nowadays, ACPI (Advanced Configuration and Power Interface) is commonly enabled within the UEFI BIOS (or Legacy BIOS) utility to allow the OS to assume full control of a computer's power management. (5) Wake-on-LAN (WoL). This BIOS setting allows a system or network administrator to wake up a computer remotely by sending data to the computer through its network adapter. However, the computer's network adapter must be functional and WoL-enabled, and the computer must be connected to the network in order for this service to work. (6) Temperature monitoring. CPU temperature can be monitored within the UEFI BIOS (or Legacy BIOS) utility. (7) Cooling fan speeds. CPU cooling fan and case fan speeds can also be monitored within the BIOS. If required, fan speeds and air flow through the computer case can be increased or decreased depending upon prevailing conditions. (8) Voltage monitoring. CPU voltage can be monitored within the BIOS. This is important in certain circumstances, especially when "overclocking" the CPU to prevent irreversible damage to the processor. (9) Monitoring CPU and RAM clock speeds. This is important in certain circumstances, especially when "overclocking" the processor. (10) Chassis intrusion detection. The BIOS utility may also be enabled to detect if the computer case (also known as the computer chassis, system unit, or, in certain circumstances, tower) has been opened and notify the PC user of such "chassis intrusion" events. (11) Virtualization Support. Virtualization only applies to computers that have an installed hypervisor – either Type 1 ("bare metal" hypervisor) or Type 2 (hosted hypervisor). To enable virtualization support in computers with Intel processors, select Intel VT option within the BIOS. Alternatively, select AMD-V option if the motherboard has an AMD processor. (12) Enable or disable USB ports and legacy devices. (13) Load BIOS defaults. If a technician makes an adjustment(s) to the BIOS that ultimately prevents the computer system from booting, the technician has the option of loading BIOS default settings that will revert the computer system to a known good BIOS configuration.

9. Correct: (ii) IEEE 802.11b. The wireless standard IEEE 802.11b has a maximum data transfer rate (DTR) of 11 Mbps and operates at a frequency of 2.4 GHz. The other wireless standards have the following respective maximum DTRs (and frequencies): (1) IEEE 802.11a: 54 Mbps (5 GHz). (2) IEEE 802.11g: 54 Mbps (2.4 GHz). (3) IEEE 802.11n: 300-600 Mbps (5 GHz and/or 2.4 GHz). (4) IEEE 802.11ac: 1.7 Gbps (5 GHz). Please note that the data throughput of an IEEE 802.11g network can potentially be doubled to 108 Mbps using Super G technology.

10. SC connector.

11. (1) Multi-mode. (2) More expensive. (3) Lower. (4) Multi-mode. (5) Larger. (6) Different angles. The completed statement should read: "There are two main types of optic fiber cables: single mode and multi-mode. Single-mode optic fiber cables are a more expensive option, but such cables can be run longer distances and offer lower signal attenuation. On the other hand, multi-mode fiber cables are the most popular amongst networking and telecommunications companies. These fiber cables have a larger diameter compared to single-mode fiber cables, and light signals are transmitted through the optic fibers at different angles. Unlike single-mode fiber cables, these fiber cables can only be run shorter distances.

12. Correct: (iii) WPA2 and (v) AES.

13. Correct: (i) The ethernet cable is disconnected (from the computer's RJ45 port), or (iii) The ethernet cable is loose.

14. Correct: (iv) Video card (or graphics card).

15. **(a)** (i) Cotton swab and (ii) Isopropyl alcohol. **(b)** The cotton swab is dipped into the isopropyl alcohol. The transfer corona wire is then identified. (The transfer corona wire is the exposed fine wire that is usually located near the paper rollers. The purpose of the transfer corona wire is to attract toner particles to the paper by conditioning the paper with a static positive charge.) Gently rub the moistened swab across the transfer corona wire, twisting the swab when one side becomes soiled.

16. **(a)** (i) PXE (Pre-Boot Execution Environment) and (v) WoL (Wake-On-LAN). **(b)** (iii) UEFI BIOS utility (or Legacy BIOS). **(c)** (i) PXE- and WoL-compliant network adapter card (or NIC).

17. Correct: (i), (iii), (iv), and (v). Gaming PCs require a HD (High Definition) audio card, a powerful multi-core processor, a high-end graphics card with a specialized GPU (Graphics Processing Unit), and high-speed RAM modules with as much memory capacity as possible. Other important system requirements include one or more eSATA or PCIe SSDs (Solid State Disks) as opposed to using conventional magnetic HDDs, advanced cooling systems (e.g. liquid-cooling for CPU, RAM heat spreaders, and powerful case fans), a large monitor or VDU (Visual Display Unit) that supports high resolutions and refresh rates, a high-speed NIC (or network adapter card), and a fast Internet connection (e.g. cable broadband as opposed to DSL which is too slow).

18. Correct: (i) Latency. Latency is directly related to the rotational speed (RPM) of a magnetic HDD. Generally speaking, the faster the HDD (or the higher the hard drive's RPM (rotations per minute) value), the lower the latency, and vice versa.

19. Correct: (iv) Phone line voltages can cause serious damage to a computer's ethernet equipment (e.g., network adapter, etc.)

20. (a) (i) Check the patch cable. Initially, the technician should ensure that the computer has a physical cabled connection to the LAN. Perhaps the computer's patch cable (or ethernet cable) has become loose or disconnected. If it transpires that the patch cable is not at issue, the technician can then use the Command Shell to run diagnostic and troubleshooting commands such as ipconfig, ipconfig /all, ping, and netstat. Moreover, the technician has the option of checking the computer's network card driver and updating the driver if necessary. **(b)** (ii) Patch cable tester. The technician should initially use a patch cable tester to check the computer's patch cable. Also, the technician has the option, if necessary, to utilize a continuity tester (or cable certifier) to diagnose longer ethernet cable runs. A loopback tester, also known as a loopback plug, is commonly used to check whether or not a local computer's network adapter (NIC) is functional.

Practice Test 15

1. A 450 W PSU is shown in *Figure 26.*

(a) Identify the parts labelled *A* to *D.*

(b) True or False: ATX motherboards receive 0 volts when the computer is powered off, even if the computer is still connected to an AC receptacle.

(c) A PC technician is troubleshooting a computer that will not power on. The computer is already plugged into an AC receptacle. The technician confirms that the power cable is securely attached to the computer and does not appear to be frayed or damaged in any way. She has also checked the AC receptacle using a multimeter. The AC outlet seems to be functioning normally.

What should the technician do next to troubleshoot this issue?

(i) Replace the PSU

(ii) Test the computer using a PSU tester

(iii) Attach a new power cord to the computer

(iv) Ensure that the CPU and RAM are seated correctly

Figure 26

2. Fill in the missing space: A CPU-intensive computer system, such as a gaming system or a multimedia system, should ideally use a ______ PSU.

3. *Figure 27* shows an I/O port cluster located on the back panel of an ATX motherboard.

Name all the connection types labelled A to K.

Figure 27

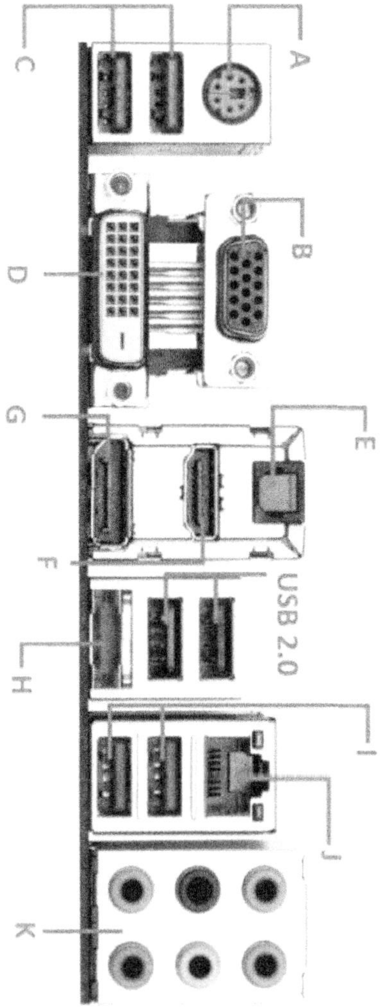

4. An administrative clerk working in an accountancy and taxation office notices that the networked laser printer is not printing to expectation. The employee observes that previous print jobs have wrinkles on some of the pages and random patterns of missing text.

What is the most likely cause of this printer problem?

(i) An ethernet cable is not securely plugged into the RJ45 jack on the laser printer

(ii) The laser printer's fuser assembly needs to be replaced

(iii) The laser printer's imaging drum is defective

(iv) The duplexing assembly is intermittently "jamming"

5. A networked printer is normally equipped with a certain type of connection jack. Which of the following indicates that a printer is connected to the network?

(i) RJ11

(ii) RJ45

(iii) RCA

(iv) mini-DIN

6. What is the maximum distance, in meters, at which a Class 2 Bluetooth device can receive signals from a Bluetooth access point or dongle?

(i) 1 m

(ii) 10 m

(iii) 100 m

(iv) None of the above

7. Fill in the missing spaces: During a computer's boot up process, ______ codes are typically generated by the ______.

8. What function is performed by the external power adapter of a laptop?

(i) Converts AC to DC

(ii) Converts DC to AC

(iii) Provides surge protection

(iv) Provides "clean" AC power

9. True or False: A 6-pin or 12-pin PCIe power connector is commonly connected to a PCIe video card (or graphics card) installed in a motherboard.

10. Name the devices shown in *Figure 28(a)* and *Figure 28(b)*.

11. Which of the following troubleshooting steps should be performed when a Bluetooth connection appears to have malfunctioned? (Select all applicable answers.)

(i) Update NIC driver

(ii) Check if the paired devices are within range

(iii) Replace the DC jack

(iv) Turn the Bluetooth connection on and off

(v) Unpair and re-pair the Bluetooth-enabled devices

Figure 28(a)

Figure 28(b)

12. Which of the following is the default port for HTTPS?

(i) 21

(ii) 80

(iii) 443

(iv) 3389

13. Fill in the two missing spaces: If a printer is giving a paper-feed error, it is highly likely that the ______ ______ require inspection and troubleshooting.

14. What type of motherboard socket incorporates "pinholes" to ensure connectivity to a CPU? (Select the best answer.)

(i) AMD-V

(ii) LGA

(iii) PGA

(iv) VT-x

15. True or False: A wireless network is occasionally referred to as a DHCP.

16. What is the maximum number of USB-compatible devices that can be daisy-chained to a USB?

(i) 25

(ii) 50

(iii) 64

(iv) 127

17. Fill in the missing space: 80 mm and ______ mm are typical sizes for case fans found in a PC.

18. Match the following names to the correct items shown in *Figure 29(a)* to *Figure 29(e).*

(i) Hub

(ii) Loopback plug

(iii) Cable certifier

(iv) Multimeter

(v) Ethernet switch

(vi) Patch panel installation

Figure 29(a)

Figure 29(b)

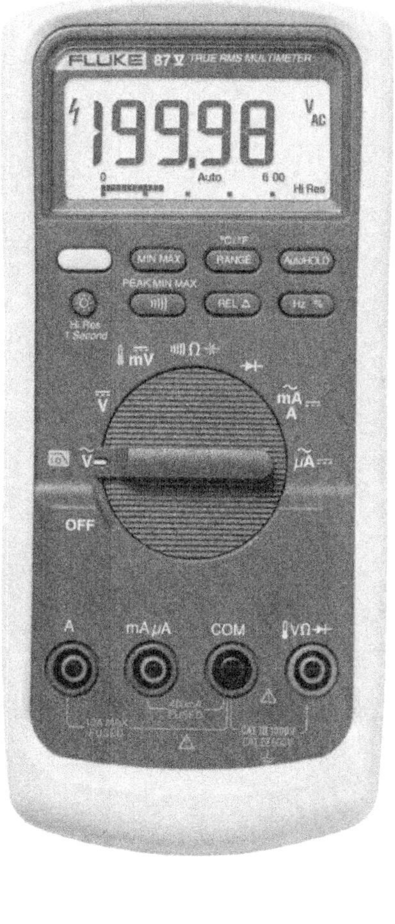
FLUKE 87 V TRUE RMS MULTIMETER
199.98
MIN MAX
RANGE
PEAK MIN MAX
REL Δ
Hz %
OFF
A
mAμA
COM

Figure 29 (c) and (d)

Figure 29(e)

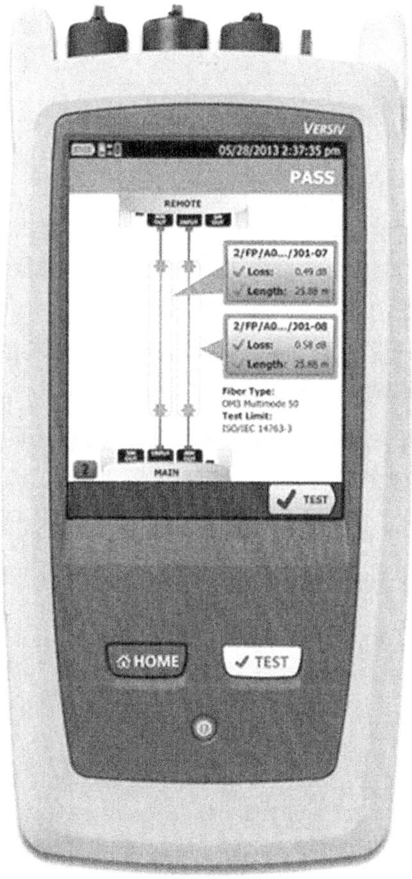
VERSIV
05/28/2013 2:37:35 pm
PASS
REMOTE
2/FP/A0.../J01-07
Loss: 0.49 dB
Length: 25.88 m
2/FP/A0.../J01-08
Loss: 0.58 dB
Length: 25.88 m
Fiber Type:
OM3 Multimode 50
Test Limit:
ISO/IEC 14763-3
MAIN
2
TEST
HOME
TEST

19. In a SOHO networked environment, the IPv4 loopback address is usually 127.0.0.1.

Answer the following questions *(a)* and *(b).*

(a) What is the IPv6 loopback address?

(i) ::1

(ii) 169.254.0.1

(iii) 255.255.255.0

(iv) FF00::/8

(b) A SOHO administrator pings a specific computer's IPv4 loopback address. However, no response is received.

What are the most likely reasons for this error? (Select two answers.)

(i) A static IP address has been assigned to the computer's network adapter

(ii) Faulty NIC on the computer

(iii) Faulty RJ45 port on the computer

(iv) The computer's TCP/IP settings have not been correctly configured

20. DVI is a common video display interface that is used to connect a video source, such as a video display controller or graphics card, to a display device such as a computer monitor. The interface is designed to transmit uncompressed digital video and is predominantly associated with computer technology. However, DVI is occasionally used in other consumer electronic products such as television sets and DVD players.

The pin outs of the many different variants of DVI are shown in *Figure 30.*

(a) Identify the DVI variants labelled A to E.

(b) DVI is designed to support either analog or digital video connections. However, some DVI variants support both analog and digital video.

State the video mode(s) (i.e., analog and/or digital) supported by DVI variants labelled A to E.

Figure 30

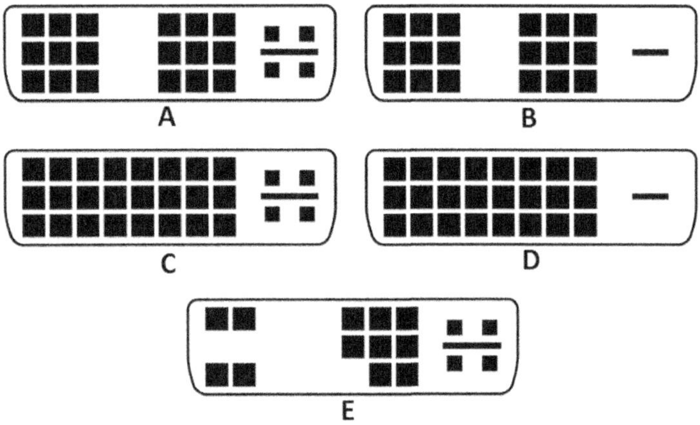

Practice Test 15			
MCQ Solutions			
1.	(a) See notes, (b) False, (c)(ii)	11.	(ii), (iv), (v)
2.	See notes	12.	(iii)
3.	See notes	13.	See notes
4.	(ii)	14.	(iii)
5.	(ii)	15.	False
6.	(ii)	16.	(iv)
7.	(i), (ii)	17.	See notes
8.	(i)	18.	See notes
9.	False	19.	(a)(i), (b)(ii)(iv)
10.	See notes	20.	(a)-(b) See notes

1. **(a)** (A) Exhaust vent (and fan). (B) Hard on/off switch. (C) C14 inlet for IEC power cable. (D) Voltage selector. **(b)** False. ATX motherboards always receive 5 volts from the PSU when the computer is powered off, assuming that the computer is still plugged into an AC outlet. **(c)** (ii) Test the computer using a PSU tester. A PSU tester will allow the technician to determine whether or not the PSU is working properly. If the PSU unit has failed, a working replacement unit can be installed. However, never open a PSU unit – this is hazardous considering that a PSU normally holds a large amount of electric charge.

2. Multi-rail. The completed statement should read: "A CPU-intensive computer system, such as a gaming system or a multimedia system, should ideally use a multi-rail PSU."

3. (A) PS/2 port. (B) 15-pin VGA (also known as DE15). (C) USB 3.0. (D) Dual-link DVI. (E) Optical S/PDIF audio port (Sony Phillips Digital Interconnect Format, otherwise simply referred to as Sony Phillips Digital Interface). (F) HDMI. (G) DisplayPort. (H) eSATA port. (I) USB 3.0. (J) RJ45 ethernet jack (or GbE (gigabit ethernet) LAN jack). (K) HD (High Definition) audio port cluster.

4. Correct: (ii) The laser printer's fuser assembly needs to be replaced.

5. Correct: (ii) RJ45 jack.

6. Correct: (ii) 10 meters (33 ft.). By way of comparison, a Class 1 Bluetooth device can receive signals from a Bluetooth access point or dongle 100 meters (or 328 ft.) away. A Class 3 Bluetooth device only has a range of 1 meter (3 ft.).

7. (i) Beep codes. (ii) POST (Power-on Self Test).

8. Correct: (i). The external power supply or adapter of a laptop converts AC (Alternating Current) power to DC (Direct Current) power.

9. False. The correct statement should read: "A 6-pin or 8-pin PCIe power connector is commonly connected to a PCIe video card (or graphics card) installed in a motherboard."

10. (A) UPS (Uninterruptible Power Supply). (B) Surge Protector.

11. Correct: (ii), (iv), and (v). If a Bluetooth connection appears to have malfunctioned, the following troubleshooting steps can be actioned: (1) Check if the paired devices are within the correct range for a specific Bluetooth class. (For example, a Class 2 Bluetooth connection has a maximum operating range of 10 meters (33 feet).) (2) Turn the Bluetooth connection on and off. (3) If applicable, unpair and re-pair the Bluetooth-enabled devices.

12. Correct: (iii) 443. FTP (File Transfer Protocol) has the default port 21, HTTP (Hypertext Transfer Protocol) corresponds to port 80, and port 3389 refers to RDP (Remote Desktop Protocol).

13. (1) Pickup. (2) Rollers. The completed statement should read: "If a printer is giving a paper-feed error, it is highly likely that the pickup rollers require inspection and troubleshooting."

14. Correct: (iii) PGA (Pin Grid Array).

15. False. The correct statement should read: "A wireless network is occasionally referred to as a SSID (Service Set Identifier)."

16. Correct: (iv) 127.

17. 120 mm. The completed statement should read: "80 mm and 120 mm are typical sizes for case fans found in a PC."

18. (A) Patch panel installation. (B) Multimeter. (C) Loopback plug. (D)Ethernet switch. (E) Cable certifier (also known as a cable tester or continuity tester). A representative image of a hub has not been included in the provided figures.

19. **(a)** (i) IPv6 loopback address is **::1** **(b)** (ii) The computer's network adapter card (NIC) is defective or faulty and/or (iv) The computer's TCP/IP settings have not been correctly configured.

20. **(a)** (A) DVI-I (Single Link). (B) DVI-D (Single Link). (C) DVI-I (Dual Link). (D) DVI-D (Dual Link). (E) DVI-A. **(b)** (A) and (C) DVI-I supports both analog and digital video. (B) and (D) DVI-D only supports digital video. (E) DVI-A only supports analog video. The pin out relating to the DVI variant known as M1 or M1-DA has not been included in the provided figure. M1-DA connections support both analog and digital video as well as USB.

Practice Test 16

1. Two corona wires, primary and transfer, respectively, are normally incorporated into the design and construction of a standard laser printer.

What is the function of these corona wires? (Select two answers.)

(i) The primary corona wire conditions the photosensitive drum (or imaging drum) with a positive charge before the drum is "written to"

(ii) The primary corona wire supplies power to the laser scanning unit during the "writing" process

(iii) The primary corona wire conditions the photosensitive drum (or imaging drum) with a negative charge before the drum is "written to"

(iv) The transfer corona wire transmits text and/or image(s) to the laser scanning unit during the "writing" step of the laser printing process

(v) The transfer corona wire imparts a positive charge to each sheet of paper, so that toner particles are attracted from the imaging drum to the paper

2. What is a phablet?

(i) A legacy device that was the forerunner to the modern tablet computer, but phablet technology is commonly regarded as being obsolete nowadays

(ii) A smartphone that has a screen size over 5.3 inches measured diagonally

(iii) A tablet computer specified with assistive technology to help users with hearing difficulties and/or visual impairment

(iv) A tablet computer that has a screen size over 10.1 inches measured diagonally

3. Using the CLI tool, what command can be used to present and review NetBIOS information?

(i) ipconfig /displaydns

(ii) nbtstat

(iii) netstat

(iv) nslookup

4. Which of the following port numbers are typically associated with SMB?

(i) 443

(ii) 445

(iii) 548

(iv) 3389

5. Select the correct options: ExpressCard is a common type of external expansion bus. ExpressCard is a (2-inch/4-inch) wide slot typically found on the side of a (laptop/tablet). This expansion bus is used to increase the host device's (RAM/storage capacity) or to add functionality such as (ethernet networking/wireless networking), 4G capability, sound cards, hard drives, etc. There are two types of ExpressCard: (24/34) and /54.

6. A small advertising consultancy and PR partnership has decided to move to a larger office space in a prestigious business center due to an unprecedented upsurge in client onboarding and new contracts.

The consultancy moves 12 PC workstations to the new office. The Dell® computers have been recently serviced and have never given any problems in the past.

However, once the Dell® computers are physically connected to the new SOHO network, it is noticed that the Cat 5e patch cables and network adapters do not seem to be functioning as normal. None of the 12 computers are able to connect to the network and there is no Internet connectivity.

(a) Which of the following is the nominal data transmission rate (and operating frequency) of a Cat 5e patch cable?

(i) 10 Mbps

(ii) 100 Mbps and 1,000 Mbps (100 MHz)

(iii) 100 Mbps and 1,000 Mbps (100 MHz/350 MHz)

(iv) 1,000 Mbps and 10 Gbps (250 MHz/500 MHz)

(b) A PC technician checks the Cat 5e patch cables and confirms that these cables are securely connected to the computers. Also, the technician tests each patch cable with a patch cable tester, and the on-screen results show that each patch cable is operating to specification.

Which of the following should the technician do next? (Select two answers.)

(i) Upgrade the patch cables with Cat 6 networking cables

(ii) Replace the network adapters

(iii) Ensure the network adapters are compatible with the installed OS

(iv) Check whether or not the relevant ports on the ethernet switch are enabled

7. A PC technician is building a customized HTPC for a client. He has successfully installed a low TDP Intel® Core™ i3 processor into an ATX motherboard. Also, he has installed a PCIe video card, SATA 3.0 HDD, 4 GB RAM (with a heat spreader), and a 600 W ATX 12 V 2.1 PSU.

(a) Explain the terms *HTPC* and *TDP.*

(b) How many pins should the main power connector to the motherboard have?

(i) 8

(ii) 15

(iii) 24

(iv) 25

(c) How many pins should the SATA power connector have?

(i) 8

(ii) 15

(iii) 20

(iv) 24

(d) Which of the following voltages are normally supplied to the SATA HDD?

(i) 3.3 V and 5 V

(ii) 3.3 V and 12 V

(iii) 3.3 V

(iv) 3.3 V, 5 V, and 12 V

(e) How many pins should the PCIe video card power connector have? (Select two answers.)

(i) 6

(ii) 8

(iii) 12

(iv) 15

(f) Why did the technician attach a heat spreader to the 4 GB RAM module? (Select two answers.)

(i) Heat spreaders must always be installed with RAM modules whenever a processor with a low TDP rating is installed in a computer system

(ii) Memory sticks with 4 GB capacity (or more) must always be installed with attached heat spreaders

(iii) To prevent intermittent shutdowns of a computer system

(iv) To prevent the RAM module from overheating

(g) When custom-building a HTPC, which internal components are the most important to ensure optimal performance of the computer system? (Select all applicable answers.)

(i) A quiet desktop case with a limited number of cooling fans

(ii) Integrated GPU

(iii) microATX

(iv) S-video port

8. A multimeter is an essential constituent of any computer technician's troubleshooting toolkit.

(a) If a technician is testing an AC outlet, which of the following multimeter settings should be selected?

(i) Continuity

(ii) Impedance

(iii) VAC

(iv) Wattage

(b) When testing an AC outlet using a multimeter, which of the following openings will display zero volts? (Select two answers.)

(i) Hot

(ii) Ground

(iii) Neutral

(iv) Live

9. A homeowner has successfully connected his newly purchased Sony® VAIO® laptop to a flat-screen TV using a HDMI connection. He then inserts a DVD movie into the optical drive. The video plays as expected, but there is no audio.

What is the most likely cause of this problem? (Select two answers.)

(i) Faulty DVD drive

(ii) HDMI audio service has not been selected

(iii) TV sound volume is muted

(iv) Damaged HDMI port

10. A network engineer has been contracted to establish a network topology for a large enterprise. A specific budget has been allocated to complete installation, configuration, and commissioning of the network. The engineer decides to create a network topology comprising a fiber optic-based backbone switch that is used to connect four different LAN switches, with each LAN switch serving a different part of the business premises.

Which of the following network topologies is described?

(i) Hierarchical star topology

(ii) Ring topology

(iii) Bus topology

(iv) Wired Mesh topology

11. An IT technician receives a troubleshooting ticket stating that journalists working in a busy newsroom for a prestigious daily newspaper are unable to access some Internet websites that are critical to the performance of their work-related assignments. However, the ticket states that employees can still access shared network resources within the LAN.

Upon visiting the newsroom, the technician confirms that all networking cables and TCP/IP settings are correct. The technician successfully pings network devices connected to the LAN, but no responses are obtained when certain Internet resources are pinged.

(a) Which of the following is the most likely cause of this connectivity issue?

(i) DHCP server is non-responsive

(ii) DNS server is non-responsive

(iii) Ethernet switch has malfunctioned

(iv) SMTP server is disconnected from network

(b) Using the CLI tool, which of the following is the next troubleshooting command to use?

(i) ipconfig /release

(ii) ipconfig /showclassid6

(iii) ipconfig /flushdns

(iv) arp -a

12. True or False: LCD computer monitors are thin-film transistor (TFT) active-matrix displays, meaning they have one transistor for each pixel on the screen. The transistors are embedded within a flexible material and are located directly in front of the liquid crystal material.

13. Which type of cache is shared by all cores of a CPU?

(i) L1

(ii) L2

(iii) L3

(iv) L4

Figure 31

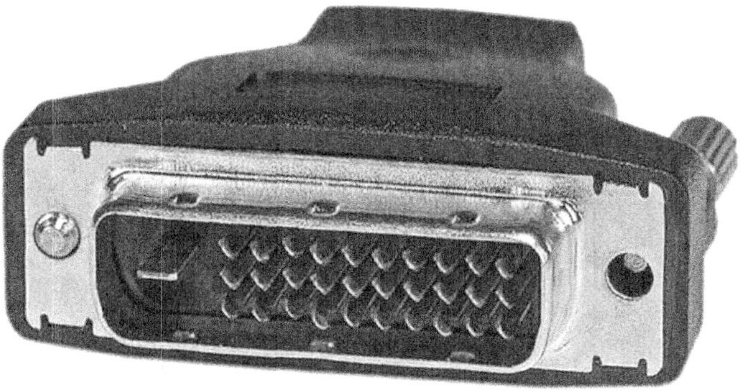

14. Which of the following motherboard form factors has maximum dimensions of 9.6 inches x 9.6 inches?

(i) microATX

(ii) ITX

(iii) ATX

(iv) Mini-ITX

15. Identify the video connector shown in *Figure 31.*

16. What is the typical latency, in milliseconds, of a standard SATA hard drive?

(i) 3.0

(ii) 4.0

(iii) 4.2

(iv) 7.2

17. Which of the following statements most accurately describes the difference between bus speed and clock speed?

(i) The clock speed refers to the speed of the processor. Bus speed is an alternative term for clock speed.

(ii) The bus speed is the internal frequency (or speed) of the CPU and is normally measured in GHz. The clock speed refers to the frequency generated by a quartz oscillating crystal that is soldered directly on to the motherboard.

(iii) The bus speed is the rate at which data is transferred between CPU and RAM. The clock speed is another term for DRAM speed.

(iv) The clock speed is the internal frequency (or speed) of the CPU and is normally measured in GHz (e.g. 1.8 GHz). The bus speed refers to the base clock of the motherboard and is the frequency generated by a quartz oscillating crystal that is soldered directly onto the motherboard.

18. A network multimeter is a very versatile multi-purpose device that can be used by network technicians to test and certify a wide range of network components, such as cables, ports, and network cards (NIC).

State three other functions of the network multimeter.

19. A computer technician has been called to troubleshoot a PC workstation on the production floor of a very busy sawmill.

The Production Manager states that the computer intermittently shuts down. When this event happens, he is able to reboot the computer as normal after a few minutes. However, after only a few hours of operation, the computer shuts down again without warning. This computer problem seems to be worsening and the Manager is hoping for a resolution.

(a) Which of the following is most likely the cause of the problem? (Select the best two answers.)

(i) SATA HDD

(ii) PSU

(iii) DIMM modules

(iv) CPU heat sink/fan assembly

(v) AC power cable

(b) The technician checks the AC power cable and inspects the exhaust vents and case fans using a flashlight. However, there does not seem to be any issues with these items.

Without opening the computer case, what should the technician do next?

(i) Upgrade device drivers

(ii) Re-install the OS

(iii) Check the CPU fan settings and temperature in the UEFI BIOS

(iv) Install an AC power conditioner

20. Which type of network connection permits high-speed data communications and is less susceptible to eavesdropping?

(i) STP

(ii) Fiber optic

(iii) Cellular

(iv) UTP

Practice Test 16			
MCQ Solutions			
1.	(iii), (v)	11.	(a)(ii), (b)(iii)
2.	(ii)	12.	False
3.	(ii)	13.	(iii)
4.	(ii)	14.	(i)
5.	See notes	15.	See notes
6.	(a)(iii), (b)(iii)(iv)	16.	(iii)
7.	(a) See notes, (b)(iii), (c)(ii), (d)(iv), (e)(i)(ii), (f)(iii)(iv), (g)(i)(ii)(iii)	17.	(iv)
8.	(a)(iii), (b)(ii)(iii)	18.	See notes
9.	(ii), (iii)	19.	(a)(ii)(iv), (b)(iii)
10.	(i)	20.	(ii)

1. Correct: (iii) and (v). The primary corona wire conditions the photosensitive drum (or imaging drum) with a negative charge before the drum is "written to". The transfer corona wire imparts a positive charge to each sheet of paper, so that toner particles are attracted from the imaging drum to the paper.

2. Correct: (ii) A phablet is a smartphone that has a screen size over 5.3 inches (134.6 mm), measured diagonally.

3. Correct: (ii) nbtstat.

4. Correct: (ii). SMB (Server Message Block) uses port 445 and/or port range 137-139.

5. Correct options: 2-inch. Laptop. Storage capacity. Wireless networking. /34.

6. **(a)** (iii) The nominal data transfer rates of a Category 5e cable are 100 Mbps and 1,000 Mbps (1 Gbps), operating at a frequency of either 100 MHz or 350 MHz. Category 3 UTP cables are rated for 10 Mbps networks. Category 5 UTP cables are rated for 100 Mbps and 1,000 Mbps (1 Gbps), operating at a frequency of 100 MHz. Category 6 and 6a UTP cables have data transfer rates of 1,000 Mbps (1 Gbps) and 10 Gbps (250 MHz or 500 MHz). Category 7 and Category 7a UTP cables are rated for 1,000 Mbps (1 Gbps) and 10 Gbps networks (600 MHz or 1,000 MHz). **(b)** (iii) and (iv). (1) The technician should initially check whether or not the relevant ports on the ethernet switch are enabled. Some routers and switches have the ability to automatically disable physical ports if the MAC (physical) addresses of the devices (e.g., a local computer) connected to the router and/or switch are not recognised. This is a built-in security measure of

some routers and switches on the market nowadays. (2) If the router and/or ethernet switch has not disabled any physical network ports, the technician can then check the network adapters to determine if they are compatible with the installed operating system (OS) version on the computers. If applicable, the technician can update the network adapter drivers to restore functionality to the network adapters (NIC).

7. (a) HTPC is an acronym for Home Theatre PC. TDP stands for Thermal Design Power. TDP signifies the quantity of heat generated by the processor during operation which the CPU's cooling system is required to dissipate. TDP is normally measured in watts (W). A common TDP rating for single-core CPUs is 200 to 250 W. However, multi-core CPUs are more efficient, generating comparatively less heat during operation. Hence, the TDP rating for multi-core processors is typically in the range 100 to 150 W. **(b)** (iii) 24 pins. There are 24 pins in the ATX 12 V 2.x power connector that supplies power to the motherboard. Historically, older generation ATX PSUs connected to the motherboard using a 20-pin connector. **(c)** (ii) 15 pins. **(d)** Correct: (iv) 3.3 V, 5 V, and 12 V. **(e)** (i) and (ii). Depending on the type of PSU, a PCIe power connector can either have 6 pins or 8 pins. With respect to an ATX 12 V 2.1 PSU, the PCIe power connector has 6 pins. For ATX 12 V 2.2 (and higher) PSUs, the PCIe power connector has 8 pins. **(f)** (iii) and (iv). Depending upon the actual purpose and usage of the PC, the RAM modules can sometimes overheat and cause intermittent shutdowns of the system. Heat sinks that are designed specifically for RAM modules can be installed to dissipate the heat generated by RAM during operation. These RAM heat sinks are made of copper or aluminum and are also known as "heat spreaders". RAM heat spreaders are commonly found in CPU-intensive computer systems, such as virtualization workstations, CAD/CAM workstations, and gaming PCs. RAM heat sinks can also be used when custom-building a HTPC, especially if the objective is to build a quiet HTPC that is more reliant on passive cooling of the processor and RAM. **(g)** (i), (ii), and (iii). The requirements for an HTPC include: (1) Small form factor (e.g., micro-ATX or mini-ATX). (2) A quiet desktop case, with a limited number of cooling fans in the case as more fans means more noise. (3) A fan controller, because motherboards oftentimes adjust fan speeds to run faster and louder than needed. (4) A silent video card. Alternatively, use an integrated GPU (Graphics Processing Unit) instead of a separate graphics card. (5) HDMI port for connectivity to big-screen TVs or projector equipment. (6) A liquid-cooled CPU (as opposed to fan-based CPU cooling). (7) SSD (Solid-State Disk) as opposed to using a conventional magnetic HDD. (8) A low TDP-rated CPU such as Intel Core i3. (9) Surround sound audio card. (10) If the HTPC is being designed for TV reception, a TV tuner needs to be installed and, if necessary, an antenna.

8. **(a)** (iii) VAC. Sometimes, this multimeter setting will be labelled as "volts AC". **(b)** (ii) and (iii). The Ground and Neutral openings in an AC outlet will normally display zero volts when tested with a multimeter.

9. Correct: (ii) and (iii). In this scenario, the most probable cause of the audio problem is that the HDMI audio service has not been selected and/or the TV's sound volume has been muted.

10. Correct: (i) Hierarchical star topology (otherwise known as a tree topology). (1) A tree topology is effectively a collection of star networks arranged in a hierarchy. (2) A ring topology is effectively a logical ring, meaning that the data is transmitted in a circular manner from one computer workstation to another on the network. However, the network design is not a physical ring topology. (3) In a star topology, all computer workstations and other networked devices are connected to a central device, either a hub or more commonly an ethernet switch. Each computer and networked device require a single cable to be connected to the hub or switch, creating a point-to-point connection between the device and the hub or switch. The star topology is by far the most widely implemented network design in use nowadays. (4) In a wired mesh topology, each computer workstation on the network connects to every other computer, creating a point-to-point connection between every computer and device on the network. The purpose of the wired mesh topology is to afford a high level of redundancy – in other words, if one ethernet cable becomes defective, data streams can always find and use an alternative path to reach their destination. Implementing a wired mesh topology can be expensive by virtue of the cabling costs involved and troubleshooting a defective cable can be problematical. In consequence, the wired mesh topology is not commonly used, but it is more popular with servers and routers.

11. **(a)** (ii) DNS server is non-responsive. **(b)** (iii) ipconfig /flushdns

12. False. The correct statement should read: "LCD computer monitors are thin-film transistor (TFT) active-matrix displays, meaning they have multiple transistors for each pixel on the screen. The transistors are embedded within a flexible material and are located directly behind the liquid crystal material."

13. Correct: (iii) L3 cache (otherwise known as Level 3 cache). L3 cache has the largest capacity compared to the other forms of CPU cache, L1 and L2. However, L3 cache has the most latency and is therefore the slowest relative to L1 and L2. If the CPU is unable to find the data it requires in L1 cache, the CPU focuses on L2, then L3, and if absolutely necessary, the CPU accesses data stored on the DRAM sticks. L3 cache is normally shared by all cores of the CPU and it is typically located "on-die" (i.e. built on to the CPU).

14. Correct: (i) microATX. microATX (otherwise referred to as mATX) is a smaller version of ATX form factor. mATX motherboards can have a maximum size of 9.6 inches x 9.6 inches (244 mm x 244 mm), but mATX can be as small as 6.75 inches x 6.75 inches (171.45 mm x 171.45 mm). mATX motherboards are square compared to ATX form factors which are rectangular (12 inches x 9.6 inches). mATX motherboards are backward compatible with ATX boards, which effectively means that most mATX boards can be installed within an ATX motherboard computer case. The ITX family of form factors vary in size from 60 mm x 60 mm to 6.7 inches x 6.7 inches depending on the type. ITX form factors are primarily designed for use in HTPCs, UMPCs (Ultra-mobile PC), and smartphones.

15. M1-DA. M1-DA (often known simply as M1) is a type of DVI video connector that incorporates dual link technology (digital and analog) with USB. M1-DA is primarily designed for use with digital display devices, such as flat-panel displays and projectors.

16. Correct: (iii). The average latency of a standard 7,200 RPM SATA hard drive is approximately 4.2 ms (milliseconds). A 10,000 RPM hard drive has an average latency of approximately 3.0 ms.

17. Correct: (iv). The correct statement should read: "The clock speed is the internal frequency (or speed) of the CPU and is normally measured in GHz (e.g., 1.8 GHz). The bus speed refers to the base clock of the motherboard and is the frequency generated by a quartz oscillating crystal that is soldered directly on to the motherboard." Please note that the "bus speed" or motherboard's base clock speed is directly related to the CPU's internal clock speed – in other words, the CPU's clock speed is based off the motherboard's base clock speed.

18. A network multimeter can be used to report the status of various network conditions, such as (1) data transmission speed of an ethernet cable, (2) length of a cable, (3) PoE (Power over Ethernet) voltage levels, and (4) duplex status – whether a cable is full duplex (permitting data transmission in both directions simultaneously) or half duplex (permitting data transmission in only one direction, at any given time).

19. (a) (ii) and (iv). The two items that could cause a computer system to shut down without warning are the PSU (or power supply) and the CPU heat sink/fan assembly. The RAM (or DIMM modules), SATA hard drive, or graphics card should not cause a computer to suddenly shut down during operation. **(b)** (iii) Check the CPU fan settings and temperature in the BIOS before opening the computer case. Perhaps the computer is automatically shutting down because the system, specifically the CPU and RAM modules to a lesser extent, are overheating. However, if the system temperature is within normal parameters, it is very likely that there is a problem with the power supply. If the PSU is starting to fail or defective, it will be necessary to replace the PSU with a working unit.

20. Correct: (ii) Fiber optic.

Practice Test 17

1. A computer user reports that the LCD display remains blank even when the computer is powered on. The power LED on the LCD display is "on". A technician has been called to investigate the matter.

(a) According to the six-step CompTIA® A+ troubleshooting methodology, which of the following should the technician do first?

(i) Establish a theory of probable cause

(ii) Identify the problem

(iii) Establish a plan of action to resolve the problem

(iv) Escalate the computer issue to another more experienced technician

(b) Which of the following are critical components to the A+ troubleshooting step referred to in (i) above?

(i) Check the maintenance log for the computer being troubleshot

(ii) Question the user of the computer being troubleshot

(iii) If necessary, consult the manufacturer's documentation

(iv) Document any actions taken so far

(v) Establish a theory of probable cause

(c) What is the second step of the A+ troubleshooting methodology?

(d) Which of the following are critical components of Step 2 of the A+ troubleshooting methodology? (Select all that apply.)

(i) Check the maintenance log for the computer being troubleshot

(ii) If necessary, consult the manufacturer's documentation

(iii) Conduct external or internal research based on the symptoms of the computer issue

(iv) Test the theory

2. True or False: DisplayPort is a type of video card connector that resembles a USB connection. DisplayPort operates in a similar manner to an ethernet connector, in that it uses data packet transmission.

3. True or False: Inkjet printers should not be connected to a UPS unit. However, PCs, LCD displays, laser printers, and speakers can be safely connected to a UPS.

4. Which of the following PCs require powerful processors? (Select all that apply.)

(i) Virtualization workstation

(ii) CAD/CAM workstation

(iii) Gaming PC

(iv) Microsoft Office 365® and VoIP PC

(v) Thin client

5. PXE is an IT industry standard client/server interface that allows a networked workstation to boot from a server on a network prior to booting the OS on the local hard drive.

Which of the following local computer hardware components is essential to PXE?

(i) Category 5e crossover cable

(ii) NIC

(iii) DRAM

(iv) L3 cache

Figure 32

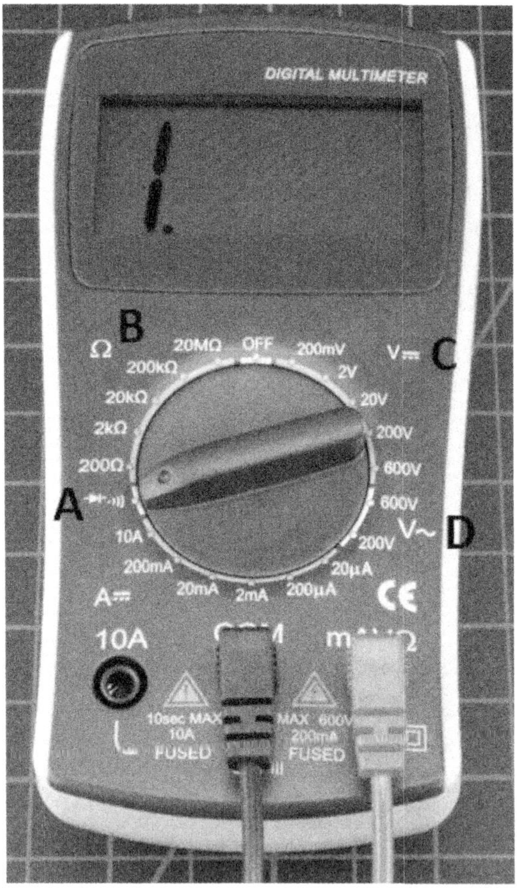
DIGITAL MULTIMETER
B
Ω
20MΩ
OFF
200mV
V⎓
C
200kΩ
2V
20kΩ
20V
2kΩ
200V
200Ω
600V
A
600V
V~
D
10A
200V
200mA
20μA
A⎓
20mA
2mA
200μA
10A
10sec MAX
10A
FUSED
MAX 600V
200mA
FUSED

6. True or False: Tablet computers and smartphones commonly use AMD®-designed CPUs and non-volatile flash memory, similar to USB flash memory, that is hard-wired to the system instead of data being stored to a magnetic HDD or SSD. These design specifications optimize the performance of tablet computers and smartphones.

7. *Figure 32* shows a typical multimeter routinely used by auto-mechanics, electricians, PC technicians, and other professionals.

Which of the following multimeter settings should only be used when there is no electrical current flowing through the computer component or part being tested? (Select two answers.)

(a) Continuity

(b) Resistance

(c) DC Voltage

(d) AC Voltage

8. The computer workstations on Floor B of an office building have no access to the LAN or the Internet. A junior network technician on duty is notified and she visits the server room. Upon locating and inspecting the relevant ethernet switch corresponding to Floor B, the technician notices that all LEDs are consistently on and not flickering.

She confirms that all ethernet cables are securely plugged into the relevant ports on the switch. Upon reviewing the maintenance logs and troubleshooting ticket history for computers on Floor B, there is no evidence of any issues affecting the computers' network adapters or network cables. All network cables seem to be securely plugged into the computer workstations.

What is the next appropriate troubleshooting step the technician should take?

(i) Update the switch's firmware

(ii) Disconnect and then re-connect all ethernet cables to the relevant switch ports

(iii) Manually reboot all the computer workstations

(iv) Manually reboot the relevant switch

9. Which of the following voltages are supplied by a Molex power connector?

(i) 0 V and 3.3 V

(ii) 5 V and 12 V

(iii) 0 V and 5 V

(iv) 3.3 V, 5 V, and 12 V

10. A customer buys an external portable Cocopa® x48 CD-ROM drive in order to access sensitive corporate data that was originally archived on a wallet of CD-ROMs.

(a) Which of the following does the x refer to in Compact Disc technology?

(i) 150 KB/s

(ii) 1.32 MB/s

(iii) 150 MB/s

(iv) 1.32 Gbps

(b) What is the maximum read speed of this CD-ROM drive?

(i) 1.32 MB/s

(ii) 7.2 MB/s

(iii) 150 MB/s

(iv) 0.01 Gbps

11. A corporate executive has a USB flash drive and an external SDHC card reader plugged into the USB 3.0 ports on her Samsung® laptop. Once she has completed her work-related assignments, she removes both devices from the laptop.

(a) What should the corporate executive have done first before physically removing the external storage media?

(i) Shut down the laptop

(ii) Log off from Windows® GUI

(iii) Click on the "Safely Remove Hardware" icon

(iv) None of the above

(b) How are most USB flash drives normally formatted by the manufacturer?

(i) FAT16

(ii) FAT32

(iii) exFAT

(iv) SCSI

12. Which of the following are possible causes of motherboard failure? (Select all applicable answers.)

(i) Normal aging and wear

(ii) Accidental impacts

(iii) Incompatible peripheral devices

(iv) Manufacturing defects

(v) Defective optical drives

13. When rebooting a Windows® OS computer workstation, a technician notices that a blue screen appears on the monitor for a few moments before the computer automatically shuts down and successfully reboots itself.

(a) What should the technician do in this specific situation?

(i) Clean the RAM slots

(ii) Do nothing

(iii) Replace the DIMM sticks

(iv) Check the Boot Device Priority in the BIOS

(b) What are the most common causes of a "blue screen" event? (Select two possible causes.)

(i) Device driver errors

(ii) Physical RAM defects

(iii) The processor is overheating

(iv) Motherboard manufacturing defect

(c) If a "blue screen" event happens persistently when the computer is booted, what should the technician do first?

(i) Replace the computer's RAM

(ii) Re-install the OS

(iii) Ensure that the CPU is seated properly

(iv) Write down the information that appears on the blue screen

14. How many pins are on a SODIMM DDR3 memory stick?

(i) 184

(ii) 200

(iii) 204

(iv) 240

15. Which of the following display resolutions is most commonly found in tablet computers?

(i) WXGA

(ii) HD 1080p

(iii) QHD

(iv) QXGA

16. A help desk technician working in the IT department of a large industrial complex receives a troubleshooting ticket from a laboratory analyst.

The analyst states that his computer workstation worked normally last week. However, upon rebooting the PC at the start of his shift, none of his plugged-in USB devices are working.

The help desk technician checks the maintenance logs and she discerns that all PC workstations in the on-site testing laboratories were serviced towards the end of last week.

What is the most likely cause of this specific IT issue?

(i) USB functionality has been disabled in the BIOS

(ii) USB functionality has been disabled in Windows® Device Manager

(iii) USB 3.0 ports are faulty

(iv) USB 3.0 controller on the motherboard is defective

17. A shared network printer in a small office has unexpectedly stopped printing. A technician has been called to troubleshoot the issue.

She verifies that the ethernet cable is securely plugged into the printer. She also verifies that the TCP/IP settings applicable to all devices on the SOHO network are correctly configured, and all patch cable connections are secure. Using the CLI tool, the technician successfully pings the default gateway, but the printer's IP address is unresponsive.

(a) What type of jack on the printer indicates that it is network-ready?

(i) RJ11

(ii) RJ45

(iii) RG-59

(iv) STP

(b) If the technician is unsure which switch of the **ping** command to use, what should she type at the command line?

(i) ping -a

(ii) ping -n

(iii) ping -t

(iv) ping /?

(c) What is the most probable cause of this particular printer issue?

(i) Computer NIC is defective

(ii) Printer NIC is defective

(iii) Loose patch cable

(iv) Obsolete printer driver

18. Which of the following memory types are found internal to the CPU?

(i) DRAM

(ii) DIMM

(iii) SODIMM

(iv) SRAM

19. During routine maintenance, a PC technician made minor adjustments to a computer's BIOS settings. However, when the computer workstation was rebooted at the start of the next shift, an employee reported that the monitor displays a black screen with a white blinking underscore on the top left hand side. The employee has rebooted the computer several times, but Windows® GUI does not load on to the screen.

What is the most likely cause of this problem?

(i) Obsolete BIOS firmware

(ii) Malware infection

(iii) WinRE has loaded on to the screen

(iv) Incorrect boot order

20. Which of the following devices is designed to test multiple wires of a PSU simultaneously?

(i) PSU tester

(ii) Multimeter

(iii) Power strip

(iv) Line conditioner

Practice Test 17			
MCQ Solutions			
1.	(a)(ii), (b)(ii), (c) See notes, (d)(i)(ii)(iii)	11.	(a)(iii), (b)(ii)
2.	True	12.	(i), (ii), (iv)
3.	False	13.	(a)(ii), (b)(i)(ii), (c)(iv)
4.	(i), (ii), (iii)	14.	(iii)
5.	(ii)	15.	(iv)
6.	False	16.	(i)
7.	See notes	17.	(a)(ii), (b)(iv), (c)(ii)
8.	(iv)	18.	(iv)
9.	(ii)	19.	(iv)
10.	(a)(i), (b)(ii)	20.	(i)

1. **(a)** (ii): Identify the problem. **(b)** (ii): Question the user of the computer being troubleshot. **(c)** Step 2: Establish a theory of probable cause. **(d)** (i), (ii), and (iii). If necessary, Step 2 of the A+ troubleshooting methodology requires the technician to carry out external or internal research based on the symptoms of the computer issue. If a technician is unable to determine the exact root cause of a specific computer issue, it may be necessary to consult the organization's documentation (e.g., computer maintenance logs) and/or the technician may need to review his own personal troubleshooting notes regarding historical computer problems. Moreover, depending upon the complexity and nature of the problem, the technician may also need to review manufacturer's documentation, research technical websites and/or contact various IT support helpdesks (over the phone or via instant messaging platforms). It may also be necessary for the technician to carry out a more extensive inspection of the internal components of the computer and check the computer's operating system (OS) as well as appropriate software-based diagnostic tools. In this way, the technician should be able to formulate a theory explaining the exact root cause of the computer issue.

2. True.

3. False. Laser printers should never be connected to a UPS. Therefore, the correct statement is: "Laser printers should not be connected to a UPS unit. However, PCs, LCD displays (and other types of computer monitor), inkjet printers, and speakers can be safely connected to a UPS."

4. Correct: (i), (ii), and (iii). Virtualization workstations, CAD/CAM workstations, and Gaming PCs all require powerful CPUs.

5. Correct: (ii) NIC. PXE (Pre-boot Execution Environment), pronounced "pixie", is reliant on a PXE-compliant NIC (Network Interface Controller, otherwise known as a network adapter card). PXE must also be supported by the local computer's BIOS (or UEFI) utility. PXE allows a computer workstation to boot from a server on a network prior to booting the operating system (e.g., Windows OS, Linux, etc.) on the local computer's hard drive. A PXE-enabled workstation connects its network adapter card to the network by means of a jumper. The purpose of the jumper is to keep the local computer connected to the network even when the computer is shut down. The main benefit of deploying PXE-enabled workstations in a LAN environment is that the network administrator is not obliged to physically visit a specific workstation to manually boot it. The booting process will be automatically performed over the network assuming that the workstation is PXE-compliant. Consequently, operating systems (OS) and other software (e.g., diagnostic applications, anti-malware software, etc.) can be loaded on to the local computer from a dedicated server over the network.

6. False. The correct statement should read: "Tablet computers and smartphones commonly use ARM-designed CPUs and non-volatile flash memory, similar to USB flash memory, that is hard-wired to the system instead of data being stored to a magnetic HDD or SSD. However, these design specifications do not optimize the performance of tablet computers and smartphones. Consequently, these devices often suffer from a lack of performance compared to laptops."

7. Correct: (a) Continuity and (b) Resistance. With reference to Figure 32, the continuity setting (labelled A) is commonly recognised as a diode symbol with propagation waves around it, resembling sound coming from a speaker. Resistance (labelled B) is denoted by the ohm symbol (Ω). DC Voltage (labelled C) is denoted by a V symbol followed by a straight/broken line combination. AC Voltage (labelled D) is denoted by a V symbol followed by a wavy line.

8. Correct: (iv). In this situation, the most sensible and easiest first troubleshooting step is to manually reboot the ethernet switch. Under normal circumstances, the LEDs on a switch should be intermittently flashing or flickering, signifying an active network. Rebooting the switch may help to restore functionality to this networking device before considering any other troubleshooting options.

9. Correct: (ii) 5 V and 12 V. Molex power connectors possess 4 pins which provide 5 V and 12 V. The Molex connector has 4 wires: 12 V (yellow), 5 V (red), and two black wires which serve as ground wires (0 volts).

10. (a) (i) 150 KB/s. The x in CD (Compact Disc) technology is equivalent to 150 KB/s. The x in DVD (Digital Versatile Disc or formerly known as Digital Video Disk) technology denotes a read/write speed of 1.32 MB/s, which is significantly faster than the read/write speeds of CD drives. (1 MB/s = 1,000 KB/s)
(b) (ii) 7.2 MB/s. To calculate the read speed of the CD-ROM drive given in the scenario, use the equation: speed rating (e.g., 48x) x 150 KB/s = 7,200 KB/s (= 7.2 MB/s).

11. **(a)** (iii) Click on the "Safely Remove Hardware" icon. This icon is usually found in the Notification Area on the Windows Desktop. Then, click "Eject" to shut down power to the device. **(b)** (ii) FAT32. FAT32 is the standard formatting system used by most USB flash drives. FAT16 (otherwise known as simply FAT) is an older file system that is predominantly used in legacy Windows operating systems. exFAT is the most common file system used by SD (Secure Digital) cards, especially SDXC (Secure Digital Enhanced Capacity). SCSI (Small Computer System Interface, pronounced "SKUH-zee") is a set of ANSI (American National Standards Institute) standard electronic interfaces that allow PCs to communicate with peripheral hardware devices such as external disk drives, tape drives, CD-ROM drives (and other external optical drives), printers, and scanners faster and more flexibly compared to previous parallel data transfer interfaces.

12. Correct: (i), (ii), and (iv). Normal aging and wear, accidental impacts to the motherboard, and manufacturing defects are common causes of motherboard failure in the field. Other possible causes of motherboard failure include: (1) Dirt, dust, debris, and pet hair can clog and block cooling fans and exhaust vents, thereby impeding air circulation that keeps the computer system cool. (2) Tar from cigarette smoke may accumulate with the computer case and cause overheating which may cause detrimental damage to the motherboard. It is recommended that the interior of a computer case is periodically cleaned at an accredited PC repair shop and try to minimise computer exposure to cigarette smoke. (3) Overheating of the motherboard can occur if multiple, CPU-intensive operations are performed simultaneously and power supply is continuous. Hence, it is recommended to give a computer system periodic rest if gaming, watching videos, etc.). Also, clogged fans and exhaust vents can lead to overheating. (4) Accidental spillage of liquids (e.g., water, coffee, etc.) can cause the motherboard to short out instantly.

13. (a) (ii) Do nothing. A single occurrence of a "blue screen" event (otherwise known as a BSOD or "Blue Screen of Death") does not necessarily mean that there is a problem with the computer's RAM or any other hardware components. Oftentimes, a BSOD occurs but there will be no recurrence. However, if a "blue screen" event repeatedly occurs, the technician will have to consider troubleshooting the root cause of the problem. **(b)** (i) and (ii). The most common causes of a BSOD event are device driver errors due to poorly written or incompatible driver code, or physical faults that affect the memory modules. **(c)** (iv) Since a BSOD event is regarded as a critical system error, recurrence of BSOD events potentially signifies a serious system problem that requires troubleshooting. In this case, a technician should initially write down or otherwise capture all the information that appears on the blue screen and cross-reference the information to the Microsoft IT Support website. Further, it may be necessary for the technician to subsequently troubleshoot the RAM modules (e.g., clean the RAM slots, re-seat the memory modules, check the RAM's BIOS settings, replace the memory sticks, upgrade the RAM, etc.).

14. Correct: (iii) 204. SODIMM (Small Outline Dual In-Line Memory Module) RAM sticks are normally inserted into laptops, while DIMM sticks are inserted into PC motherboards. SODIMM DDR3 modules have 204 pins. SODIMM DDR and DDR2 have 200-pins. SODIMM DDR4 has 260 pins.

15. Correct: (iv) QXGA. QXGA (Quad Extended Graphics Array) has a display resolution of 2048 x 1536 and a 4:3 aspect ratio.

16. Correct: (i) USB functionality has been disabled in the BIOS. If none of the USB devices connected to the PC are working, it is very likely that the maintenance technician disabled USB functionality in the BIOS during routine PC servicing. The company may have revised its AUP (Acceptable User Policy) regarding computer use by employees, so that PC users cannot use USB flash drives (e.g., to copy commercially sensitive data, etc.) or boot PCs to personal USB drives that may be compromised (e.g., infected with malware, etc.). Even if the USB 3.0 controller on the motherboard has failed or the USB 3.0 ports are somehow faulty, the PC user can still use the USB 2.0 ports assuming that the USB 2.0 controller is still working as normal. Using Windows Device Manager to disable all USB ports, although possible, is seldom seen in practice – therefore, this option is irrelevant.

17. **(a)** (ii) RJ45 jack. **(b)** (iv) ping /? **(c)** (ii) It is highly likely that the printer's network adapter card (NIC) has become defective.

18. Correct: (iv) SRAM. SRAM (Static Random Access Memory) is faster and more expensive compared to DRAM (Dynamic Random Access Memory). SRAM is typically located within the CPU where it is used as CPU cache memory (viz. L1, L2, and L3 cache). In comparison, DRAM is used as a computer's main memory (or RAM).

19. Correct: (iv) Incorrect boot order. Whenever a black screen with a white blinking underscore appears on the screen, it is very likely that the BIOS boot order is incorrect. For instance, the BIOS boot order may have been changed by the maintenance technician to boot from removable media such as a CD-ROM or DVD-ROM during routine maintenance (e.g., OS or other software upgrade, security patch installation, etc.). However, once the PC maintenance/servicing was completed, the technician may have inadvertently neglected to change the BIOS settings to ensure that the hard drive is selected first in the Boot Device Priority screen, hence the inability to load Windows GUI (Graphical User Interface). WinRE refers to Windows Recovery Environment.

20. Correct: (i) PSU tester (otherwise known as a power supply tester). A line conditioner is sometimes referred to as an AC power conditioner.

Practice Test 18

1. Fill in the missing spaces: The data transmission rate of a Thunderbolt 1.0 connection is faster than ______, which in turn is faster than Firewire 400 and 800, which in turn is faster than ______. However, the data transmission rate of a Thunderbolt 1.0 connection is equivalent to ______.

2. The laser printing process is occasionally referred to as an imaging process.

Answer the following questions *(a)* to *(d)*.

(a) What process occurs first in the laser printing process? Briefly explain what happens during this phase.

(b) What process occurs immediately after the charging (or conditioning) of the photosensitive drum by a negative charge? Briefly describe what happens during this step.

(c) What process occurs last in the laser printing sequence? Briefly explain what happens during this final laser printing process.

(d) Which of the following components are normally incorporated into the design and construction of a typical laser printer? (Select all applicable answers.)

(i) Fuser assembly

(ii) Imaging drum

(iii) PCL driver

(iv) Transfer roller

3. A Faraday cage has recently been installed in a secure room within a US government office complex. The room is normally used to archive confidential PII data of a sensitive nature pertaining to former military personnel.

(a) Explain the term "PII".

(b) Which of the following items does a Faraday cage prevent the use of?

(i) USB flash drives

(ii) Smartphones

(iii) Smart cameras

(iv) Bluetooth 2.0 headsets

4. Which of the following items should be initially checked when a laptop does not power on? (Select all applicable answers.)

(i) AC/DC adapter

(ii) Hibernate status

(iii) Power LED

(iv) LCD resolution settings

(v) RJ45 jack

5. UDP and TCP are common networking protocols.

Which of the following statements describe the main characteristics of these protocols? (Select two answers.)

(i) TCP establishes an end-to-end connection

(ii) UDP maintains the integrity of the data packets being transmitted

(iii) UDP is oftentimes used for media streaming

(iv) UDP is the main protocol that is used to support common user activities such as browsing the Internet and sending email correspondence

Figure 33

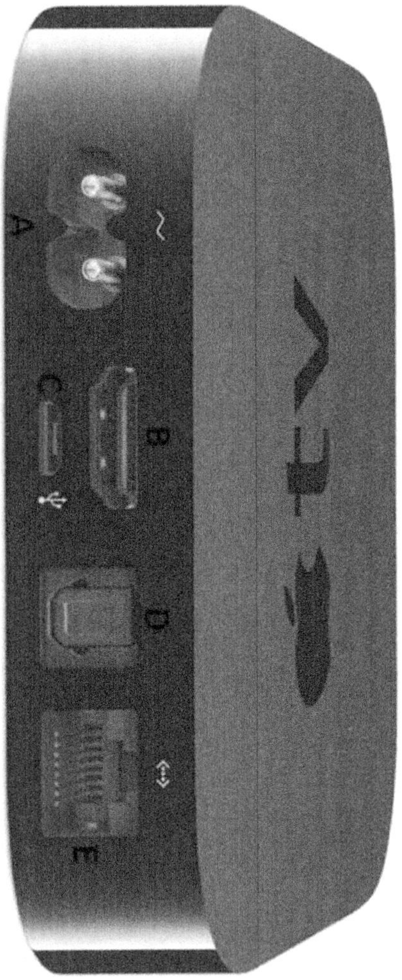

6. *Figure 33* shows the rear of an Apple® TV STB.

(a) Identify the items labelled A, B, C, D, and E.

(b) Briefly explain the term *STB.*

(c) A customer has recently purchased an Apple® TV STB from her local consumer electronics store. She eventually returns to the store and complains to a retail assistant on duty that there is a red laser-like light being emitted from one of the ports on the rear of the device.

She explains that none of the other ports emit a red light, and she is concerned that the device is defective. She also states that there is no audio when she connects the STB to her HD widescreen television.

The retail assistant visually confirms that a red light is being emitted from port D (see *Figure 33*) once the device is powered on.

Which of the following best describes what is happening with respect to the preceding scenario?

(i) Manufacturing fault

(ii) Apple® TV device's sound card is defective

(iii) Warning LED indicating that the device is about to fail

(iv) Optical audio cable is not connected to the sound card

7. Which of the following are essential features of a Home Server PC? (Select all applicable answers.)

(i) GbE network adaptor

(ii) Liquid cooling system

(iii) Embedded RAID controller

(iv) Windows® OS HomeGroup

(v) RAID array

(vi) Powerful multi-core processor

8. Which of the following is the CPU's second fastest cache memory in a PC?

(i) L1

(ii) L2

(iii) L3

(iv) L4

9. A manufacturing engineer working for a large consumer electronics company sends a PDF document to a shared network Xerox® laser printer. When he goes to the printer to collect his print job, he notices that the printer is generating only blank pages.

An IT technician subsequently confirms that the ethernet cable is securely attached to the printer's RJ45 jack and that the printer settings are correct.

What is the most likely cause of this particular problem?

(i) Photosensitive drum is defective

(ii) No power is being supplied to transfer corona wire

(iii) Primary corona wire is frayed and faulty

(iv) Fusing assembly is not getting sufficiently hot

10. *Figure 34 (a)* to *(e)* shows twisted-pair cabling tools that are commonly used by telecommunication and network technicians.

(a) Name the cabling tools labelled A to E.

(b) Briefly state the purpose and function of each cabling tool labelled A to E.

Figure 34(a)

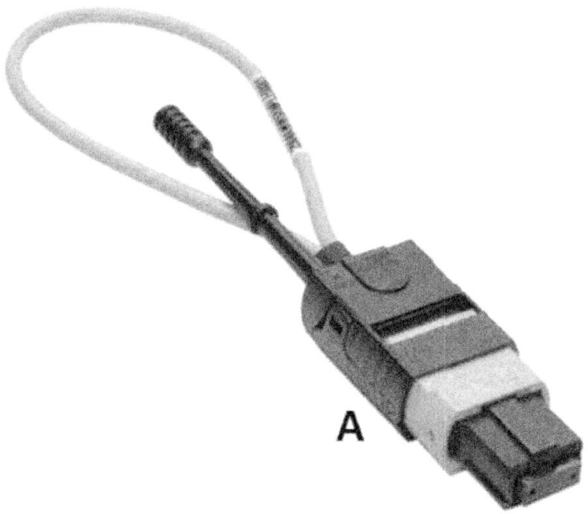

Figure 34(b)

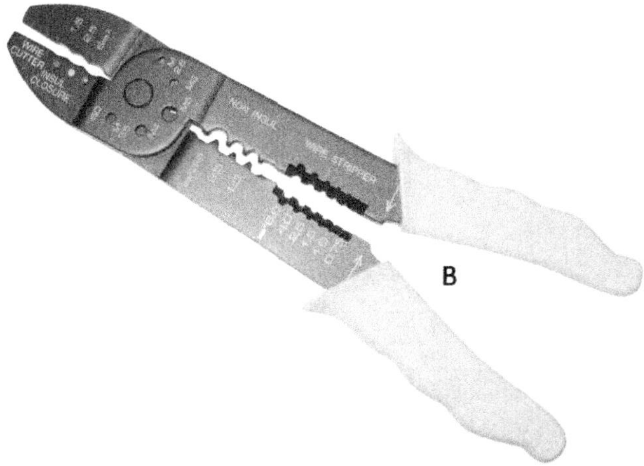

Figure 34(c)

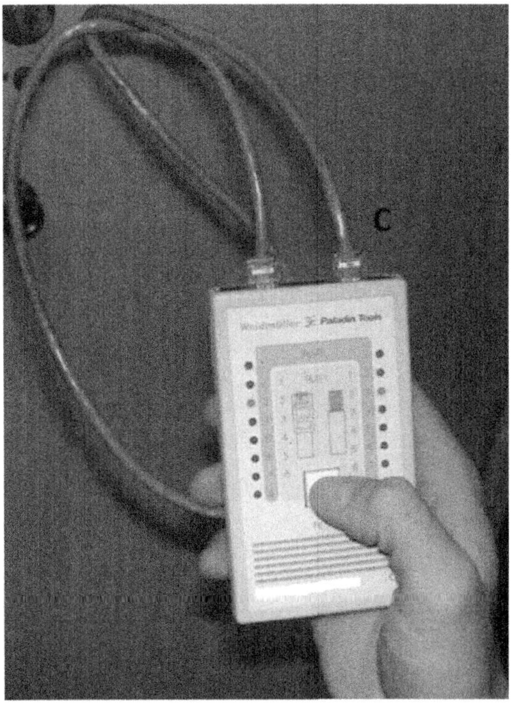

Figure 34(d)

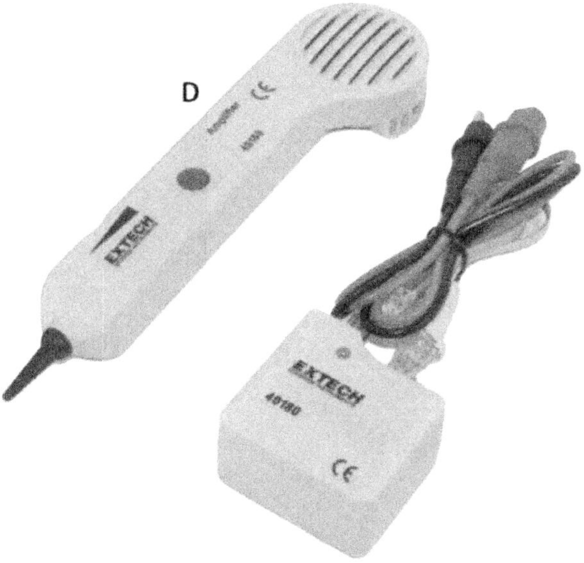

Figure 34(e)

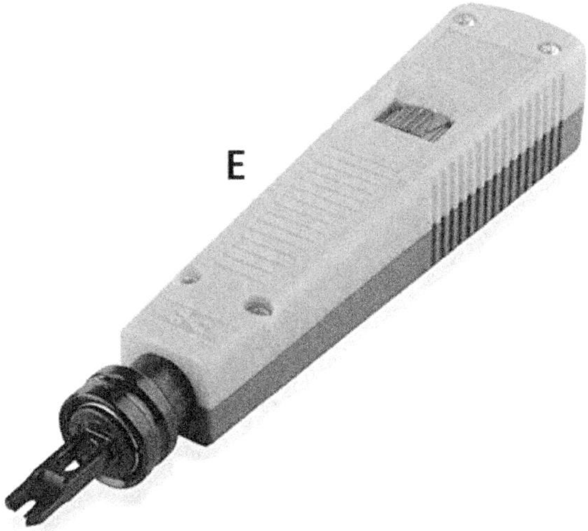

11. Fill in the missing spaces: To create a RAID ______ array, at least two mirrored HDD pairs must be used. Hence, the minimum number of drives in this RAID configuration must be ______. If ______ drives in a RAID ______ configuration fail, it is ______ to recover data. However, data recovery is dependent upon which ______ ______ become defective.

12. Which of the following motherboard form factors is specifically designed for use in UMPCs and smartphones?

(i) mATX

(ii) ATX

(iii) AMD

(iv) ITX

13. How many pins are on a DIMM DDR4 memory stick?

(i) 200

(ii) 204

(iii) 240

(iv) 288

14. What should a technician do to optimize the performance of a HDD labelled as a C: volume that is acting in a slow and sluggish manner? (Select two answers.)

(i) Use the format command with the /p switch

(ii) Run Disk Defragmenter

(iii) Use the Disk Cleanup utility

(iv) Update the AV definitions

(v) Enter defrag C: /d at the command prompt

15. Which of the following devices can be used to access triple- and quadruple-layer Blu-ray discs?

(i) BD-R

(ii) BD+R

(iii) BD-X

(iv) BD-XL

16. A junior PC technician has been requested by his supervisor to install a new security patch to an old Toshiba® Windows® 8.0 OS computer. The security patch is loaded on to a DVD-ROM disc.

The technician inserts the disc into the DVD-ROM drive and re-boots the computer. However, the security patch fails to load from the DVD-ROM and the computer boots as normal into Windows® GUI.

(a) What should the technician have done initially before inserting the disc into the DVD-ROM drive?

(i) Change the Boot Device Priority

(ii) Run the Disk Defragmenter utility

(iii) Wipe the disc with a clean, lint-free cloth

(iv) Un-install Windows® 8.0 OS

(b) Upon realizing his mistake, the technician presses the DVD-ROM drive's "Eject" button in an attempt to remove the disc. However, the drive's tray is unresponsive and seems to be jammed.

What should the technician do next?

(i) Use a plastic shim to prise open the drive tray

(ii) Reboot the computer

(iii) Shut down the computer and open the case to remove the optical drive

(iv) Use a paper clip to eject the drive tray

17. Which of the following describes the process of inserting SODIMMs into a laptop's motherboard?

(i) Insert the module on a 45-degree angle using gentle force

(ii) Insert the module on a 90-degree angle using gentle force

(iii) Plug the module into the relevant socket on the motherboard

(iv) Insert the module by pressing straight down

18. Which of the following represents the typical refresh rate for a standard laptop's LCD monitor?

(i) 6 Hz

(ii) 60 Hz

(iii) 60 MHz

(iv) 60 GHz

(v) None of the above

19. What is the maximum theoretical data transfer rate of DIMM DDR3-2133?

(i) 8,500 MB/s

(ii) 17,000 MB/s

(iii) 12,800 MB/s

(iv) 1.7 GB/s

20. The IT team of an up-and-coming web hosting and IaaS company is planning to install and commission a new powerful computer system that will have the ability to host numerous different virtual operating systems.

The team intends to install multiple versions of Windows® OS, Linux®, Apple® OS X, and Windows® Server 2012™ on the same host computer system. It is also anticipated that powerful CPU-intensive applications will be installed on this computer system to fulfil the business requirements of the company's growing client base.

(a) Briefly explain the term *IaaS.*

(b) What type of computer system is the IT team planning to install?

(i) HTPC+

(ii) Virtualization system

(iii) CAD/CAM workstation

(iv) VM

(v) EDGE system

(c) True or False: A critical component of this computer system is a Type 2 hypervisor.

(d) Which of the following are essential hardware requirements for this type of computer system? (Select all applicable answers.)

(i) Powerful multi-core CPU

(ii) HD audio card

(iii) Fast RAM

(iv) Compatible motherboard BIOS/UEFI

(v) IEEE 1394 and Thunderbolt connectivity

(vi) OLED

Practice Test 18			
MCQ Solutions			
1.	See notes	11.	See notes
2.	(a)-(c) See notes, (d) (i)(ii)(iv)	12.	(iv)
3.	(a) See notes, (b)(ii)	13.	(iv)
4.	(i), (ii), (iii)	14.	(ii), (v)
5.	(i), (iii)	15.	(iv)
6.	(a)-(b) See notes, (c)(iv)	16.	(a)(i), (b)(iv)
7.	(i), (iii), (iv), (v)	17.	(i)
8.	(ii)	18.	(ii)
9.	(ii)	19.	(ii)
10.	(a)-(b) See notes	20.	(a) See notes, (b)(ii), (c) False, (d)(i)(iii)(iv)

1. (1) USB 3.0. Bluetooth 1.2, (2) 2.0, and (3) 3.0. USB 3.1 Gen 2. Full correct statement: "The data transmission rate of a Thunderbolt connection is faster than USB 3.0, which in turn is faster than Firewire 400 and 800, which in turn is faster than Bluetooth 1.2, 2.0, and 3.0. However, the data transmission rate of a Thunderbolt connection is equivalent to USB 3.1 Gen 2."

2. (a) Processing. (The text and/or image to be printed is transmitted to the laser printer, where an in-built processor reassembles the text and/or image and stores it in the printer's memory (RAM).) **(b)** Exposing (also referred to as "writing"). During this process, the laser is activated and "writes" the text and/or image to be printed to the photosensitive drum as it spins. Where the laser beam hits the spinning drum, it displaces the negative charge on the surface of the drum towards the center of the drum which is grounded. As a result, the laser-treated areas of the drum now have a lesser negative charge. **(c)** Cleaning. During this phase, a rubber blade removes any surplus toner from the photosensitive drum as it spins. Furthermore, a special lamp removes any residual negative charge on the drum, bringing the surface of the drum to zero volts. Once the cleaning process is completed, the photosensitive drum is ready for another print job. **(d)** (i), (ii), and (iv). The hardware components of a typical laser printer include photosensitive drum (or imaging drum), fuser assembly, transfer belt, transfer roller, pickup rollers, separation pads, and in some cases, duplexing assembly. A laser printer will also have a primary corona wire and a transfer corona wire.

3. (a) PII is an acronym for Personally Identifiable Information. PII is any data that could potentially identify a specific individual. Any information that can be utilized to distinguish one person from another and can be used for de-anonymizing strictly confidential and otherwise "anonymous" data can be deemed to be PII. **(b)** (ii) Smartphones. Smartphones and other cell phones cannot obtain a signal when used within a Faraday cage because of its in-built shielding. The primary purpose of a Faraday cage is to block signals from inside or outside the cage. Therefore, data and other communications cannot be wirelessly transmitted outside the cage.

4. Correct: (i), (ii), and (iii). If a laptop does not power on, the following items need to be checked first: (1) Power LED. (2) AC/DC adapter. (3) "Power-on" button. (4) Hibernate mode. It is possible that the laptop is currently in hibernation mode (S4 state) and needs to be activated using the appropriate keystroke, etc.

5. Correct: (i) and (iii). (1) The main characteristics of TCP (Transfer Control Protocol) are: (a) TCP maintains the integrity of data being transmitted. (b) TCP establishes an end-to-end connection. (c) TCP can be used for web browsing and email transmission/receipt. (2) The main characteristics of UDP (User Datagram Protocol) are: (a) Data packets may arrive out of order. (b) UDP is connectionless. (c) UDP is oftentimes used for media streaming.

6. (a) (A) Power connection. (B) HDMI connection. (C) USB port. (D) S/PDIF port (or optical audio port). (E) RJ45 ethernet port. **(b)** The term STB is an acronym for set-top box. This device (otherwise known as a set-top unit or STU) is used by cable and satellite TV providers respectively to provide customers or subscribers with access to digital television. It can also be used as a hybrid I/O device that not only provides digital television, but Internet connectivity as well. **(c)** (iv) In this scenario, it is apparent that a red, laser-like light is being emitted by the sound card's port (or optical audio port) because no optical audio cable has been plugged into this port. This would also help explain why the customer is complaining that there is no audio when she connects the STB to her HD (High Definition) widescreen TV.

7. Correct: (i), (iii), (iv), and (v). Home Server PCs require a fast network adapter, preferably a GbE (Gigabit Ethernet network adapter) to ensure rapid transfer of files and other data over the SOHO network, a RAID array (preferably with fault tolerance) to permit fast and reliable access to data and other network resources, and a properly configured Windows OS HomeGroup to facilitate file and printer sharing as well as media streaming. A Home Server PC can also be set up using Apple Mac with OS X installed, or most desktop variants of Linux.

8. Correct: (ii) L2 cache (otherwise referred to as Level 2 cache). L1 is the fastest CPU cache memory and is located within the CPU's core. The second fastest cache memory is L2. L3 cache has the largest capacity of CPU cache but is the slowest of the three types of CPU cache. L4 cache is not as common in PCs but it is occasionally located on more powerful computer workstations and servers.

9. Correct: (ii) No power is being supplied to transfer corona wire. Under normal circumstances, power supplied to the transfer corona wire gives it a positive charge. In many laser printers, paper slides between the photosensitive drum (imaging drum) and the positively charged transfer corona wire. The transfer corona wire applies its positive charge to the paper.

Because the paper now has a positive charge and the toner particles on the imaging drum have a negative charge, the toner particles are attracted to the paper thereby creating text and/or graphics on the paper. If no power is being supplied to the transfer corona wire, the "transferring" step of the laser printing process is unable to execute and all pages generated by the printer are blank.

10. (a) (A) Loopback plug (or loopback tester). (B) RJ45 crimper (incorporating a wire stripper). (C) Patch cable tester. (D) Tone generator and probe kit. (The tone generator is located on the right-hand-side of the figure and the probe is located on the left-hand-side of the figure.) (E) Punch down tool. **(b)** (A) Function of loopback tester: (1) The insertion of a loopback tester into the RJ45 (ethernet) port on a computer simulates a network connection, thereby allowing the technician to test and verify the functionality of the network card. This loopback test also allows the technician to verify if the TCP/IP settings of the network card are correctly configured. Once the loopback tester has been inserted, the technician can open the Command Shell and enter the command ping 127.0.0.1. Alternatively, the technician can ping the actual IP address of the local computer. The responses generated by the Command Shell can be used to determine if the network card is functional or not. (2) A loopback tester can be used to test the functionality of network ports found on an ethernet switch. A loopback tester can also be used to determine which port on a switch a particular patch cable is connected to in situations where a patch cable has not been labelled and/or a patch cable is being troubleshot. (B) Function of RJ45 crimper: An RJ45 crimper can be used to make patch cables. This tool is used by telecommunication and network technicians to permanently attach RJ45 plugs to the ends of patch cables. Patch cables connect the various network ports of a patch panel to an ethernet switch and they are also used to connect RJ45 jacks to computers. (C) Function of patch cable tester: A patch cable tester is used to test patch cables. Before connecting patch cables to a network installation or device, a technician should check these cables with a patch tester. This hand-held device has two RJ45 jacks. Each end of the patch cable is plugged into the two RJ45 jacks on the patch cable tester. A test button can then be pressed to verify the functionality of the patch cable. (D) Function of tone generator and probe kit: A tone generator and probe kit can be used to test network cables. The tone generator unit is connected to one end of a network cable and sends a tone along the length of the cable. The probing device (or probe) can then be used to detect the tone anywhere along the length of the cable run and also at the cable termination point. However, most telecommunication and network technicians use a network cable tester (also known as a continuity tester or cable certifier) instead of a tone generator and probe kit to carry out this cable testing task. In this connection, the network cable tester is more accurate and reliable compared to the tone generator/probe kit and, consequently, is more commonly used for cable certification. (E) Function of punch down tool: A punch down tool (also known as a krone tool) is a hand-held tool used by telecommunication and network technicians to physically connect telecommunication and network wires to the clips of an RJ45 jack, patch panel, punch down block, keystone module, or surface mount box.

11. (1) 10. (2) Four. (3) Two. (4) 10. (5) Possible. (6) Two drives. The completed statement should read: "To create a RAID 10 array, at least two mirrored HDD pairs must be used. Hence, the minimum number of drives in this RAID configuration must be four. If two drives in a RAID 10 configuration fail, it is possible to recover data. However, data recovery is dependent upon which two drives become defective."

12. Correct: (iv) ITX. The ITX family of motherboard form factors are specifically designed for HTPCs, UMPCs (Ultra-mobile PC), and smartphones. ITX form factors are small, low-power motherboards ranging in size from 60 mm x 60 mm to 6.7 inches x 6.7 inches. The ITX family comprises Mini-ITX, Nano-ITX, Pico-ITX, and Mobile-ITX.

13. Correct: (iv) 288. DIMM (Dual In-Line Memory Module) RAM modules are normally inserted into PC motherboards. DIMM DDR has 184 pins. DIMM DDR2 and DDR3 have 240 pins. DIMM DDR4 has 288 pins.

14. Correct: (ii) and (v). Run the Disk Defragmenter utility. Since the HDD in the scenario is only occupied by a C: volume, you can also enter the command **defrag C: /d** in the Command Shell to achieve the same outcome. Updating the AV definitions means updating the computer's anti-malware or anti-virus settings before running a routine scan.

15. Correct: (iv) BD-XL drive.

16. (a) (i) Change the Boot Device Priority. In the scenario, we are told that the security patch is loaded on to a DVD-ROM disc and it is highly likely that the relatively old Toshiba computer must initially boot to the DVD-ROM drive so that the security patch can be installed. Since this is apparently the situation, the technician should have configured the BIOS settings so that the DVD-ROM optical drive boots first. The BIOS boot order can be altered within the Boot Device

Priority section of the BIOS utility. Once the security patch has successfully installed on to the system, the technician can then change the Boot Device Priority so that the hard drive always boots first. **(b)** (iv) Use a paper clip to eject the tray drive. By far, it is the easiest and most sensible solution. A PC technician should always have a packet of paper clips in his/her computer repair toolkit.

17. Correct: (i) Insert the module on a 45-degree angle using gentle force. In comparison, DIMM DDRx memory is installed in a PC's motherboard by pressing straight down at a 90-degree angle to the horizontal. In both cases, the technician should touch the computer case chassis before picking up the RAM modules (to ensure he is adequately grounded) and the modules should be held by the edges only without touching any of the chips, components, pins, or other circuitry on the module. Whenever the technician needs to put the module down, carefully place it on an antistatic mat (or into an antistatic bag).

18. Correct: (ii) 60 Hz.

19. Correct: (ii) 17,000 MB/s. Using the information provided, DIMM DDR3-2133 has a data transfer rate of 2133 MT/s (mega-transfers per second). To calculate the maximum theoretical data transfer rate (DTR), measured in MB/s (megabytes per second), use the equation: MT/s x 8 bytes = DTR. Hence, 2133 x 8 = 17,064 MB/s. Since the answers given in the question are only approximate values, the most suitable answer is (ii) 17,000 MB/s. Since DDR versions are designed with a 64-bit wide bus, this means that only 8 bytes of data can be transferred per cycle. Since the DDR3-2133 module is designed to allow 2133 cycles (or mega-transfers) per second, the maximum data transfer rate in megabytes is 2133 x 8 bytes = 17,000 MB/s (approx.). Answer (iv) 1.7 GB/s is incorrect because this value is only equivalent to 1,700 MB/s (1 GB/s = 1,000 MB/s).

20. (a) IaaS stands for Infrastructure as a Service. IaaS is a form of cloud computing that provides virtualized computing resources over the Internet. IaaS offers computing networking, data backup, data storage, data partitioning, routing, VM (virtual machine) hosting, as well as other networking services. Common examples of IaaS include Amazon Web Services (AWS), Cisco Metapod, Google Compute Engine (GCE), and Microsoft Azure. IaaS is one of three main categories of cloud computing services alongside SaaS (Software as a Service) and PaaS (Platform as a Service). **(b)** (ii) Virtualization system. A virtualization system is a computer system that runs one or more virtual operating systems. In a virtual environment, these operating systems are known as VMs. **(c)** False. The correct statement should read: "A critical component of this computer system is a Type 1 hypervisor." Since Type 1 hypervisors (otherwise known as "bare metal" hypervisors) are much faster and more efficient compared to Type 2 hypervisors (also called hosted hypervisors), Type 1 hypervisors are normally employed by virtual servers used by web-hosting companies and companies that offer cloud-computing services. **(d)** (i), (iii), and (iv). Any computer system that is designed to host and operate a virtual computing environment and is specified to support either a Type 1 or Type 2 hypervisor has the following hardware requirements: (1) A powerful multi-core processor, or multiple multi-core CPUs. (2) High-speed RAM. (3) As much RAM capacity that can be accommodated by the system. (4) A powerful, compatible motherboard. (5) The motherboard's BIOS/UEFI and CPU should be able to support virtualization. In summary, virtualization computing systems are very reliant on maximum RAM capacity and CPU cores.

Practice Test 19

1. True or False: HDMI, DVI, and USB 3.1 Gen 2 are all examples of video ports.

2. A copyeditor working for a large publishing house sends a 500-page manuscript to a network laser printer. When she collects a portion of the printed manuscript from the laser printer, she sees a distinct dark smudge that repeats itself every few inches down the right-hand-side of each printed page.

The copyeditor decides to stop the printing, but the laser printer is non-responsive. She then returns to her computer and tries to delete the large print job by double-clicking on the printer icon and selecting the delete option. However, the laser printer continues to print the cosmetically flawed manuscript.

(a) Which of the following hardware components of the laser printer most likely needs to be replaced?

(i) Pickup rollers

(ii) Imaging drum

(iii) Developer roller

(iv) Transfer corona wire

(b) What is the best and most sensible course of action to terminate the print job?

(i) Unplug the laser printer from the AC receptacle

(ii) Clear the print spooler

(iii) Update the PostScript driver

(iv) Deactivate the duplexing assembly

3. An IT technician has installed a new computer workstation in a SOHO environment. Using the relevant tools in Windows® OS, the technician assigns a static IP address of 192.168.0.12 to this computer. Windows® OS then automatically allocates a default subnet mask to the computer workstation.

(a) Which of the following IP classes does 192.168.0.12 belong to?

(i) Class A

(ii) Class B

(iii) Class C

(iv) Class D

(b) Which of the following subnet masks is assigned to 192.168.0.12 by default?

(i) 127.0.0.1

(ii) 255.0.0.0

(iii) 255.255.0.0

(iv) 255.255.255.0

(c) What is the Gateway IP address for this specific SOHO network?

(i) 169.254.0.1

(ii) 192.0.0.1

(iii) 192.168.0.1

(iv) None of the above

4. Which of the following motherboard components does a PCIe x16 slot directly communicate with? (Select two answers.)

(i) DRAM

(ii) Northbridge

(iii) Southbridge

(iv) CPU

5. Which of the following has the second largest theoretical storage capacity?

(i) CD-RW

(ii) DVD-18

(iii) Blu-ray

(iv) SATA HDD

6. A customer of a computer sales shop in a small provincial town has just purchased a reconditioned HP® laptop. When she takes the laptop home and plugs the AC adapter into mains electricity, the customer is unable to power on the laptop. The power LED on the front of the laptop is un-lit.

(a) Which of the following are two possible reasons for the inability of the laptop to power on? (Select two answers.)

(i) The Li-ion battery is completely discharged

(ii) An incorrect AC adapter

(iii) The boot files are missing

(iv) ACPI settings in the BIOS are incorrect

(b) Upon returning to the computer sales shop, the irate customer explains the issue to the PC technician on duty. The technician successfully powers on the laptop. However, only after a few minutes of normal operation, the laptop's LCD display suddenly and without reason goes blank.

Which of the following are two possible reasons for this sudden display outage? (Select two answers.)

(i) Defective inverter

(ii) Faulty LCD display

(iii) Burned-out backlight

(iv) Incorrect LCD resolution settings

(c) Following on from part *(b)* above, what should the technician do to confirm his suspicion regarding the cause of the problem?

(i) Open the laptop display casing using a plastic shim

(ii) Adjust the LCD cut-off switch

(iii) Adjust the display's resolution settings

(iv) Shine a flashlight directly at the LCD screen

7. A computer technician is troubleshooting a CAD/CAM workstation in a busy electronics manufacturing facility.

A design engineer has previously reported that the graphics rendering software has started to become very slow and sporadically freezes. The technician confirms her theory that the high-end video card is malfunctioning and needs to be replaced.

According to the CompTIA® A+ troubleshooting methodology, what should the technician do next? (Select two answers.)

(i) Test the theory

(ii) Establish a plan of action

(iii) Implement preventative measures

(iv) Implement a solution

(v) Document the actions taken so far

8. Select the correct options: (RAID 0/RAID 1) and RAID 5 are HDD arrays that provide fault tolerance. However, (RAID 0/RAID 5) provides both fault tolerance and (mirroring/striping with parity).

9. Shortly after a custom-built gaming PC is switched on, a burning odor seems to be coming from the exhaust vents.

(a) Which of the following is the most likely source of the burning odor?

(i) NIC

(ii) DRAM

(iii) Thermal interface material

(iv) PSU

(b) Upon noticing the burning odor, what should the PC do?

(i) Power off the computer immediately

(ii) Reboot the computer

(iii) Test the integrity of the computer's internal components using a POST card

(iv) Upgrade the cooling fans

10. A computer technician is trying to diagnose a network issue. He types a command into the Command Shell and the information as depicted in *Figure 35* displays on the screen.

(a) What command did the technician type into the Command Shell?

(i) nbtstat

(ii) netstat

(iii) ping /?

(iv) ping -t

(b) What is the purpose of this command? (Select the best two answers.)

(i) This command can be used to query the Domain Name System to obtain a specific domain name

(ii) This command displays all active network connections between a local computer and remote computers using TCP/IP

(iii) This command can be used to show IPv4 and IPv6 routing tables

(iv) The primary function of the command referenced in part *(a)* above is to show and change the parameters of the network interface

Figure 35

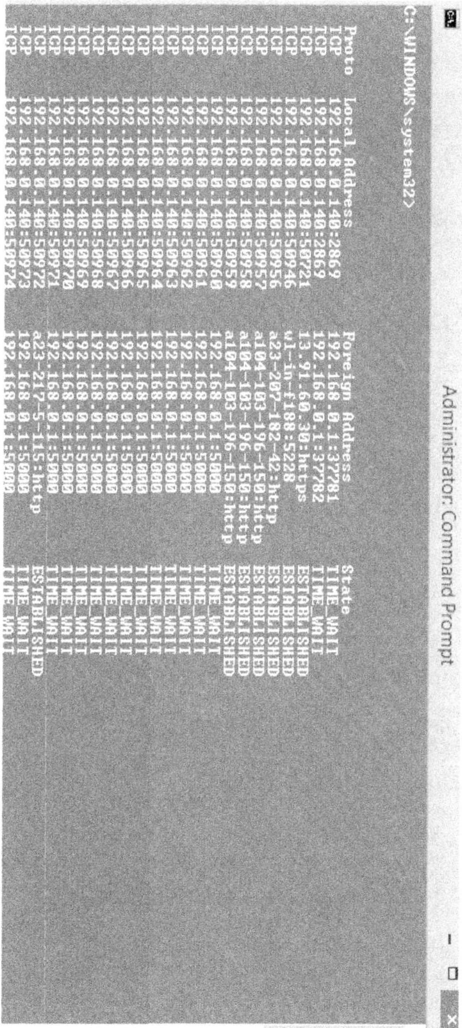
Administrator: Command Prompt
C:\WINDOWS\system32>
Proto Local Address Foreign Address State
TCP 192.168.0.140:2869 192.168.0.1:37781 TIME_WAIT
TCP 192.168.0.140:2869 192.168.0.1:37782 TIME_WAIT
TCP 192.168.0.140:50721 13.91.60.30:https ESTABLISHED
TCP 192.168.0.140:50946 wl-in-f188:5228 ESTABLISHED
TCP 192.168.0.140:50956 a23-207-182-42:http ESTABLISHED
TCP 192.168.0.140:50957 a104-103-196-150:http ESTABLISHED
TCP 192.168.0.140:50958 a104-103-196-150:http ESTABLISHED
TCP 192.168.0.140:50959 a104-103-196-150:http ESTABLISHED
TCP 192.168.0.140:50960 192.168.0.1:5000 TIME_WAIT
TCP 192.168.0.140:50961 192.168.0.1:5000 TIME_WAIT
TCP 192.168.0.140:50962 192.168.0.1:5000 TIME_WAIT
TCP 192.168.0.140:50963 192.168.0.1:5000 TIME_WAIT
TCP 192.168.0.140:50964 192.168.0.1:5000 TIME_WAIT
TCP 192.168.0.140:50965 192.168.0.1:5000 TIME_WAIT
TCP 192.168.0.140:50966 192.168.0.1:5000 TIME_WAIT
TCP 192.168.0.140:50967 192.168.0.1:5000 TIME_WAIT
TCP 192.168.0.140:50968 192.168.0.1:5000 TIME_WAIT
TCP 192.168.0.140:50969 192.168.0.1:5000 TIME_WAIT
TCP 192.168.0.140:50970 192.168.0.1:5000 TIME_WAIT
TCP 192.168.0.140:50971 192.168.0.1:5000 TIME_WAIT
TCP 192.168.0.140:50972 a23-217-5-115:http ESTABLISHED
TCP 192.168.0.140:50973 192.168.0.1:5000 TIME_WAIT
TCP 192.168.0.140:50974 192.168.0.1:5000 TIME_WAIT

11. An IT technician working for a substantial logistics and distribution center receives a troubleshooting ticket stating that a computer workstation in the Stock Controller's office is not booting correctly.

According to the ticket, "When the computer is powered on, the VDU remains blank and the computer generates a series of loud beeps. The computer has not been known to give any problems before."

What should the technician do next?

(i) Check that the VDU is connected to AC power

(ii) Check that the VDU is connected to the video port

(iii) Find the PC's vendor documentation

(iv) Remove the graphics card and replace it with a working unit

12. The I/O clock speed of a DDR3 memory module is 933 MHz. What is the maximum data transfer rate, in megabytes per second, of this memory module?

(i) 1,860

(ii) 3,700

(iii) 7,400

(iv) 14,900

13. A number of computer workstations connected to a surge protector in an open-plan office are unable to be powered on at the start of the working day. After a cursory inspection of the computer workstations and the shared surge protector by an experienced IT technician, it is suspected that there may be a problem with the AC outlet.

(a) Which tool should the technician use to confirm his suspicion?

(i) Loopback plug

(ii) PSU tester

(iii) Line conditioner

(iv) Multimeter

(b) Using the relevant tool to test the AC outlet, the technician confirms that there is an electrical problem. Once the AC outlet is safely quarantined, what should the technician do next? (Select two answers.)

(i) Replace the AC outlet

(ii) Connect the surge protector to a known working AC outlet

(iii) Install a UPS

(iv) Contact the building supervisor or manager

14. Which of the following devices is "hot-swappable"?

(i) DLT

(ii) HDD

(iii) DVD+R

(iv) BD-R

15. A computer technician is configuring the wireless settings on a Linksys® router used by a thriving web app development company in Philadelphia. The company shares office floor space in an enterprise center with two other small firms.

The router is responsible for operating a 2.4 GHz frequency IEEE 802.11 b/g/n wireless network throughout the entire building. Each company has been assigned its own unique SSID and Channel. The microelectronics design company uses Channel 3 and the data analytics firm uses Channel 6.

(a) To minimise the possibility of interference with the other 2.4 GHz wireless networks in the office building, which of the following channels should the technician select for the web app development company?

(i) 5

(ii) 8

(iii) 10

(iv) 11

(b) If the Linksys® router had been set up to provide a 5 GHz IEEE 802.11ac wireless network to the entire office building, which of the following channel ranges would the router use?

(i) 1 to 11

(ii) 1 to 48

(iii) 48 to 165

(iv) 48 to 180

16. With reference to the computer component shown in *Figure 36,* answer the following questions.

(a) State the name of the computer component shown in the figure.

(b) True or False: For optimal functionality and performance, the component shown in the figure is normally installed in computers used by gaming enthusiasts and graphics designers, as well as CAD/CAM workstations.

Figure 36

17. SRAM is a type of computer memory that does not need to be periodically refreshed, unlike DRAM. What are the primary uses of SRAM? (Select all answers that apply.)

(i) Cache memory for CPUs

(ii) Temporary storage for LCD displays

(iii) Used as buffers on the motherboard or within hard drives

(iv) Can be used as EEPROM storage

18. True or False: Unlike USB flash drives and SD cards, CF cards have an integrated SCSI controller that makes these cards appear as a hard drive to Windows® OS. In other words, these cards are displayed as a volume within Windows® Explorer.

19. Which of the following are considered to be I/O devices?

(i) Printer, scanner, and speakers

(ii) Keyboard, mouse, and STB

(iii) Smart card reader, fingerprint reader, and touchscreen

(iv) KVM switch, Smart TV, STB, and touchscreen

(v) Microphone, Smart TV, and STB

20. Identify the fiber optic connectors labelled A and B which are shown in *Figure 37.*

Figure 37

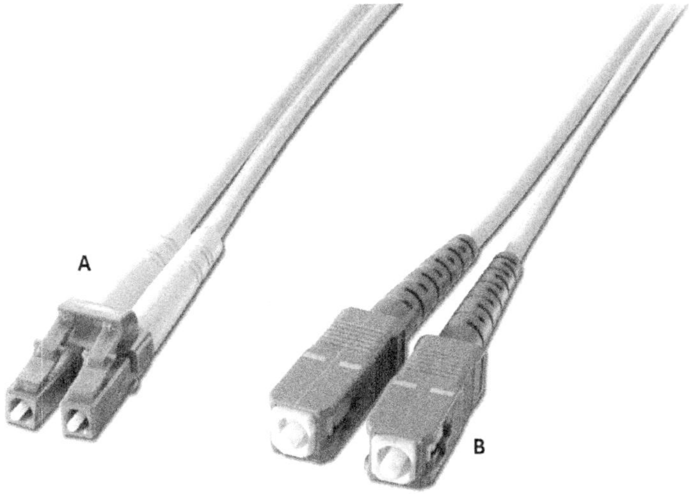

Practice Test 19			
MCQ Solutions			
1.	False	11.	(iii)
2.	(a)(ii), (b)(ii)	12.	(iv)
3.	(a)(iii), (b)(iv), (c)(iii)	13.	(a)(iv), (b)(ii)(iv)
4.	(ii), (iv)	14.	(ii)
5.	(iii)	15.	(a)(iv), (b)(iii)
6.	(a)(i)(ii), (b)(i)(iii), (c)(iv)	16.	(a) See notes, (b) True
7.	(ii), (iv)	17.	(i), (ii), (iii)
8.	See notes	18.	False
9.	(a)(iv), (b)(i)	19.	(iv)
10.	(a)(ii), (b)(ii)(iii)	20.	See notes

1. False. HDMI, DVI, DisplayPort, S-video, Component Video, BNC/RCA, and VGA are all examples of video ports. USB 3.1 Gen 2 is not regarded as being a video port per se.

2. **(a)** (ii) Imaging drum (otherwise known as the photosensitive drum). **(b)** (ii) The best and most sensible course of action is to clear the print spooler. This can be achieved by entering the relevant commands into the Command Shell.

3. **(a)** (iii) Class C. IP addresses that belong to the range 192 to 223 are designated as Class C IP addresses, and such addresses are normally associated with SOHO (Small Office/Home Office) networks. Other IP address classifications include Class A (1 to 126) which normally apply to large corporations and ISPs (Internet Service Providers), and Class B (128 to 191) which are typically assigned to companies, universities, and other organisations. **(b)** (iv) 255.255.255.0. Class A IP addresses (1 to 126) are normally assigned a default subnet mask of 255.0.0.0 (net.node.node.node). Class B IP addresses (128 to 191) have a default subnet mask of 255.255.0.0 (net.net.node.node), and Class C IP addresses for SOHO networks are assigned 255.255.255.0 (net.net.net.node). **(c)** (iii) On the basis of the information provided in the scenario, the Gateway IP address for this SOHO network is 192.168.0.1.

4. Correct: (ii) and (iv). The PCIe x16 slot directly communicates with the Northbridge chipset on AMD-supported motherboards and older Intel-compatible form factors. Nowadays, the PCIe x16 slot is directly connected to the processor on newer Intel CPU-compatible motherboards.

5. Correct: (iii) Blu-ray. A standard Blu-ray disk (single layer) has a storage capacity of 25 GB and a dual-layer Blu-ray disk has a storage capacity of 50 GB. A typical CD can theoretically hold 700 MB of data. DVD-18 has a maximum storage capacity of 17 GB (2 sides/4 layers), while the most common DVD format, DVD-5, has a maximum storage capacity of 4.7 GB (1 side/1 layer). SATA hard drives normally have storage capacities that are substantially greater than any of the other options listed in the question.

6. (a) (i) and (ii). The laptop's lithium-ion (Li-ion) battery may have completely discharged, therefore the laptop will not power on if it is not connected to an AC outlet. Also, the customer may be using an incorrect AC adapter; therefore, the laptop will not receive any power if an incorrect model of AC adapter is connected to the laptop. **(b)** (i) and (iii). Defective inverter or burned-out backlight. A damaged inverter or burned-out backlight is usually responsible for a laptop's LCD screen to suddenly go blank during normal operation. **(c)** (iv). The technician can verify if it is a faulty inverter or burned-out backlight issue by shining a flashlight directly at the LCD screen. When the technician does this, he should be able to faintly see Windows GUI.

7. Correct: (ii) and (iv). Step 4: Establish a plan of action to resolve the problem and then implement a solution.

8. (1) RAID 1. (2) RAID 5. The correct statement should read: "RAID 1 and RAID 5 are HDD arrays that provide for fault tolerance. However, RAID 5 provides for both fault tolerance and striping with parity."

9. (a) (iv) PSU (Power Supply Unit). **(b)** (i) The PC user should power off the computer immediately. In this scenario, it is very probable that the PSU is faulty and there is a distinct risk of electrical fire. Ultimately, the PSU needs to be replaced with a working unit of the correct wattage rating.

10. **(a)** (ii) netstat. **(b)** (ii) and (iii). The command netstat shows the network statistics for a local computer. More specifically, netstat displays all active network connections between a local computer and remote computers using TCP/IP (Transmission Control Protocol/Internet Protocol), as well as IPv4 and IPv6 routing tables. Netstat can also be used to provide useful information and statistics concerning other network protocols in use.

11. Correct: (iii) Find the PC's vendor documentation. Considering that the PC is generating a series of beep codes during POST and the VDU (Visual Display Unit) or monitor remains blank, the most sensible first troubleshooting step is to find and review any vendor documentation that relates to the motherboard. The technician may need to access the manufacturer's IT Support website for the relevant troubleshooting information. The technician may also need to determine the computer's BIOS/UEFI version before carrying out any additional research. The technician can also utilize a POST card to ascertain the exact nature of the problem. A POST card is a plug-in interface card that displays progress and error codes generated during the POST (Power-on Self Test) of a computer. A POST card can be very useful when troubleshooting computers that do not start up, for whatever reason.

12. Correct: (iv) 14,900 MB/s. The maximum data transfer rate (DDR) is calculated as follows: I/O clock speed x 8 bytes x 2 = DDR (in MB/s). All versions of DDR permit only 8 bytes of data to be transferred per cycle.

The number "2" is used considering that DDR is an acronym for Double Data Rate, meaning that twice the data is transferred but at the same clock speed. Therefore, 933 MHz x 8 bytes x 2 = 14,928 MB/s. The closest approximate answer listed in the question is (iv) 14,900 MB/s, and this is considered to be the correct answer.

13. **(a)** (iv) Multimeter. **(b)** (ii) and (iv). (1) Since it is the start of the working day and office employees may need to use the affected computer workstations, it will be necessary to plug the shared surge protector into another known working AC outlet. (2) In the case of an electrical fault (e.g., a defective AC outlet), the technician is obliged to contact the building supervisor, facilities engineer, or relevant manager so that a licensed electrician can be contacted to remedy the problem. Only suitably qualified and authorized persons such as licensed electricians should rectify any electrical problems involving mains electricity.

14. Correct: (ii) HDD. "Hot swapping" is a term that is used to describe the process whereby computer hardware components can be replaced or added to the system without stopping or shutting down the system. With the appropriate software installed on the computer system, a technician can plug in and unplug such hardware components without rebooting. PCIe and SATA hard drives can be "hot-swappable", especially when they are used in NAS (Network Attached Storage) devices and advanced server systems. However, hot-swappable HDDs are not commonly found in PCs and laptops. Tape drives such as LTO (Linear Tape-Open) and DLT (Direct Linear Tape) are not hot swappable. Also, BD-Rs (Blu-ray drives) and DVD drives are not hot swappable.

15. **(a)** (iv) 11. To minimise the possibility of interference with the other 2.4 GHz wireless networks, the technician should select channel 11 for the web app development firm. In the United States, 2.4 GHz wireless networks operate on the basis of a channel range from 1 to 11. Moreover, the 2.4 GHz frequency spectrum is divided into three discrete channel sub-ranges: (1) channels 1 to 5, (2) channels 6 to 10, and (3) channel 11. Therefore, to avoid interference with other 2.4 GHz wireless networks, select a channel in either 1-5, 6-10, or 11, depending on what channels are available in each sub-range. Considering the above scenario, since one company is using channel 3 (within range 1 to 5) and another firm is using channel 6 (within range 6 to 10), the technician should select channel 11 for the web app development company to minimise wireless interference. **(b)** (iii) 48 to 165. In the United States, routers operating on the basis of a 5 GHz wireless network typically use channels between 48 and 165. (Other countries may use slightly different channel ranges for a 5 GHz wireless network.)

16. **(a)** A video card (or graphics card) including a built-in GPU (Graphics Processing Unit), air cooling system, and memory (RAM). **(b)** True. CAD is an acronym for Computer-Aided Design and CAM means Computer-Aided Manufacturing.

17. Correct: (i), (ii), and (iii). SRAM is an acronym for Static Random Access Memory. SRAM can be used as cache memory for CPUs, as buffers on the motherboard or within HDDs, and as temporary storage for LCD monitors. EEPROM stands for Electrically Erasable Programmable Read Only Memory.

18. False. The correct statement should read: "Similar to USB flash drives and SD cards, CF (Compact Flash) cards have an integrated ATA controller that makes these cards appear as a hard drive to Windows OS. In other words, these cards are displayed as a volume within Windows Explorer." ATA is an acronym for Advanced Technology Attachment. ATA is a type of disk drive that integrates the drive controller directly on the disk drive itself. Computers can use ATA hard drives without a specific controller on the motherboard to support the disk drive. However, the motherboard must still support an ATA connection, but a separate card (such as a SCSI card for a SCSI hard drive) is not required.

19. Correct: (iv). KVM switches, Smart TVs, STBs, and touchscreens are all considered to be both input and output (I/O) devices. STB is an acronym for Set-top box. This device is used by cable TV and satellite TV companies to allow customers (or subscribers) access digital television channels. STBs can also be used as hybrid devices, offering both conventional TV and Internet access.

20. (A) LC connector. (B) SC connector.

Practice Test 20

1. True or False: CMOS is the volatile memory for storing a motherboard's BIOS settings. If the CMOS is not receiving power from some source, this memory device loses its stored contents.

2. A network administrator working for a large corporation has received reports that several employees in the Planning Office are unable to access the Internet and network resources while using their work laptops. However, employees using PC workstations in the same office do not have any difficulty accessing the Internet or sharing files and documents over the network.

Which of the following devices is most likely causing this particular problem?

(i) Cable modem

(ii) DNS server

(iii) WAP

(iv) Firewall

(v) Router

3. Answer the following networking protocol questions *(a)* to *(d)*.

(a) What does the acronym SLP mean?

(i) Server Location Protocol

(ii) Service Link Protocol

(iii) Service Location Protocol

(iv) None of the above

(b) Which port number is commonly associated with this networking protocol?

(i) 25

(ii) 427

(iii) 445

(iv) 3389

(c) Which of the following statements most accurately reflects the function of this protocol?

(i) SLP is mainly used to facilitate email routing between mail servers

(ii) SLP is a networking protocol that enables computers and other devices to access network resources on a LAN without prior configuration

(iii) SLP is primarily used by servers to detect incoming client connections over a network

(iv) SLP is used to support direct TCP/IP networking access without the need for a NetBIOS layer on a Microsoft®-based LAN

(d) What is the primary transport mechanism used by SLP? (Select the best answer.)

(i) IP

(ii) TCP

(iii) UDP

(iv) URL

Figure 38

000
HOLD/TEST
LIGHT
AUTO
MANUAL
66B7000
20A
mA
COM
V Ω
USB
RJ45
RJ12
RJ11

4. Answer the following questions *(a)* and *(b)*.

(a) Identify the device shown in *Figure 38.*

(b) A very busy accounting and taxation consultancy has a multi-part form printer. However, the taxation team has noticed that recent print jobs are quite faint. An IT technician has been called to investigate the matter.

What will most likely resolve this printer issue?

(i) Install a maintenance kit

(ii) Print a test page

(iii) Replace the fusing assembly

(iv) Replace the print ribbon

5. True or False: In a RAID 5 array of 6 HDDs, only two drives can become defective before you lose the entire HDD array.

6. A design engineer working for an automotive components manufacturer is using a recently refurbished CAD/CAM workstation.

The engineer launches AutoCAD® and begins working on a new design project. However, after a while, he notices that the 3D images displayed on the LCD monitor start to rotate very slowly and occasionally become distorted.

An IT technician is informed regarding the issue and commences the troubleshooting process.

(a) What is the most probable cause of this particular issue?

(i) Display resolution is incorrect

(ii) The graphics card is not powerful enough

(iii) AutoCAD® needs to be re-installed

(iv) CPU is overheating

(b) What corrective action can the technician implement to prevent recurrence of the aforementioned issue?

(i) Apply more thermal paste between the heat sink and the processor before re-seating the heat sink/cooling fan assembly

(ii) Modify the contrast settings on the VDU

(iii) Overclock the CPU

(iv) Upgrade the graphics card

(c) Which of the following do CAD/CAM workstations require the most to ensure optimal performance?

(i) Liquid cooling system

(ii) Type 1 hypervisor

(iii) Powerful CPU and RAM

(iv) High-speed NIC

7. Which of the following is classified as being a parallel technology?

(i) USB

(ii) IEEE 1394

(iii) PCI

(iv) PCIe

8. A computer technician is servicing a PC on behalf of a client who wants to optimize the computer's performance.

The technician decides to expand the memory capacity of the motherboard. Hence, he successfully seats 4 GB Micron® DDR3 modules into the relevant RAM slots.

According to the technician's research, these DIMM sticks are compatible with the motherboard and processor. However, when the computer is powered on, the BIOS does not recognize the new memory.

What should the technician do next?

(i) Clean the RAM slots

(ii) Replace the RAM modules

(iii) Flash the BIOS

(iv) Re-seat the DIMM modules

9. Which type of memory is required to increase the storage capacity of an Android™ smartphone?

(i) LPDDR3

(ii) CF card

(iii) HHD

(iv) microSD

10. Which of the following commands can be entered at the command prompt to temporarily disable the print spooler?

(i) net disable spooler

(ii) net stat spooler

(iii) net stop prn spooler

(iv) net stop spooler

11. Which of the following network devices is responsible for moving data packets between a source computer and a destination computer on the basis of their respective MAC addresses?

(i) Hub

(ii) Patch panel installation

(iii) Switch

(iv) Router

12. T568A and T568B are TIA/EIA standards applicable to network cabling and wiring. Generally speaking, the most common standard is T568B.

(a) Which of the following represents the color sequence for each of the wires (or pins) with respect to the T568B standard?

(i) (1) White/Green (2) Green (3) White/Orange (4) Blue (5) White/Blue (6) Orange (7) White/Brown (8) Brown

(ii) (1) White/Brown (2) Brown (3) White/Orange (4) Blue (5) White/Blue (6) Orange (7) White/Green (8) Green

(iii) (1) White/Orange (2) Orange (3) White/Green (4) Blue (5) White/Blue (6) Green (7) White/Brown (8) Brown

(iv) (1) White/Orange (2) Orange (3) White/Blue (4) Blue (5) White/Green (6) Green (7) Brown (8) White/Brown

(b) What impact tool is used by telecommunication and network technicians to insert T568B-compliant wires into insulation/displacement connectors on patch panels?

(i) Crimper

(ii) Loopback plug

(iii) RJ45 plug

(iv) Punch-down tool

(v) Punch-in tool

13. An employee working in a graphic design studio plugs a USB 3.0-enabled Lexmark® scanner into a USB 2.0 port on the front panel of a PC. However, the scanner remains inactive.

(a) What is the most likely cause of this problem? (Select two possible answers.)

(i) The scanner is incompatible with the USB 2.0 port

(ii) The front panel connectors have become loose

(iii) The USB 2.0 controller on the motherboard has failed

(iv) The scanner is not plugged into an AC outlet

(b) The employee desperately needs to use the scanner to complete an important assignment on behalf of a prestigious client.

What should the employee do next? (Select the best option.)

(i) Plug the scanner into the back-panel USB 3.0 port

(ii) Reboot the computer

(iii) Update the scanner's driver in Windows® OS

(iv) None of the above

14. Which of the following display resolutions is most commonly found in Android™ smartphones?

(i) QHD

(ii) QXGA

(iii) HD Ready

(iv) WSXGA+

15. Which type of video cable is mainly used with a computer (as opposed to a Smart TV) and is designed to carry both analog and digital signals?

(i) DVI-I

(ii) DVI-A

(iii) DVI-D

(iv) DP

16. A PC repair shop has received an order from a prestigious corporate client to custom build a virtualization workstation.

The technician has installed a powerful Intel® Quad Core™ i7 processor and heat sink/fan assembly. Once all relevant hardware components are installed, he powers on the virtualization workstation. However, the POST generates a series of beep codes and the system is unable to complete the booting process.

(a) After the technician had seated the processor into the CPU socket and installed the heat sink/fan assembly, what should he have done next? (Select two answers.)

(i) Boot the computer system

(ii) Apply thermal paste

(iii) Plug in the CPU fan

(iv) Check all motherboard cable connections

(b) What is the most likely cause of the beep codes and the computer system's inability to boot? (Select two possible answers.)

(i) The computer system is overheating

(ii) The processor is not properly seated

(iii) The BIOS firmware is incompatible

(iv) RAM modules are not seated properly

17. Which of the following are possible symptoms of a failing or malfunctioning HDD? (Select two answers.)

(i) BIOS no longer recognizes the HDD

(ii) Frequent computer system "freezes" or lockups

(iii) Boot files do not execute

(iv) BSOD

(v) Sudden system shutdowns

18. Which type of RAID utilizes only two HDDs?

(i) RAID 0

(ii) RAID 1

(iii) RAID 5

(iv) None of the above

19. A technician is troubleshooting a network issue. As part of his troubleshooting exercise, he opened the Command Shell and entered a command. The information as depicted in *Figure 39* then displayed on the screen.

(a) Which of the following commands did the technician enter at the command prompt?

(i) arp -a

(ii) nbtstat -A

(iii) netstat -n

(iv) ping -n

(b) What is the function of this command?

(i) This command can be used to conduct DNS queries in order to obtain a specific domain name

(ii) This command can be used to show the networking services running on a local computer or a remote computer in a format known as the NetBIOS Name Table

(iii) This command translates IP addresses into MAC addresses

(iv) None of the above

Figure 39

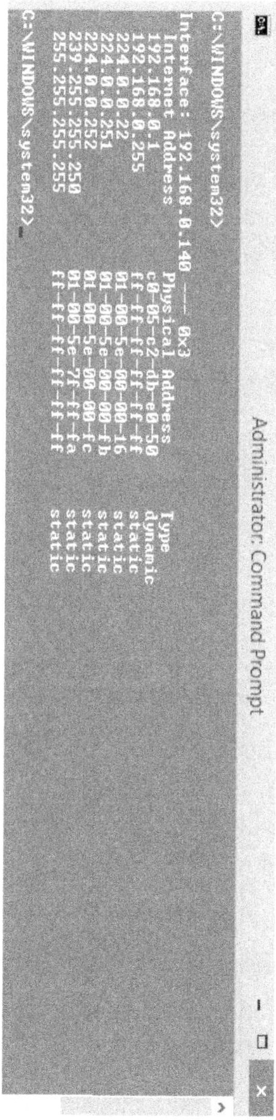
Administrator: Command Prompt
C:\WINDOWS\system32>
Interface: 192.168.0.140 --- 0x3
Internet Address Physical Address Type
192.168.0.1 c0-05-c2-db-e0-50 dynamic
192.168.0.255 ff-ff-ff-ff-ff-ff static
224.0.0.22 01-00-5e-00-00-16 static
224.0.0.251 01-00-5e-00-00-fb static
224.0.0.252 01-00-5e-00-00-fc static
239.255.255.250 01-00-5e-7f-ff-fa static
255.255.255.255 ff-ff-ff-ff-ff-ff static
C:\WINDOWS\system32>

20. A computer technician has been requested by the company's IT department to make several newly purchased Acer® PCs network ready. The PC workstations have not yet been connected to the network.

The technician needs to make a couple of patch cables by securely attaching an ethernet plug to the end of each UTP cable. As per company policy, she then needs to test and verify the functionality of each new computer's NIC before connecting the computers to the network.

(a) Which type of plug does the technician need to attach to the end of each twisted-pair cable?

(i) Loopback

(ii) RJ11

(iii) RJ45

(iv) SSL

(b) Which of the following tools should the technician employ to create a networking patch cable?

(i) Continuity tester

(ii) Crimper

(iii) Punch down tool

(iv) Torx screwdriver

(c) Which of the following tools should the technician use to test and verify the functionality of the NIC before a local computer is connected to the network?

(i) Continuity tester

(ii) Loopback tester

(iii) Multimeter

(iv) Tone and probe kit

Practice Test 20			
MCQ Solutions			
1.	True	11.	(iii)
2.	(iii)	12.	(a)(iii), (b)(iv)
3.	(a)(iii), (b)(ii), (c)(ii), (d)(iii)	13.	(a)(ii)(iii), (b)(i)
4.	(a) See notes, (b)(iv)	14.	(i)
5.	False	15.	(i)
6.	(a)(ii), (b)(iv), (c)(iii)	16.	(a)(ii)(iii), (b)(ii)(iv)
7.	(iii)	17.	(ii), (iii)
8.	(iii)	18.	(ii)
9.	(iv)	19.	(a)(i), (b)(iii)
10.	(iv)	20.	(a)(iii), (b)(ii), (c)(ii)

1. True.

2. Correct: (iii) WAP (Wireless Access Point).

3. **(a)** (iii) SLP means Service Location Protocol. **(b)** (ii) 427. **(c)** (ii) SLP is a networking protocol that enables computers and other devices to access network resources on a LAN without prior configuration. This is achieved through the use of a URL (Uniform Resource Locator), which allows computers to access specific network services provided the user knows the URL pathway to that service, e.g., service:printer://hostname. **(d)** (iii) SLP mainly uses UDP (User Datagram Protocol) as its mode of transport across the network, but it can also use TCP if necessary.

4. **(a)** Network multimeter. **(b)** (iv) Replace the print ribbon. The multi-part form printer is an example of an impact printer. In this scenario, the print ribbon is worn or defective. Replacing the print ribbon will most likely resolve the matter.

5. False. The correct statement should read: "In a RAID 5 array of 6 HDDs, only <u>one</u> drive can become defective before you lose the entire HDD array."

6. **(a)** (ii) The graphics card is not powerful enough. Since the CAD/CAM workstation was recently refurbished, we can only assume that some of the internal components of the system were replaced by more powerful equivalents, compatible with the motherboard and CPU. However, it is probable that the maintenance technician inadvertently installed a less powerful graphics card. Software such as AutoCAD is CPU-intensive and requires a high-end graphics card to support 3D design and rendering. **(b)** (iv) The graphics card needs to be upgraded by the technician to ensure that the 3D images rotate quickly and smoothly. **(c)** (iii) Powerful CPU and RAM. In general, a CAD/CAM computer requires a powerful, multi-core processor, a high-end video card, and as much RAM capacity as feasible. High-speed RAM is also preferable. A compatible motherboard for all these components is also necessary.

7. Correct: (iii) PCI. PCI is classified as being a 32-bit parallel technology with maximum data transfer rates of 133 MB/s and 266 MB/s, respectively. All of the other technologies listed in the question (viz. USB, IEEE 1394, and PCIe) are serial technologies.

8. Correct: (iii) Flash the BIOS. Since the technician in the scenario has confirmed that the new RAM modules are compatible with the motherboard and processor, yet the new memory is not recognised by the BIOS during POST (or the BIOS screen does not show the correct RAM capacity), it may be necessary to upgrade the BIOS firmware ("flashing"). It is possible that the RAM modules represent a newer generation DDRx technology that the motherboard's BIOS firmware is unable to identify.

9. Correct: (iv) microSD card (assuming that the smartphone has a suitably sized slot available for memory add-ons or upgrades).

10. Correct: (iv) The command **net stop spooler** turns off the print spooler service in Windows OS.

11. Correct: (iii) Switch. (1) The basic function of an ethernet switch is to receive data packets from any source network device (e.g., a computer workstation) connected to it and transmit that information to the appropriate destination device only. The switch performs this role by identifying the MAC addresses of the source and destination devices. (2) A hub, on the other hand, obtains information from a source network device and transmits the data to every other device attached to the network. The computer or network device that the information is intended for accepts the data; the rest of the networked devices ignore the information. Hence, a hub is less efficient than a switch. (3) A router is a networking device that wirelessly transmits data packets between computer networks (i.e., from one LAN to another LAN) and it can also transmit signals from all computers connected to a LAN out to the Internet. In essence, a data packet is transmitted from one router to another router until the data packet reaches its destination node or device.

12. (a) (iii) The T568B wiring standard has the following wiring color code: (1) White/Orange (2) Orange (3) White/Green (4) Blue (5) White/Blue (6) Green (7) White/Brown (8) Brown. Less commonly, a telecommunication or network technician will see the T568A wiring standard in the field: (1) White/Green (2) Green (3) White/Orange (4) Blue (5) White/Blue (6) Orange (7) White/Brown (8) Brown. The TIA/EIA wiring standards are devised by the Telecommunications Industry Association and Electronic Industries Alliance, respectively. **(b)** (iv) Punch-down tool. A punch-down tool is a small hand impact tool that is used by telecommunication and network technicians. It is used for inserting T568-compliant wires into insulation/displacement connectors on punch down blocks, patch panels, keystone modules, and surface mount boxes.

13. (a) (ii) and (iii). A USB 3.0 (or higher) device will work normally in a USB 2.0 port but at the lower USB 2.0 speed. Contrariwise, a USB 2.0-enabled device will operate normally at USB 2.0 speed even when plugged into a faster USB 3.0 (or higher) port. On the basis of what we are told in the scenario, it is very probable that the front panel connectors have become loose or are not plugged into the motherboard. It is also possible that the USB 2.0 controller on the motherboard has failed, rendering all USB 2.0 ports on the PC defective. **(b)** (i) The easiest and most sensible option is to plug the scanner into the back panel USB 3.0 ports, assuming that the USB 3.0 controller on the motherboard is still operational and that the back panel USB 3.0 ports are not faulty.

14. Correct: (i) QHD. QHD (Quad High Definition) has a 2560 x 1440 resolution and a 16:9 aspect ratio. HD Ready, which is similar to WXGA 720p (Widescreen Extended Graphics Array), is primarily used on laptops and has a display resolution of 1366 x 768. QXGA (Quad Extended Graphics Array) 1536p is mainly used in tablet computers.

15. Correct: (i) DVI-I. DP refers to DisplayPort video connector.

16. (a) Correct: (ii) and (iii). (1) After installing the CPU into the corresponding motherboard socket, the technician should apply thermal paste (or thermal compound) to fill and therefore eliminate any microscopic crevices and gaps that naturally occur when a metal heat sink is placed over the CPU. The application of thermal paste aids with heat transference from the CPU to the heat sink. (2) After installing the heat sink/fan assembly, the technician should plug in the CPU fan to the appropriate connector on the motherboard. **(b)** Correct: (ii) and (iv). In this scenario, it is very likely that the processor is not properly seated in the CPU socket or there is a problem with the installed RAM modules (e.g., not properly seated). The POST normally generates a series of beep codes (or on-screen display codes) if there are problems with the CPU and RAM.

17. Correct: (ii) and (iii). Frequent system "freezes" and boot files that fail to execute during boot-up, as well as disproportionately long waiting times to access folders and files, are all possible signs of a failing or malfunctioning hard drive. Other possible warning signs of HDD failure include: (1) Frequent and cryptic error messages while performing common operations such as moving files or folders. (2) Folder and file names that have been scrambled and changed. (3) Disappearing folders and files. (4) Hard drive is non-responsive for a relatively long time after you request data by clicking on a file or folder. (5) Garbled or unintelligible output from open files or print jobs. (6) Hard drive constantly makes grinding sounds by virtue of noisy bearings.

18. Correct: (ii) RAID 1. RAID 1 (otherwise known as "mirroring") uses two HDDs only. RAID 0 ("striping") uses two disks or more. RAID 5 ("striping with parity") uses a minimum of three disks or more.

19. (a) (i) arp -a. **(b)** (iii) ARP is an acronym for Address Resolution Protocol. The arp command translates IP addresses into MAC (physical) addresses. This protocol operates by default on Windows OS computers and it can be viewed and/or configured by entering the arp command (or one of its switches) into the Command Shell. The arp -a switch displays the IP addresses and MAC addresses of all devices connected to the network.

20. (a) (iii) RJ45 plug. **(b)** (ii) Crimper. The technician should use a crimper (otherwise known as a crimping tool) to permanently attach an RJ45 plug to the end of a twisted pair ethernet cable. **(c)** (ii) Loopback tester. To test a network adapter or network interface card (NIC) without a network connection, the technician should use a loopback tester (also known as a loopback plug). The insertion of a loopback tester into the RJ45 (ethernet) port on a computer simulates a network connection, thereby allowing the technician to test and verify the functionality of the network card. A loopback tester can also be used to test the functionality of network ports found on an ethernet switch. SSL is an acronym for Secure Sockets Layer. SSL is a standard security protocol that is almost ubiquitously used to establish an encrypted link between a server and a client computer – typically, a web server hosting a specific website and a browser (e.g., Microsoft Edge, Apple Safari, etc.), or a mail server and a mail client (e.g., Microsoft Outlook, Google Gmail, etc.). SSL allows sensitive data such as credit card numbers, social security numbers, and log-in credentials to be securely transmitted over the Internet. Under normal circumstances, data sent between browsers and web servers is transmitted in plain, intelligible text and numbers, rendering this data susceptible to unauthorized eavesdropping. If a cyber-attacker or intruder is able to intercept these data transmissions, the attacker can see and use that information in a potentially malicious manner. SSL technology helps to prevent such an eventuality, thereby ensuring the integrity and security of transmitted data streams.

Practice Test 21

1. What is the correct sequential order of a PC or laptop's booting sequence?

(i) Boot Loader, CPU, POST, OS

(ii) CPU, Boot Loader, OS, POST

(iii) CPU, POST, Boot Loader, OS

(iv) OS, CPU, Boot Loader, POST

2. Which of the following power connectors is used to supply power to an x16 video card?

(i) 4-pin Molex

(ii) 4-pin EATX12V

(iii) 8-pin EATX12V

(iv) 6-pin PCIe

(v) None of the above

3. Wireless networks that operate on the basis of wireless standard IEEE 802.11ac have a maximum data transfer rate of 1,700 Mbps.

What does the *b* in 1,700 Mbps stand for?

(i) beta

(ii) bit

(iii) byte

(iv) None of the above

4. What term is used to describe the process by which the BIOS or UEFI prepares a computer system before the OS is initialized and loaded on to the computer during Startup?

(i) Booting

(ii) Bootstrapping

(iii) POST

(iv) Initialization sequence

5. A regular customer of a PC sales shop has just bought a new ASUS® laptop. When the customer takes the laptop home and starts typing on the integrated keyboard, a strange combination of alpha-numeric characters appear on the LCD display instead of only letters.

Which of the following is the most likely cause of this issue?

(i) Scroll Lock key is enabled

(ii) Incompatible word processing application

(iii) Fn key is stuck

(iv) Num Lock key is enabled

6. A gaming enthusiast buys a reconditioned Nvidia® GeForce™ high-end graphics card from his local computer sales store.

When he removes the graphics card from the box, he notices that the manufacturer's DVD-ROM containing the card's driver and other documentation is missing. He successfully installs the card into his custom-built Windows® OS gaming PC to replace a pre-existing video card.

(a) Where should the gaming enthusiast obtain a compatible driver for his newly installed graphics card?

(i) support.microsoft.com

(ii) Any reputable website that sells generic video card drivers

(iii) Use the old video card's driver

(iv) Download the correct driver from the manufacturer's website

(b) When the gaming PC is rebooted post-installation of the Nvidia® graphics card, Windows® OS installs a generic video card driver. However, the driver installation does not finish and an error message appears on the screen.

What should the gaming enthusiast do next? (Select two answers.)

(i) Re-install the generic driver

(ii) Roll back the generic driver

(iii) Reboot the gaming PC

(iv) Visit nvidia.com to download the correct driver

(v) Return the graphics card to the computer store

7. Which type of active matrix LCD technology allows for better color reproduction and wider viewing angles?

(i) OLED

(ii) TFT

(iii) TN

(iv) IPS

8. The proprietor of a small graphics design studio has recently launched a website that is used primarily to showcase the products and services provided by the studio, as well as to manage online orders and customer queries.

For cybersecurity reasons, the proprietor has set up an effective firewall on the SOHO router.

What service on the router can be configured to ensure that all external network traffic to the studio's website is directed through the firewall to the correct web server?

(i) DNS

(ii) NAT

(iii) Port forwarding

(iv) Port triggering

9. Fill in the missing spaces: Liquid cooling systems can be used in certain circumstances to dissipate the heat generated by the ______. Liquid cooling is oftentimes employed by gaming enthusiasts. However, this heat dissipation method may also be seen in other ______-intensive computer systems, such as ______ systems, ______ workstations, ______ computers, and sometimes server systems.

10. The Procurement and Contracts Office of a prestigious American university has recently purchased a number of HP® laptops for academic staff in the School of Biomedical Engineering.

However, the School's associate professor contacts the university's IT department complaining that the touchpad of his laptop is not working. All other academic staff working in the School report that they have encountered no issues with the new laptops.

An IT technician has been sent to troubleshoot the laptop.

What should the technician do first to try to resolve the matter?

(i) Update the laptop's touchpad driver

(ii) Clean the touchpad with isopropyl alcohol

(iii) Replace the touchpad

(iv) Contact the manufacturer to raise an RMA

(v) Ensure that the touchpad has not been accidentally disabled

Figure 40(a)

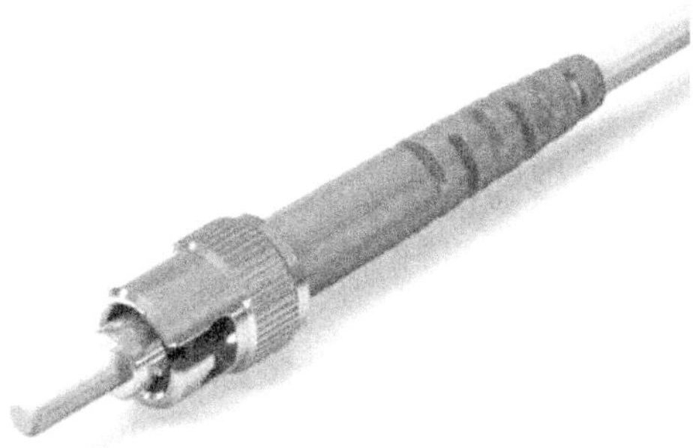

Figure 40(b)

11. True or False: The data transmission speed of Thunderbolt 1.0 is faster than USB 3.1 Gen 2.

12. SMTP and POP3 are common networking protocols.

Answer the following questions *(a)* to *(d)*.

(a) What do the acronyms SMTP and POP3 mean?

(i) Server Message Transfer Protocol, Post Office Protocol 3

(ii) Simple Mail Transfer Protocol, Post Office Protocol 3

(iii) Simple Mail Transfer Protocol, Principal Order Protocol 3

(iv) Simple Messaging Transfer Protocol, Principal Owner Protocol 3

(b) What port numbers are typically associated with the protocols SMTP and POP3, respectively?

(i) 25, 110

(ii) 21, 427

(iii) 23, 443

(iv) 25, 443

(c) What is the function of SMTP?

(i) SMTP is mainly used to receive email messages

(ii) SMTP is predominantly used by servers to detect incoming client connections over a network

(iii) SMTP is predominantly used by servers to facilitate outgoing client connections

(iv) The primary function of SMTP is to send email correspondence

(d) What is the function of POP3?

(i) POP3 is a networking protocol that is used by email clients to access incoming email messages from a mail server

(ii) POP3 is a networking protocol that utilizes "secret key" cryptography to authenticate client-server applications

(iii) POP3 is primarily used by email clients to route outgoing email correspondence to the correct mail server before being dispatched to the intended recipient

(iv) None of the above

13. Identify the fiber optic connectors displayed in *Figure 40(a)* and *Figure 40(b).*

14. A junior technician is building and customizing an ASUS® PC for gaming enthusiasts. Prior to customization, the PC operated as normal.

The technician has successfully upgraded the CPU and he has also installed a newer, more powerful video card with an embedded GPU and air cooling system. The computer already has a 400 W PSU.

However, upon switching on the revamped computer, the ASUS® PC shuts down before completing its booting sequence.

What is the most likely reason for the computer's inability to successfully complete boot up?

(i) Corrupt video card driver

(ii) PSU is not providing sufficient wattage

(iii) PSU is providing too much wattage

(iv) None of the above

15. A computer workstation in a LAN environment is experiencing intermittent connectivity to a specific online corporate portal. A technician troubleshooting the issue wants to check the status of the connectivity to the aforesaid website's web server over the course of 30 minutes.

Which of the following commands should the technician enter at the command prompt?

(i) netstat

(ii) ping -l

(iii) ping -n

(iv) ping -t

(v) ping /?

16. True or False: A modem connects a device, such as a computer, to an Internet Service Provider (ISP) by way of fiber optic cables. Modems convert light signals to digital signals that computers can interpret and vice versa, in a process termed rectification/de-rectification.

17. A PC user working in a LAN environment reports that the OLED display of a computer workstation remains blank when the computer is powered on. The power LED and HDD LED on the front panel of the computer case are active.

A PC technician has been requested to troubleshoot the issue. The technician asks the PC user a sequence of questions. He then makes some notes with respect to the apparent symptoms of the issue.

(a) Explain the term OLED display.

(b) State one advantage of OLED displays compared to LED monitors.

(c) With reference to the preceding scenario, what should the technician do next?

(i) Establish a plan of action to resolve the problem

(ii) Escalate the problem to another technician

(iii) Establish a theory of probable cause

(iv) Implement a solution to the computer issue

(d) Which of the following internal components should the technician investigate initially when troubleshooting this particular computer issue? (Select two possible answers.)

(i) Network interface controller

(ii) Video card

(iii) CPU

(iv) Hypervisor

18. What expansion bus uses "lanes" to transfer data?

(i) eSATA

(ii) PCI

(iii) PCIe

(iv) USB 3.0

19. Which of the following signifies the speed of a processor?

(i) CFM

(ii) TDP

(iii) Clock speed

(iv) Bus speed

20. A computer enthusiast is planning to upgrade the Intel® Core™ i3 1.8 GHz processor in her HP® laptop to a faster Intel® processor.

Which of the following should she do first? (Select two answers.)

(i) Remove the system board

(ii) Employ appropriate antistatic measures

(iii) Upgrade the BIOS firmware

(iv) Visit the manufacturer's website to ascertain if the new processor is compatible with the system

(v) It is not possible to upgrade a laptop's CPU

Practice Test 21			
MCQ Solutions			
1.	(iii)	11.	False
2.	(iv)	12.	(a)(ii), (b)(i), (c)(iv), (d)(i)
3.	(ii)	13.	See notes
4.	(ii)	14.	(ii)
5.	(iv)	15.	(iv)
6.	(a)(iv), (b)(ii)(iv)	16.	False
7.	(iv)	17.	(a) See notes, (b) See notes, (c)(iii), (d)(ii)(iii)
8.	(iii)	18.	(iii)
9.	See notes	19.	(iii)
10.	(v)	20.	(ii), (iv)

1. Correct: (iii) CPU, POST, Boot Loader, and OS (Operating System).

2. Correct: (iv) 6-pin PCIe. An x16 video card is normally supplied by either a PCIe 6-pin power connector (for ATX 12 V 2.1 power supplies) or a PCIe 8-pin power connector (for ATX 12 V 2.2 or higher power supplies).

3. Correct: (ii) bit (as opposed to byte, which refers to a different quantity of data).

4. Correct: (ii) Bootstrapping. Bootstrapping is normally accomplished by the BIOS or UEFI (Unified Extensible Firmware Interface).

5. Correct: (iv) Num Lock key is enabled. The Number Lock (Num Lock) key is used to enable or disable the numeric keypad. Given the scenario, it is very likely the customer inadvertently pressed the Num Lock key while typing. Consequently, the keys on the keyboard that have a dual function (i.e., can be used to generate either numbers or letters) are now only active as numbers, thus leading to a combination of letters and numbers on the screen when the customer types.

6. (a) (iv) Download the correct driver from the manufacturer's website. The manufacturer's website is invariably the best place to download the correct driver version for the graphics card. A disc is usually supplied with the graphics card by the manufacturer that contains the relevant driver, but since the disc is missing in this particular scenario the gaming enthusiast needs to visit the manufacturer's website. Downloading a generic video card driver or using the old video card's driver is not advisable. **(b)** (ii) and (iv). The gaming enthusiast needs to un-install the generic driver and then visit the graphic card manufacturer's website to download the correct version of the driver.

7. Correct: (iv) IPS. IPS (In-plane switching) is a type of active-matrix LCD technology that offers a wider viewing angle and relatively better color reproduction compared to TN (Twisted Nematic). IPS-based LCD monitors use more power than TN-based LCD displays. Less expensive LCD monitors usually feature TN technology, whereas more expensive LCDs are specified with IPS.

8. Correct: (iii) Port forwarding. The studio owner needs to set up port forwarding on the router and configure this service correctly. In essence, port forwarding is used to forward external network ports to an internal IP address or port on a computer that is attached to a SOHO network or LAN. Port forwarding is sometimes referred to as DNAT (Destination Network Address Translation). On the other hand, port triggering is a service that allows a technician (or SOHO administrator) to specify outgoing ports that a computer attached to a SOHO network or LAN can use for special applications (e.g., IP phones, online games and IM (Instant Messaging) applications). When the online sessions are established (e.g., two PC users communicating with each other in real time using IM), the corresponding inbound ports automatically open.

9. (1) CPU. (2) CPU. (3) CAD/CAM. (4) Virtualization. (5) Audio/video editing. The completed statement should read: "Liquid cooling systems can be used in certain circumstances to dissipate the heat generated by the CPU. Liquid cooling is oftentimes employed by gaming enthusiasts. However, this heat dissipation method may also be seen in other CPU-intensive computer systems, such as CAD/CAM systems, virtualization workstations, audio/video editing computers, and sometimes server systems."

10. Correct: (v) Ensure that the touchpad has not been accidentally disabled. Most laptops have a button or function key to enable or disabled the touchpad. If the touchpad is not working, the first troubleshooting step to take is to ensure that the touchpad is not disabled. The acronym RMA means Return Merchandise Authorization. Raising an RMA with a manufacturer is part of the process of returning a defective or damaged product to receive a refund, replacement, or repair during the product's warranty period.

11. False. Thunderbolt 1.0 and USB 3.1 (also called USB 3.1 Gen 2) both have a theoretical data transfer speed of 10 Gbps.

12. **(a)** (ii) SMTP (Simple Mail Transfer Protocol). POP3 (Post Office Protocol Version 3). **(b)** (i) SMTP uses inbound port 25. POP3 uses port 110. **(c)** (iv) The main function of SMTP is to send email. **(d)** (i) The main function of POP3 is to receive email. POP3 is used by email clients to access incoming email messages from an email server. The email server uses port 110 to send email messages to the clients.

13. (A) ST connector. (B) SC connector.

14. Correct: (ii) The installed 400 W PSU (Power Supply Unit) is not providing sufficient wattage for the new high-end video card. Hence, the computer in the scenario powers down before it can complete the booting process. Most mid-range gaming PC builds can operate using PSUs in the range 450 to 600 W, depending on the type and specifications of the GPU

(Graphics Processing Unit), but the ideal wattage range for a PSU used in gaming PCs is 500 to 550 W.

15. Correct: (iv) ping -t. The technician should type ping <IP address> -t into the CLI tool. This command continuously pings a specified IP address until such time that the command is terminated using the **Ctrl+C** keystroke. The technician can therefore use the on-screen results of this command to monitor the computer workstation's connectivity to a particular website over a period of time.

16. False. The correct statement should read: "A modem connects a device, such as a computer, to an Internet Service Provider (ISP) by way of traditional telephone cables. Modems convert analog signals to digital signals that computers can interpret and vice versa, in a process termed modulation/de-modulation."

17. **(a)** OLED is an acronym for Organic Light-Emitting Diode. OLED displays may be used in a computing environment as an alternative to LCD displays, LED (Light Emitting Diode) monitors, and plasma displays. OLED displays utilize a film of organic semiconductor material that emits light in response to an electric current. The organic-colored LEDs are situated between electrodes. An electrically conductive layer comprising plastic molecules allows the organic-colored molecules to emit light. **(b)** Main OLED advantages: Because the light-emitting layers of an OLED display are lighter, the substrate of an OLED display can be flexible instead of rigid. OLED substrates can be plastic as opposed to the glass used for LED and LCD monitors. OLEDs tend to be brighter than LED displays. **(c)** (iii) Establish a theory of probable cause. **(d)** (ii) Video card and (iii) CPU. Since the power LED and HDD LED on the front panel of the computer case are active, it is obvious that the computer is receiving power and that the hard drive seems to be active. Since the computer definitely has a power source, yet the screen remains blank, it will be necessary for the technician to check all of the following internal components in order: (1) video card, (2) RAM stick(s), (3) CPU, and (4) motherboard.

18. Correct: (iii) PCIe (Peripheral Component Interconnect Express).

19. Correct: (iii) Clock speed. The clock speed refers to the speed of a CPU (e.g., 1.8 GHz).

20. Correct: (ii) and (iv). When upgrading a CPU in a laptop to a newer, faster generation processor, it is imperative to check the laptop manufacturer's documentation or visit the laptop manufacturer's website to determine if the faster CPU is supported by the system. If it transpires that the processor is supported, then the next most appropriate step would be to employ ESD prevention measures.

Assessment Tests

Assessment Test I

Assessment Test I comprises 90 multiple-choice questions. Each question is worth 10 points. The passing score is 675 points out of 900 (i.e., 75.0%).

1. Which of the following networking protocols use port 21?

(a) AFP

(b) FTP

(c) SSH

(d) Telnet

2. What is the minimum category networking cable required for a 1000Base-T network?

(a) Cat 3

(b) Cat 5

(c) Cat 5e

(d) Cat 7a

3. What is user-replaceable memory in a PC called?

(a) SRAM

(b) DRAM

(c) SODIMM

(d) Cache

4. Which of the following hardware components is the least likely to be replaced on a laptop?

(a) Keyboard

(b) LCD display

(c) SODIMM

(d) CPU

5. A small architectural design firm has a color laser printer that was purchased a few years ago. Historically, the printer has seldom given any problems, normally being fast and efficient. The printer is mainly used to print out large architectural schematics and large documents occasionally embedded with color images.

Recently, one of the architects has reported that the printer spontaneously pauses and resumes printing several times when large print jobs are sent to the printer.

What is the most likely cause of this issue?

(a) The printer's memory is not sufficient to handle large print jobs

(b) The cable connections to the printer are loose

(c) The printer is overheating

(d) The pickup rollers are partially "jammed"

6. A PC repair technician has been requested to service a number of PCs that are used for inventory management and order processing purposes in a large grain storage depot. Warehouse staff report that the computers tend to shut down unexpectedly and this phenomenon has been occurring frequently over the last few weeks.

The technician notices that the PC cases are full of dust, with a lot of dust having accumulated in the exhaust vents. Also, the technician observes that some of the computers have no card slot covers.

What are the most likely reasons for the warehouse computers shutting down unexpectedly? (Select two answers.)

(a) Computers are connected to faulty AC receptacles owing to an intermittent, undiagnosed problem with an electrical circuit (or circuits) within the warehouse facility

(b) Inadequate air circulation within the computer cases

(c) Malfunctioning or defective power supplies

(d) Overheating CPUs

7. Which of the following connection types provides the fastest data transfer rates? (Select one answer.)

(a) Firewire 800

(b) Firewire 400

(c) eSATA

(d) USB 2.0

8. What CLI command allows a network technician to view the current network sessions between a PC and the Internet?

(a) nbtstat -A

(b) netstat

(c) ipconfig /all

(d) None of the above

9. While investigating the cause of a network issue, a technician notices that one set of LED lights on an ethernet switch is blinking rapidly. All other LED lights on the switch are blinking at a normal, intermittent rate.

Which of the following are the most likely reasons for the rapidly blinking LED lights on the switch? (Select two answers.)

(a) A network adapter card in a networked computer is defective

(b) The firmware on the switch needs to be updated

(c) A port on the switch is faulty

(d) High-speed data transmission over the network

10. A network technician is troubleshooting a Lenovo® PC workstation. The PC workstation's network connection seems to be operating at a slower speed than usual.

Using the Command Shell, he has already run an **ipconfig /all** statement and he has determined that the TCP/IP configuration settings for this workstation seem to be normal. He now wants to know how many SMB data packets are currently being received by this workstation.

What command should he enter at the command line?

(a) arp -a

(b) nbtstat

(c) netstat

(d) ping -t

11. What troubleshooting command is very useful when a technician is trying to determine connectivity problems on a Windows® OS computer that is unable to connect to the Internet?

(a) ipconfig

(b) nbtstat

(c) netstat

(d) None of the above

12. DisplayPort is a type of video card connector. Which of the following video connectors was DisplayPort originally designed to replace? (Select two answers.)

(a) Component RGB

(b) DVI

(c) HDMI

(d) VGA

13. A technician receives a call from a client who is attempting to set up a home theatre stereo system. The client has stated that she is unsure how to connect her HTPC's sound card to the stereo system.

What types of audio connections would you recommend to the client? (Select two answers.)

(a) Component RGB

(b) M1-DA

(c) TOSLINK™ optical audio

(d) RCA

14. What should be used to clean a laser printer's transfer corona wire? (Select two answers.)

(a) Cotton swab

(b) Isopropyl alcohol

(c) Small sponge

(d) Urea

15. What is the standard printing resolution stated in DPI?

(a) 24

(b) 72

(c) 300

(d) 600

16. Sound does not emanate from a HTPC's integrated speakers. Which of the following are possible reasons for this specific issue? (Select two answers.)

(a) The sound card's driver needs to be installed

(b) The volume is turned down or muted

(c) Faulty speakers

(d) Defective sound card

17. Which chipset determines where data will be stored in a computer's RAM?

(a) Southbridge

(b) Northbridge

(c) EEPROM

(d) PROM

18. A junior computer technician is troubleshooting a virtualization workstation that is unable to complete the booting process. He has devised a series of theories regarding the probable cause of the issue and he has tested the theories. However, his endeavors to identify the root cause of the booting problem have been unsuccessful.

What should the technician do next?

(a) Establish another theory of probable cause

(b) Document findings, actions taken, and outcomes

(c) Implement a temporary solution

(d) Escalate the matter to a more experienced technician

19. Which tool is normally used to test the actual amount of voltage that emanates from a 24-pin ATX 12V power connector?

(a) Receptacle tester

(b) PSU tester

(c) Ohmmeter

(d) Multimeter

20. What tool can be used to numerically display the amount of voltage that comes from an AC outlet?

(a) Power supply tester

(b) AC receptacle tester

(c) Cable certifier

(d) Multimeter

21. Which of the following cards is normally plugged into a PCIe x16 adapter card slot?

(a) ExpressCard

(b) Network adapter card

(c) RAID controller card

(d) Video card

22. A technician working in a large distribution center has been asked to connect wireless earpieces to company-issued smartphones. This is to ensure that drivers can operate their articulated vehicles safely while speaking on the phone.

Which technology would you advise the technician to use in this situation?

(a) Wi-Fi

(b) Bluetooth

(c) NFC

(d) WiMAX

23. What port number is typically associated with IMAP?

(a) 23

(b) 143

(c) 443

(d) 3389

24. A PC user intends to expand the peripheral devices of his Acer® Aspire™ desktop computer. However, the system does not have sufficient on-board ports.

What type of card should be installed to remedy this problem?

(a) SATA card

(b) USB card

(c) SDXC

(d) SDHC

25. A graphics designer sends a 3D image to the network laser printer. However, when collecting the printout, she notices that the printout only shows a ghosted image. An IT technician confirms that there are no networking issues to be concerned about.

What is the most likely cause of the ghosted image?

(a) Depleted toner cartridge

(b) Faulty photosensitive drum

(c) Transfer corona wire is not receiving sufficient voltage

(d) Fusing assembly is not getting sufficiently hot

26. How many colors approximately does a 32-bit Windows® OS have?

(a) 256

(b) 65,536

(c) 16.78 million

(d) 4.29 billion

27. Which of the following encryption protocols offer the strongest form of wireless encryption? (Select two answers.)

(a) WEP 64

(b) WPA

(c) WPA2

(d) TKIP

(e) AES

(f) WEP 128

28. You are the senior IT technician for a large transnational company. The Director of IT has asked you if there are viable alternatives to the standard username and password when employees log on to their workstations.

Which of the following peripherals could potentially be used as alternative log-on methods for employees? (Select two answers.)

(a) Biometric device

(b) KVM switch

(c) Smart card reader

(d) USB key

29. A computer technician has installed a new NIC into an ASUS® laptop. What physical tool can the technician use to test NIC functionality?

(a) KVM switch

(b) LAN adapter

(c) Loopback plug

(d) POST card

30. An Apple® iPad™ Air tablet is wirelessly connected to a local Bluetooth-enabled printer.

What is the name of the app on the tablet that permits the user to print documents?

(a) AirPrint™

(b) APNS

(c) Bonjour™

(d) None of the above

31. Which of the following environmental factors is most likely to affect a thermal printer?

(a) Cold weather

(b) High ambient temperatures

(c) ESD

(d) Moisture

32. Which of the following networking protocols use port 53?

(a) DNS

(b) HTTPS

(c) SSH

(d) TLS

33. A very successful design studio located in London, England allows its employees to use their own mobile devices to carry out work-related tasks.

What is this organizational policy known as?

(a) BYOD

(b) DRM

(c) EULA

(d) SSO

34. Which of the following is the maximum data transfer rate of SATA 3.0?

(a) 150 MB/s

(b) 300 MB/s

(c) 6 Gbps

(d) 16 Gbps

35. Which fiber optic cable connector has a bayonet tip?

(a) F-connector

(b) LC

(c) RJ45

(d) ST

36. A computer technician has installed a new NIC into an ASUS® laptop.

What CLI command can the technician use to test the functionality of the new NIC? (Select two answers.)

(a) netstat -a FF::/8

(b) ping ::1

(c) ping 127.0.0.1

(d) ping FE80::/10

37. What component on a motherboard typically supplies power to the CMOS after a computer is shut down?

(a) Li-ion battery

(b) Li-ion polymer battery

(c) NiCd battery

(d) CR2032 battery

38. Which motherboard technology divides the RAM slots into different colors?

(a) Single channel

(b) Dual channel

(c) Full duplex

(d) FM2+

39. What type of network can be created by means of a Bluetooth connection?

(a) LAN

(b) MAN

(c) PAN

(d) WLAN

40. A technician in a PC repair shop has been asked by a customer to add a second SODIMM memory module to his laptop. When the technician opens the memory compartment on the undersurface of the laptop, he notices that there is already a 2 GB DDR3 memory module installed to the only available slot. However, this laptop is specified to accommodate a maximum of 4 GB RAM.

Where should the technician look for a second memory slot?

(a) Underneath the keyboard

(b) Behind the Li-ion battery compartment

(c) Underneath the optical drive

(d) Underneath the touchpad

41. A SOHO network environment in a small real estate office comprises 5 Dell® PC workstations, 2 Samsung® laptops, and a wireless Samsung® Xpress® laser printer. However, the office administrator has noticed that connectivity to the wireless printer seems to be intermittent during peak times when employees are using all available computer workstations, including the portable devices.

An IT technician has been called to troubleshoot the issue and he discovers that only 7 IP addresses have been set up on the router. The office administrator tells the technician that the SOHO network has never given any problems in the past, with the exception of the recurrent connectivity issues affecting the wireless printer.

What is the most likely cause of the intermittent wireless connectivity affecting the printer?

(a) Faulty RJ45 jack on the printer

(b) Insufficient physical memory installed on the printer

(c) There is no available IP address to assign to the printer during peak office times

(d) Wrong virtual COM port has been assigned to the printer

42. Which of the following connection types is the slowest in terms of its data transfer rate?

(a) USB 3.0

(b) Thunderbolt 1.0

(c) USB 2.0

(d) Firewire 400

43. A company's LAN is set up on the basis of DHCP networking. Recently, new PC workstations have been added to the network. One user has reported to the IT department that her computer has generated a system error message:

Error: There is an IP conflict with another device on the network. Unable to access network resources. Please try again later.

The user also confirmed that her workstation operated properly up until recently.

What is the most likely cause of this networking error? (Select the best answer.)

(a) DHCP server has "crashed" and needs to be power cycled

(b) DNS resolver cache has become corrupt

(c) The local computer's NetBIOS settings have become misconfigured

(d) There is a duplicate IP address registered on the network

44. A computer technician is upgrading an ATX motherboard. He has successfully installed new DDR3 memory modules and a high-end graphics card. The technician has also flashed the BIOS to ensure that the reconditioned motherboard is compatible with Intel® processors. Finally, he installs an Intel® Core™ i5 CPU into the processor socket.

However, upon booting the computer, the technician hears a sequence of high and low beeps. Eventually the computer automatically shuts down.

Which of the newly installed components are most likely the cause of this particular issue?

(a) BIOS

(b) CPU

(c) Graphics card

(d) RAM

45. A large university hospital campus in New York is very reliant upon the computer resources provided by its dedicated server room.

The Chief Technical Officer (CTO) of the hospital board is formulating a plan to gradually replace the hard disk drives used by the servers with SSDs. Very confidential patient medical records and other sensitive hospital data are stored on the servers. Hence, the CTO wants to configure RAID arrays that will ensure data security and minimise the risk of data corruption or loss.

Which of the following options would an IT consultant most likely recommend to the hospital board? (Select one answer.)

(a) IPsec

(b) RAID 5

(c) RAID 10

(d) TLS/SSL

46. What is the typical rotational speed of a SATA HDD?

(a) 5,400 RPM

(b) 7,200 RPM

(c) 10,000 RPM

(d) 10,800 RPM

47. Which wireless technology requires an unobstructed "line of sight" between devices?

(a) IR

(b) NFC

(c) Bluetooth

(d) GSM

48. What type of computer display has the highest contrast ratio?

(a) LCD

(b) LED

(c) OLED

(d) Plasma

49. Which of the following is a common charging port that is built into an Android™ smartphone?

(a) USB Type B

(b) Micro USB Type B

(c) Mini USB Type B

(d) Lightning

50. An employee working for a prestigious software development firm reports that she is unable to decrypt email messages using her company-issued mobile device. The firm's IT technician has noticed that her mobile device does not have the correct digital certificate.

What else could be potentially missing from the user's mobile device? (Select one answer.)

(i) POP3

(ii) Private key

(iii) Public key

(iv) SSL certificate

51. What are the Intel® and AMD® names for CPU virtualization using a hypervisor, respectively? (Select two answers.)

(a) AM3+

(b) AMD-V

(c) FM2+

(d) VT-x

52. A computer technician has installed a new 2 GB Corsair® DDR3 SODIMM module into a Samsung® Chromebook™ laptop which already has a pre-existing older generation 2 GB Corsair® memory stick. She confirms that the new SODIMM module is compatible with the motherboard.

However, when the computer is eventually rebooted and the technician reviews the BIOS settings, she discovers that the BIOS still only recognizes 2 GB RAM.

What do you think the technician should do to resolve the issue?

(a) Upgrade the CPU

(b) Replace the RAM modules

(c) Flash the BIOS

(d) Re-seat the RAM modules

53. Which of the following is the most important item of information required to connect to a specific wireless network?

(a) QoS

(b) Channel

(c) SSID

(d) MAC

54. Which type of external connection permits the fastest hard drive data transfer rate?

(a) HDMI

(b) HHD

(c) eSATA

(d) USB 3.0

55. A network technician is troubleshooting a newly installed Dell® desktop PC. The computer does not have any access to shared resources on the network or Internet connectivity. The technician observes that the ethernet port light on the rear of the computer case is not active.

Which of the following indicates the most likely cause of this networking issue? (Select two answers.)

(a) The ethernet cable is disconnected

(b) The network adapter is faulty

(c) The ethernet cable is loose

(d) BIOS firmware does not recognize the NIC

56. What type of laptop display uses a backlight?

(a) CRT

(b) LCD

(c) Plasma

(d) VDU

57. How many pins are normally found in the print head of a high-quality dot matrix printer?

(a) 15

(b) 20

(c) 24

(d) 34

58. A PC technician is troubleshooting a computer and he has opened the case. In the event of an unexpected power surge or electrical discharge, which of the following tools may be helpful in protecting the technician?

(a) Antistatic strap

(b) Antistatic bag

(c) Antistatic mat

(d) Multimeter

59. According to an ipconfig statement, a computer workstation in a LAN environment has been assigned the IP address 169.254.0.140. This Windows® OS computer is unable to access shared resources on the network or the Internet. Other computers on the network also have limited or no Internet connectivity.

What is the significance of the IP address 169.254.0.140?

(a) The default gateway address applicable to the network is 169.254.0.140

(b) The local computer has been previously configured to use a static IP address as opposed to using a dynamic IP address

(c) The IP address 169.254.0.140 indicates that the local computer can no longer implement the APIPA protocol because it is unable to access the relevant server system

(d) The IP address 169.254.0.140 indicates that Windows® OS on the local computer has implemented APIPA

60. What term is used to describe the practice of sharing a mobile device's Internet connection with other Wi-Fi capable USB-connected devices?

(a) PAN

(b) Synchronization

(c) Wi-Fi tethering

(d) None of the above

61. Which type of video connector is primarily used with a computer (as opposed to a Smart TV) and carries an analog signal?

(a) DVI-A

(b) DVI-I

(c) HDMI Type A

(d) M1-DA

62. Which of the following internal components of a computer could cause the POST to fail during boot up? (Select two answers.)

(a) CPU

(b) LCD

(c) Windows® OS

(d) RAM

63. Which of the following allows a mobile device (e.g., smartphone) to access 4G signals?

(a) Wi-Fi card

(b) Cellular card

(c) Bluetooth dongle

(d) NIC

64. A networking installation and engineering company has recently been awarded a US federal contract to install the Cat-6 networking cables in a purpose-built government research center.

An experienced network engineer and a team of technicians have also been appointed by the regional government to monitor the installation and commissioning work carried out by the network cabling company. The purpose of the audit is to ensure that all Cat-6 cable runs do not exceed a maximum length of 100 meters (328 feet) and that data transmission rates over the network will be within specified parameters.

What tool can be used by the audit team to carry out their assigned tasks in the most efficient manner possible?

(a) Use a patch cable tester to verify cable distance

(b) Use a tone generator and probe to verify cable distance

(c) Use a network multimeter to verify cable distance

(d) None of the above

65. A technician is configuring a router for an accountancy practice. In the interests of network security, the technician wants to ensure that the router assigns its public IP address to all data packets heading to external networks (e.g., Internet), thereby ensuring that the originating sources of data packets on the network (e.g., client workstations) remain hidden.

Which feature of the router should be enabled to enhance network security?

(a) Channel

(b) NAS

(c) NAT

(d) WEP

66. Which connector can transmit uncompressed digital video?

(a) VGA

(b) DVI

(c) S-video

(d) HDMI

67. Which of the following CLI tools can be used by a network technician to determine which router between his PC workstation and another computer on the network has failed?

(a) tracert

(b) arp -a

(c) nbtstat -a

(d) ipconfig /?

68. A Dell® PC workstation's memory is being upgraded. The PC workstation already has a 4 GB Corsair® memory module installed in Bank 1. A technician installs a new 4 GB Corsair® DIMM stick into the correct slot in Bank 2 on the ATX motherboard. However, when the computer workstation is rebooted, a memory error notification is displayed on the monitor.

Which of the following is the most likely explanation for this error?

(a) BIOS does not recognise the newly installed DIMM

(b) The new memory module operates at a lower speed compared to the pre-existing DIMM in Bank 1

(c) The new memory module is overheating

(d) The RAM slot is dirty

69. A laser printer is printing lighter in random areas of each page. What should a maintenance technician do to resolve this printer issue?

(a) Clean the primary corona wire

(b) Clean the fusing assembly

(c) Clean the rubber rollers

(d) Replace the toner cartridge

70. A very experienced PC technician is installing a new kit of 2 Kingston® 2 GB DDR4 memory sticks into a Lenovo® laptop on behalf of a customer. The customer purchased the laptop almost 2 years ago.

According to the laptop manufacturer's website, the new memory sticks are compatible with the laptop's motherboard. However, when the technician boots the laptop, an error message appears on the screen:

Memory not recognised. Press any key to continue.

What is the most likely cause of the memory error?

(a) New RAM modules not correctly seated

(b) Dirty RAM slots

(c) Memory modules were damaged by ESD during installation

(d) UEFI BIOS does not recognize newly installed RAM

71. Laptops can communicate with other computers using wired connections such as ethernet cables and dial-up (RJ11) connections.

Which wireless connections enable laptops to communicate with other computers and devices? (Select all applicable answers.)

(a) Bluetooth

(b) WLAN

(c) NFC

(d) Cellular WAN

(e) USB 3.0

72. A computer operates normally for a few minutes, but then the system "freezes" or "crashes". What is the most likely cause?

(a) Case cooling fans are starting to fail

(b) Device driver errors

(c) Physical DIMM faults

(d) Motherboard manufacturing defects

73. A network technician working for a large BPO company has been requested by the Director of IT to create additional mapped network drives to support the business's ongoing client onboarding process. The technician opens the Command Shell and types a series of commands.

What command should the technician enter at the command prompt to view any currently mapped network drives set up on the company's LAN?

(a) net use

(b) net view

(c) netstat

(d) net start

74. An internationally renowned Internet technology company is planning to construct a new state-of-the-art data center in Finland. Ultimately, the data center will comprise a multitude of secure server rooms. A team of network engineers have been contracted to design these server rooms.

Which of the following devices should the engineers include in the design of each server room to ensure ease of administration for data center personnel?

(a) Ethernet switch

(b) KVM switch

(c) Linux® workstation

(d) MIDI

75. An inkjet printer is printing streaks on documents. What is the best first troubleshooting step to resolve this issue?

(a) Manually wipe the print heads with a clean, lint-free cloth

(b) Replace the print ribbon

(c) Use the printer's "Clean" option

(d) Power cycle the printer

76. A computer technician is troubleshooting a networking issue. She types ping 193.168.10.05 -l 1500 into the command shell. What does this command do?

(a) This command pings the specified IP address with 1,500 bytes of data 10 times

(b) This command pings the specified IP address with 1,500 bytes of data 4 times

(c) This command pings the specified IP address with 1 byte of data 1,500 times

(d) This command pings the specified IP address with 1,500 bytes of data only once

(e) This command is incorrect. The correct command is: ping 193.168.10.05 -L 1500

77. What is the typical storage capacity of DVD-5 and DVD-18 formats, respectively? (Select two answers.)

(a) 4.7 GB

(b) 5 GB

(c) 9.4 GB

(d) 17 GB

(e) 18 GB

78. Which statement most accurately describes the purpose and function of the netstat -n command? (Select two answers.)

(a) If a computer technician intends to submit a request to a DNS server to determine DNS details, including the IP address of host computers, he/she would enter netstat -n at the command prompt

(b) Netstat -n displays network protocol statistics for a local computer that use NetBIOS over TCP/IP connections

(c) Netstat -n shows the network statistics for a local computer in a numerical format only

(d) The netstat -n command specifies the number of active connections open on a network at any given point in time

79. A company's IT technician is working on a Windows® 8.1 OS desktop computer in the main office. The office administrator asks the technician to securely erase the SATA hard drive so that the company can recycle it.

What should the technician do to securely erase this hard drive?

(a) Perform a low-level format on the hard drive

(b) Use the **format** command with the **/p** parameter

(c) Run Disk Cleanup utility

(d) Use **defrag -f** command

80. Which of the following ethernet physical media would support the use of a fibre optic connection? (Select two answers.)

(a) An ethernet cable that supports a data transmission rate of 100 Mbps

(b) A networking cable that supports a data transmission rate of 1,000 Kbps

(c) An ethernet cable that is designed to a 1,000 Mbps specification

(d) A networking cable that can transmit 10 Gbps

81. Which one of the following IEEE 802.11 wireless standards has a maximum data transmission rate of 11 Mbps and uses the 2.4 GHz frequency range?

(a) 802.11a

(b) 802.11b

(c) 802.11g

(d) 802.11n

(e) 802.11ac

82. Which networking device has a demodulator?

(a) Hub

(b) Modem

(c) Switch

(d) WAP

83. The optical drive in a computer is no longer working. The PC user has decided to buy and install a new drive.

Which optical drive variety can be purchased to allow the user to record the most data on a single disc?

(a) BR-D

(b) DVD-RW

(c) DVD+RW

(d) CD-ROM

84. A technician is troubleshooting a laptop. He decides to boot the computer into VGA mode from the ABOM.

What is the default display resolution for this mode?

(a) 1280 x 800

(b) 1366 x 768

(c) 640 x 480

(d) 1920 x 1080

85. Which cable type is used for carrying satellite television signals?

(a) Coaxial

(b) UTP

(c) STP

(d) Plenum-rated

86. While troubleshooting a network issue, a computer technician types *net view* into the Command Shell.

What type of information does this command present on the screen?

(a) Net view displays network protocol statistics and current TCP/IP connections that use NetBIOS

(b) Net view is used to show a list of computers and network devices connected to a specific network

(c) The command net view specifies the number of active connections open on a network at any particular moment in time

(d) None of the above

87. A technician is installing a new touchscreen monitor for a Windows® 8.0 OS workstation in a small bank branch.

Which of the following cable connections will be required to ensure that the touchscreen monitor will function properly? (Select three answers.)

(a) Ethernet

(b) Power

(c) USB

(d) Video

88. Which of the following is the most common indication that a PC's PSU is starting to fail? (Select all applicable answers.)

(a) Smoke emanating from the computer case

(b) The computer system repeatedly "freezes" or "crashes"

(c) BSOD event

(d) Repeated failure of the computer system's hard drives

89. When a user turned on his computer workstation, the LCD monitor started to flicker and then became blank, and smoke started to come out of the PC case.

However, the user notices that the case fans are still working because he can hear their signature sound.

What is the most likely cause of this PC issue?

(a) Faulty inverter

(b) Failed video card

(c) Defective PSU

(d) Faulty LCD monitor

90. A network technician working for a large BPO company has been requested by the Director of IT to create additional mapped network drives to support the business's ongoing client onboarding process. The technician opens the Command Shell and types a series of commands.

Which of the following commands should the technician enter at the command prompt if he wants to map a network drive S: to a shared resource called data$, located on a remote computer called PC-140?

(a) net use C: \\PC-140\data$

(b) net start S: PC-140\data$

(c) net use S: \\PC-140\data$

(d) net view S: \\PC-140\data$

Assessment Test I			
MCQ Solutions			
1.	b	17.	b
2.	c	18.	d
3.	b	19.	d
4.	d	20.	d
5.	c	21.	d
6.	b, d	22.	b
7.	c	23.	b
8.	b	24.	b
9.	a, c	25.	b
10.	c	26.	d
11.	a	27.	c, e
12.	b, c	28.	a, c
13.	c	29.	c
14.	a, b	30.	a
15.	d	31.	b
16.	a, b	32.	a

33.	a	51.	b, d
34.	c	52.	c
35.	d	53.	c
36.	b, c	54.	c
37.	d	55.	a, c
38.	b	56.	b
39.	c	57.	c
40.	a	58.	a
41.	c	59.	d
42.	d	60.	c
43.	d	61.	a
44.	b	62.	a, d
45.	c	63.	b
46.	b	64.	c
47.	a	65.	c
48.	d	66.	b
49.	b	67.	a
50.	b	68.	b

69.	d	80.	c, d
70.	d	81.	b
71.	a, b, d	82.	b
72.	a	83.	a
73.	a	84.	c
74.	b	85.	a
75.	c	86.	b
76.	b	87.	b, c, d
77.	a, d	88.	b, d
78.	c, d	89.	b
79.	b	90.	c

Assessment Test II

Assessment Test II comprises 90 multiple-choice questions. Each question is worth 10 points. The passing score is 675 points out of 900 (i.e., 75.0%).

1. Which type of cable connector is primarily used with a computer (as opposed to a Smart TV) and carries only a digital signal?

(a) DVI-D

(b) DVI-I

(c) HDMI Type A

(d) M1-DA

2. On which of the following computers is RAM capacity a very important consideration?

(a) AV workstation

(b) Virtualization workstation

(c) HTPC

(d) Gaming PC

3. What is the third step of the CompTIA® A+ troubleshooting methodology?

(a) Question the user of the computer equipment being troubleshot

(b) Establish a theory of probable cause

(c) Verify full system functionality and, if applicable, implement preventative measures

(d) Test the theory to determine cause

4. What two steps can be performed to optimize an IR connection between a laptop and a HP® LaserJet Pro® printer? (Select two answers.)

(a) Install an IR booster

(b) Maintain a clear and direct "line of sight" between both devices

(c) Modify the laptop's power scheme to ensure that the laptop does not enter S3 state whilst using the IR-enabled printer

(d) Shorten the distance between the laptop and the IR-enabled printer

5. Which networking device can be used to connect multiple network segments?

(a) Router

(b) Switch

(c) Cable modem

(d) NAS

6. A junior network technician is in the process of installing a new patch panel in a server room. A senior technician is supervising the installation and commissioning activities. Once the patch panel framework has been installed, the various ethernet cables must be attached to the relevant 110 punch blocks.

Which of the following tools should the senior technician recommend to his subordinate when carrying out the cabling attachment activity?

(a) RJ45 crimper

(b) Punch down tool

(c) Punch-in tool

(d) Torx screwdriver

7. Which of the following should a technician check first when a Windows® OS PC is unable to connect to the Internet?

(a) Patch cable

(b) NIC driver

(c) TCP/IP settings

(d) Windows® Firewall settings

8. A router is a networking device that connects a SOHO network or LAN to other networks. Routers can also be used to connect a WAN (or WANs) to a LAN or connect dissimilar networks together.

Which of the following are other notable functions of a router? (Select all applicable answers.)

(a) Limits network broadcasts

(b) Segments IP address ranges

(c) Allows different networked devices to communicate

(d) Interconnects different physical media

(e) Filters and isolates network traffic

9. Which of the following RAID arrays is fault tolerant and permits mirroring combined with striping?

(a) RAID 0

(b) RAID 1

(c) RAID 5

(d) RAID 10

10. Motherboards normally contain a component known as CMOS.

What is the primary function of this component?

(a) CMOS is an alternative name for the Southbridge chipset and therefore controls all of a computer system's I/O functions, such as USB, audio, serial, ISA bus, interrupter controller, and IDE channels

(b) The CMOS manages data transmissions between the CPU, RAM, and PCIe video card

(c) The CMOS stores the BIOS settings

(d) The CMOS temporarily stores data required by the CPU

11. A senior partner in a prestigious law office wants to rip the contents of an audio CD to a compressed file format that can be easily read using Windows® OS PCs, Linux® computers, and Apple® Mac™ computers.

Which file format should be selected in this situation?

(a) *.bmp

(b) *.docx

(c) *.jpeg

(d) *.mp3

12. Which of the following connections provide the fastest data transfer rates? (Select one answer.)

(a) SuperSpeed USB

(b) USB 3.1 Gen 2

(c) eSATA

(d) Bluetooth 3.0

13. Which of the following tools can be used by a computer technician to test an AC outlet? (Select two answers.)

(a) Multimeter

(b) POST card

(c) PSU tester

(d) Receptacle tester

14. What is the main difference between a router and an ethernet switch?

(a) An ethernet switch is designed to interconnect computers on the same network so that they can communicate with each other. A router interconnects one or more networks

(b) A router is designed to interconnect computers on the same network so that they can communicate with each other. An ethernet switch interconnects one or more networks

(c) Both an ethernet switch and a router are designed to interconnect computers on the same network so that they can communicate with each other

(d) An ethernet switch is simply a router that is equipped with multiple ports

15. What port number is used by HTTP?

(a) 23

(b) 80

(c) 427

(d) 443

16. Which type of memory do most mobile devices, such as tablet computers and smartphones, store long-term data to?

(a) SATA HDD

(b) SCSI

(c) SoC

(d) Solid-state flash memory

17. A CPU socket is an electrical interface between the processor and the motherboard. LGA and PGA are two common types of socket.

What are the main functions of a CPU socket? (Select two answers.)

(a) A CPU socket insulates and therefore protects the processor from drastic changes in ambient temperatures

(b) A CPU socket physically supports an installed processor and heat sink assembly

(c) A CPU socket protects the processor from EMI and extraneous signal interference

(d) The main function of a CPU socket is to house the processor on the motherboard without the necessity to solder the CPU in situ

18. A PC user observes that the lights on her computer's keyboard repeatedly flicker during POST.

What would this sequence of events tell a technician?

(a) Keyboard's USB cable is loose

(b) BIOS firmware is automatically updating

(c) Hardware error

(d) Corrupt keyboard driver

19. An IT help desk receives a call from an irate customer. The customer angrily explains that he has recently purchased a relatively expensive wireless inkjet printer. However, when he attempts to print a document using an application on his laptop, the wireless printer produces unintelligible text.

The customer confirms that the laptop and printer are correctly paired via Bluetooth connectivity, and that the printer is in close proximity to the laptop.

Which of the following options is the best first troubleshooting step to effectively resolve this issue? (Select one option.)

(a) Update the printer's driver

(b) Clean the print heads

(c) Ensure that the inkjet printer is correctly paired to the laptop

(d) Power cycle the printer

20. Using the CLI tool, which command displays a NIC's MAC address?

(a) arp -a

(b) ipconfig

(c) ipconfig /all

(d) netstat -a

21. A PC technician is in the process of installing a newly purchased ATX motherboard in a PC case. Before installing the motherboard, what would you recommend the technician to do first?

(a) Verify that the new motherboard is compatible with the specifications of the PC case

(b) Install the CPU into the LGA socket before installing the motherboard into the PC case

(c) Employ appropriate ESD prevention methods and tools

(d) Test the motherboard with a multimeter

22. Which of the following is the default subnet mask for the IP address 192.162.1.10?

(a) 255.0.0.0

(b) 255.255.255.0

(c) FE80::/10

(d) FF00::/8

23. How many pins does a SATA HDD data connector have?

(a) 4

(b) 7

(c) 15

(d) 24

24. AFP is a common networking protocol that is employed by Apple® Mac™ computers and associated devices.

What port number is normally associated with AFP?

(a) 25

(b) 443

(c) 548

(d) 3389

25. Which of the following are possible symptoms of a failing CPU? (Select all applicable answers.)

(a) System lockups

(b) Singular BSOD event

(c) CPU temperature in BIOS is beyond its recommended range

(d) Beeping codes during POST

(e) Recurrent video card failure

(f) CPU is operating beyond its recommended voltage range

26. A PC repair technician is replacing the LCD screen of a laptop.

What tool should the technician use to minimise the risk of damage to the plastic casing when removing the LCD screen?

(a) Crimper

(b) Phillips-head screwdriver

(c) Plastic shim

(d) Torx screwdriver

27. Which type of form factor is commonly found in HTPCs?

(a) ATX

(b) micro-ATX

(c) mobile-ITX

(d) nano-ITX

28. Which of the following is <u>not</u> a possible reason explaining why a laptop's keyboard ceases to function? (Select one answer.)

(a) A damaged or defective Esc key

(b) A loose keyboard ribbon cable

(c) A warped keyboard

(d) Liquid spillage over the keyboard

29. An IT technician working for a large pharmaceutical company is reviewing several troubleshooting tickets at the start of her 12-hour shift.

One of the tickets reports that an employee in the Operations Team is having problems with the LCD display on his work laptop. The employee states that the LCD display shows intermittent lines on the screen while he is working, and that these lines become more pronounced when he moves his laptop around during shift.

The technician notes that the maintenance log shows that laptops used by the Operations Team were recently serviced.

What is the most likely reason for the issue raised in the ticket?

(a) Defective video card

(b) LCD display cable is loose

(c) Faulty LCD monitor

(d) PSU is starting to fail

30. What is the maximum data transfer rate of USB 3.0?

(a) 400 Mbps

(b) 480 Mbps

(c) 5 Gbps

(d) 10 Gbps

31. Which of the following items has the fastest data throughput?

(a) CD-ROM

(b) USB 3.0

(c) SATA HDD

(d) RAM

32. A large manufacturing facility predominantly relies on its server room installations for computing resources and, as a result, is less dependent upon the computing power of its client workstations.

In this scenario, what term is commonly used to describe these client workstations?

(a) Thin clients

(b) Thick clients

(c) Virtual machines

(d) Heavy clients

33. An IT technician working for a prominent contract manufacturing company is notified that a critical server system in one of its manufacturing facilities is frequently rebooting itself without being instructed to do so. The exhaust vent fans are operating as normal. The technician determines that the fault is a hardware issue.

Which two components of the server system are most likely responsible for this fault?

(a) CPU cooling fan

(b) KVM switch

(c) RAID controller

(d) PSU

34. An IT technician has finished servicing a company laptop and he has certified that the Windows® 8.1 OS laptop is in perfect working condition. However, one week later, the Director of Quality Systems reports to the company's IT helpdesk that the laptop cannot access the wireless network. No other users within the company have reported experiencing any networking issues with their mobile devices.

What are the possible reasons for the laptop's inability to access the wireless network? (Select three answers.)

(a) Faulty network adapter

(b) Airplane mode is on

(c) "Forgotten" wireless network

(d) WAPs are out of range

(e) Function key for wireless connectivity was accidentally pressed

35. What is the primary function of the Northbridge chipset on an ATX motherboard?

(a) The Northbridge chipset handles communications between the CPU, RAM, and PCIe (or AGP) video cards

(b) The Northbridge is the chip that controls all of a computer's I/O functions, such as USB, audio, serial, ISA bus, interrupt controller, and IDE channels

(c) The primary function of the Northbridge is to handle and store the BIOS configuration settings of the motherboard

(d) None of the above

36. What is the standard connection type of a contemporary Apple® smart device?

(a) HDMI

(b) micro-USB

(c) USB Type C

(d) Thunderbolt

37. The IT department in a large pharmaceutical manufacturer has purchased a new high-end computer system for the Operations Team. The computer will be mainly used for data analytics and temporary storage of batch manufacturing records. The computer has several HDDs already installed.

The IT technician has been asked to configure the HDDs into a "striped set" for faster read/write speeds.

What type of RAID configuration has the technician been asked to set up?

(a) RAID 0

(b) RAID 1

(c) RAID 5

(d) RAID 10

38. What is the name of the RAM module that is normally installed in tablet computers and smartphones?

(a) LPDDR

(b) SODIMM

(c) eMMC

(d) SRAM

39. What type of cable should be used to directly connect a laptop to a PC?

(a) Cat 5e crossover cable

(b) SMF

(c) USB 3.1 cable

(d) None of the above

40. A maintenance technician has recently installed a duplexing assembly into an office laser printer.

What does the duplexing assembly enable the printer to do?

(a) A duplexing device enables a black-and-white laser printer to produce color printouts

(b) High-speed data transmission between a network computer and a laser printer is permitted via the use of a duplexing assembly installed in the laser printer, thereby facilitating comparatively faster printing

(c) A duplexing assembly enables a laser printer to print on both sides of paper

(d) None of the above

41. Which of the following encryption protocol combinations offers the most secure form of wireless encryption?

(a) WPA2-PSK (TKIP)

(b) WPA-PSK (TKIP)

(c) WPA2-PSK (AES)

(d) WEP

42. A computer technician is reviewing the settings in a PC's BIOS. Which of the following changes can the technician make within the Integrated Peripherals section of the BIOS?

(a) Adjust the CPU's operating voltage

(b) Change the CPU's permitted temperature threshold

(c) Enable or disable on-board devices

(d) Enable or disable virtualization support

43. Which networking protocol uses port 3389?

(a) Telnet

(b) RDP

(c) SMTP

(d) SSH

44. According to the CompTIA® A+ troubleshooting methodology, what should a technician do initially before making any adjustments to a computer system? (Select two answers.)

(a) Identify the problem

(b) Establish a theory of probable cause

(c) Implement effective anti-ESD measures

(d) Perform a system backup

(e) Consult the manufacturer's documentation

45. Which of the following hardware cards enables the full functionality of Windows® Media Centre™ "Live TV" option?

(a) Network Adapter Card

(b) GPU video card

(c) TV tuner card

(d) SDXC card

46. Which of the following connections allow devices to be connected to a PC at distances greater than 20 feet (6 meters) using a single cable? (Select two answers.)

(a) IEEE 1394

(b) Thunderbolt

(c) USB 2.0

(d) USB 3.0

47. Which of the following network devices allows a remote device (e.g., VoIP phone) to receive both data connectivity and electrical power?

(a) PoE injector

(b) Repeater

(c) Router

(d) WAP

48. A power outage occurs due to an electrical storm. The computer workstations in the administrative center shut down in an orderly manner because UPS units had been previously deployed. All 50 workstations connected to the LAN are configured to use a DHCP server.

However, upon rebooting the workstations, an IT technician notices that two computers are unable to reconnect to the network. Rebooting these two computers does not resolve the matter.

What do you think is the most likely cause of the network issue? (Select three answers.)

(a) The two computer workstations were previously assigned Static IP addresses

(b) The ports on the switch connected to these two workstations have become defective

(c) The ethernet cables connecting the two workstations to the switch have either become defective or loose

(d) The DHCP server is not working properly

(e) The NIC drivers on the affected workstations need to be updated

49. Which of the following IEEE Wi-Fi standards are most likely to be affected by the activity of wireless phones, Bluetooth devices, and microwaves?

(a) 802.11a

(b) 802.11a and 802.11b

(c) 802.11b and 802.11g

(d) 802.11b, 802.11g, and 802.11n

50. Which of the following actions helps to secure a router in a SOHO environment? (Select all correct answers.)

(a) Enable SSID broadcasting

(b) Enable MAC filtering

(c) Enable WEP 128 encryption

(d) Change the SOHO router's default password

(e) Disable SSID broadcasting

(f) Enable WPS

(g) Select IEEE 802.11 b/g/n standard

51. A technician has been requested to troubleshoot a computer workstation that will not boot. However, the technician notices that the case fans are running as normal.

What is the most likely cause of this issue? (Select two possible answers.)

(a) Defective PSU

(b) 24-pin ATX 12V 2.1 power connector is loose

(c) Faulty CMOS battery

(d) 24-pin ATX 12V 2.1 power connector is not seated properly

52. Which of the following devices or installations is linked to a network and has the sole purpose of providing data to client workstations?

(a) Patch panel

(b) Switch

(c) NAS

(d) Bridge

53. Which statement regarding LGA and PGA sockets is correct? (Select one answer.)

(a) LGA is a type of CPU socket on a motherboard that uses "lands" to connect the socket to the CPU

(b) LGA is a type of CPU socket on a motherboard that uses a series of moveable "levers" to embed the CPU in the motherboard

(c) PGA sockets have a multitude of tiny protrusions that facilitate connectivity between the processor and the motherboard

(d) PGA sockets are a type of specialized motherboard socket into which the Northbridge chipset is installed

54. Which of the following is the maximum speed of a USB 3.0-compatible ExpressCard device that uses a USB 2.0 bus?

(a) 400 Mbps

(b) 480 Mbps

(c) 5 Gbps

(d) 10 Gbps

55. What command can be entered at the command prompt to find out which ports are open in Windows® Firewall?

(a) arp -a

(b) ipconfig /all

(c) netstat -an

(d) ping /?

56. Computer workstations in a small office are connected to a surge protector. All PC workstations seem to be operating as normal. During the course of the working day, a brownout event occurs. When the SOHO administrator subsequently checks to determine if any workstations are affected, he observes that only one PC's monitor has no display. However, the LED light on the monitor appears to be functional.

What is the first action to be taken to troubleshoot the monitor issue?

(a) Modify the ACPI settings in the BIOS

(b) Open the computer case and inspect the PCIe video card connection

(c) Reboot the PC

(d) Use a multimeter or PSU tester to validate the voltages supplied by the power supply

57. A Windows® 8.0 OS computer is unable to access the Internet. However, all other PC users in the office report no difficulties connecting to the Internet.

Which of the following is the first step an IT technician should take when investigating this particular issue?

(a) Check Windows® firewall settings

(b) Check the NIC driver

(c) Check the patch cable

(d) Check the NIC

58. A color laser printer has recently produced images that are tinted green.

What would you do initially to troubleshoot this specific issue?

(a) Calibrate the laser printer

(b) Clean the imaging drum with a dry lint-free cloth

(c) Replace the laser printer's duplexing assembly

(d) Use isopropyl alcohol or another suitable solvent to clean the primary corona wire

59. Which media type is the best choice for large backups in a corporate environment?

(a) Blu-ray

(b) CD-ROM

(c) DVD

(d) Tape

60. A Python developer working for a prestigious software development firm in London contacts the IT helpdesk explaining that his Dell® PC workstation requires additional memory. Frequently, the developer has numerous PaaS applications open on the screen, and he has noticed that the Dell® PC occasionally becomes non-responsive for a few moments or its performance is marginally slower than normal.

An IT technician confirms that the computer most likely needs additional DDR3 memory to be installed.

According to the BIOS settings, the computer already has 4 GB Kingston® DDR3 memory installed. Also, the motherboard has dual-channel RAM architecture.

After prepping a vacant RAM slot on the motherboard, the technician carefully seats a new 4 GB Kingston® DDR3 memory module. However, when the computer is booted, a memory error is displayed on the display.

What is the most probable reason for a memory error occurring upon booting the computer?

(a) The new memory module has not been seated correctly in the corresponding slot

(b) The new memory module is defective and needs to be replaced

(c) The new memory module has been inserted into the incorrect RAM slot on the motherboard

(d) Dirty RAM slot

61. A PC user in a SOHO environment is installing a wireless keyboard to a computer.

What type of dongle does the PC require to enable connectivity to the wireless keyboard?

(a) Bluetooth

(b) NFC

(c) WiMAX

(d) None of the above

62. Which type of networking cable would be the best choice to use underneath the floor of a building?

(a) Cat 3 UTP

(b) Coaxial

(c) Plenum-grade Cat 5e UTP

(d) STP

63. What is the name of the networking device that connects multiple computer workstations together in a wired LAN environment?

(a) Cat 6

(b) Ethernet switch

(c) Network interface controller

(d) Router

64. A Xerox® maintenance technician is servicing a laser printer in a large open-plan office. There is one other laser printer in the office which is currently being used by staff. However, one member of staff is very annoyed because this other laser printer has mildly creased some pages in her printout.

What should the maintenance technician do to resolve this printer issue? (Select the best two answers.)

(a) Replace the pickup rollers

(b) Adjust the humidity level to 5%

(c) Adjust the humidity level to 35%

(d) Inspect the laser printer and remove any unnoticed paper jams

65. What is the minimum number of HDDs necessary to set up a RAID 5 array?

(a) Two

(b) Three

(c) Five

(d) None of the above

66. An IT engineer has set a new BIOS "Supervisor Password" for two web servers in a client's server room after carrying out routine maintenance. A few weeks later, the web servers are shut down and re-started as part of a security patch installation. However, the client's Senior Technician has mislaid the password and he is unable to boot the web servers into Windows® Server 2012 R2™.

How should the technician reset the BIOS password?

(a) Update BIOS firmware

(b) Remove CMOS battery

(c) Remove Northbridge chipset

(d) Un-install and re-install Windows® Server 2012 R2™

67. Which of the following connections offer the fastest data transfer rates? (Select one answer.)

(a) Thunderbolt

(b) SuperSpeed USB

(c) Firewire 800

(d) Thunderbolt 3.0

68. What precautionary step should be performed before removing a paper jam in a network printer?

(a) Employ appropriate anti-ESD measures

(b) Reduce the fuser assembly's temperature

(c) Disconnect the patch cable from the printer's RJ45 jack

(d) Switch off the printer

69. What is the term that is used to describe the transmission and receiving of data at the same time?

(a) Duplexing

(b) Half duplex

(c) Full duplex

(d) Simultaneous transfer

(e) None of the above

70. Which of the following are examples of cellular technologies? (Select all applicable answers.)

(a) GSM

(b) TDMA

(c) CDMA

(d) TDP

71. What network cabling variety has four twisted pairs?

(a) EMI

(b) MMF

(c) SMF

(d) UTP

72. UDP is a networking protocol. Which of the following statements regarding UDP are correct? (Select all applicable answers.)

(a) Data packets may arrive out of order

(b) UDP sessions are known as "connection-less sessions"

(c) UDP sessions are known as "connection-oriented sessions"

(d) UDP is used in streaming media sessions

(e) Every data packet sent is tracked and acknowledged

73. Which connection type is primarily used with a computer (as opposed to a TV) and carries both a digital and analog signal?

(a) DVI-A

(b) DVI-D

(c) DVI-I

(d) micro-HDMI

74. A documentation specialist working for a pharmaceutical company has noticed that when she prints short documents, the network laser printer is very efficient and fast. However, when she tries to print larger SOP manuals, the printer is non-responsive.

An IT technician has confirmed that all printer cables and settings are correct. Also, the technician has verified the spooler settings are properly configured.

What is the most likely cause of this particular problem?

(a) Obsolete or corrupted printer driver

(b) Printer's in-built memory is inadequate

(c) Faulty RJ45 jack on printer

(d) Defective imaging drum

75. What type of form factor normally uses a single 24-pin power connector?

(a) ATX

(b) HTPC

(c) Mobile-ITX

(d) Pico-ITX

76. Which of the following commands will ping a specified IP address continuously until such time that a technician terminates the command?

(a) ping -t

(b) ping -a

(c) ping -6

(d) ping -l

77. To prevent damage to a computer system and other sensitive electronic equipment, a computer should be connected to which of the following devices?

(a) Power strip

(b) Power inverter

(c) UPS unit

(d) AC power conditioner

78. The thermal printer module that forms part of a cash register at a service station has started to print light and barely readable text.

What is the most likely cause of this issue?

(a) High humidity

(b) Moisture

(c) Dirty heating element

(d) Worn print ribbon

79. A customer has informed their local PC repair shop that their flat panel LCD monitor has several faulty pixels. The customer complains that the faulty pixels are affecting her concentration as she can see them in her peripheral visual field as she works on an important project.

Which pixel color will most likely require the LCD display to be replaced?

(a) Black

(b) Blue

(c) Green

(d) Yellow

(e) None of the above

80. What should be used to clean a laser printer's rubber rollers? (Select two answers.)

(a) Diluted boric acid

(b) Lactic acid

(c) Lint-free cloth

(d) Isopropyl alcohol

(e) Vinegar

81. An Apple® MacBook™ user recently purchased a new external SATA HDD. The user intends to back up important files and documents to this external HDD. However, he does not recognize the connector type.

What type of connector would the user most likely have encountered?

(a) eSATA

(b) Thunderbolt

(c) HDMI Type D

(d) micro USB

82. What is the maximum data transfer rate of a SATA 3.2 HDD?

(a) 1.5 Gbps

(b) 5 Gbps

(c) 6 Gbps

(d) 16 Gbps

83. Which unit of measurement is typically used to demonstrate the effectiveness and throughput speed of computer air cooling systems?

(a) CDMA

(b) CFM

(c) DTR

(d) TDP

84. Liquid cooling systems are sometimes employed in CPU-intensive computer systems to dissipate the heat generated by the processor.

Which of the following are typical components of a liquid-based cooling system? (Select all applicable answers.)

(a) CR2032 battery

(b) Hollow metal block

(c) Pump

(d) PVC tubing

85. The LAN in a large workplace needs to be set up using the most common cabling and wiring standard.

What is the name of this TIA/EIA network standard?

(a) ANSI

(b) T568A

(c) T568B

(d) 802.3af

86. A Dell® Inspiron™ laptop user receives an on-screen notification stating "No connections are available" when he is trying to locate his usual wireless network.

What is the most likely cause as to why the laptop user is not finding the correct network?

(a) Hidden SSID

(b) Wireless turned off

(c) Disabled wireless NIC

(d) Incorrect firewall settings

87. Which CLI tool can be used to determine the MAC address of a computer's NIC?

(a) netBIOS

(b) netstat

(c) ipconfig

(d) ping -a

88. An English Literature student has noticed that whenever she puts her Android™ smartphone too close to her wallet, the smartphone makes a beeping sound. The student is concerned that her new smartphone is faulty, and therefore she visits a mobile phone repair shop for advice.

What do you think the technician is going to tell the student?

(a) Android™ OS is intermittently updating

(b) NFC is enabled

(c) NFC is disabled

(d) Smartphone's antenna is faulty

89. A marketing executive has recently relocated from Europe to the United States as part of a corporate restructuring program. However, the executive has been unable to power up his PC since his arrival in Seattle. The PC never posed any problems to the executive when he was working in Frankfurt, Germany.

What is the most likely issue with the PC?

(a) PSU has become defective

(b) Dual voltage selector is improperly set

(c) IEC cable has become loose

(d) 24-pin ATX motherboard power connector is damaged

90. A PC user in a large open-plan office is attempting to connect to a shared network printer designated as "printer 20" using the UNC path **\74.125.126.100\printer20.** Upon executing the said UNC path, an error message appears on the monitor.

Which of the following UNC paths would enable the PC user to successfully connect to "printer 20"? (Select two answers.)

(a) //74.125.126.100/printer20

(b) http://74.125.126.100/printer20

(c) https://74.125.126.100/printer20

(d) ipp://74.125.126.100/printer20

Assessment Test II			
MCQ Solutions			
1.	a	17.	b, d
2.	b	18.	c
3.	d	19.	d
4.	b, d	20.	c
5.	a	21.	c
6.	b	22.	b
7.	a	23.	b
8.	a, b, d, e	24.	c
9.	d	25.	a, c, d, e
10.	c	26.	c
11.	d	27.	b
12.	b	28.	a
13.	a, d	29.	b
14.	a	30.	c
15.	b	31.	d
16.	d	32.	a

33.	a, d	51.	b, d
34.	b, c, e	52.	c
35.	a	53.	a
36.	d	54.	b
37.	a	55.	c
38.	a	56.	c
39.	a	57.	c
40.	c	58.	a
41.	c	59.	d
42.	c	60.	c
43.	b	61.	a
44.	c, d	62.	c
45.	c	63.	b
46.	a, b	64.	c, d
47.	a	65.	b
48.	a, b, c	66.	b
49.	c	67.	d
50.	b, d, e	68.	d

69.	c	80.	c, d
70.	a, b, c	81.	b
71.	d	82.	d
72.	a, b, d	83.	b
73.	c	84.	b, c, d
74.	b	85.	c
75.	a	86.	a
76.	a	87.	c
77.	c	88.	b
78.	c	89.	b
79.	a	90.	c

Printed in Great Britain
by Amazon

26924379R00268